D0242722

Dewey

A Beginner's Guide

ONEWORLD BEGINNER'S GUIDES combine an original, inventive, and engaging approach with expert analysis on subjects ranging from art and history to religion and politics, and everything in between. Innovative and affordable, books in the series are perfect for anyone curious about the way the world works and the big ideas of our time.

anarchism
ruth kinna

anti-capitalism
simon tormey

artificial intelligence
blay whitby

the bahá'í faith
moojan momen

the beat generation
christopher gair

biodiversity
john spicer

bioterror & biowarfare
malcolm dando

the brain
a. al-chalabi, m. r. turner
& r. s. delamont

christianity
keith ward

cloning
aaron d. levine

criminal psychology
ray bull *et al.*

daoism
james miller

democracy
david beetham

energy
vaclav smil

evolution
burton s. guttman

evolutionary psychology
r. dunbar, l.barrett &
j. lycett

fair trade
jacqueline decarlo

genetics
a. griffiths, b.guttman,
d. suzuki & t. cullis

global terrorism
leonard weinberg

hinduism
klaus k. klostermaier

life in the universe
lewis dartnell

mafia & organized crime
james o. finckenauer

marx
andrew collier

NATO
jennifer medcalf

oil
vaclav smil

**the palestine–israeli
conflict**
dan cohn-sherbok &
dawoud el-alami

paul
morna d. hooker

philosophy of mind
edward feser

postmodernism
kevin hart

quantum physics
alastair i. m. rae

religion
martin forward

the small arms trade
m. schroeder, r. stohl
& d. smith

sufism
william c. chittick

SELECTED FORTHCOMING TITLES:

astronomy	**feminism**	**modern slavery**
british politics	**globalization**	**philosophy of religion**
censorship	**history of science**	**political philosophy**
civil liberties	**humanism**	**psychology**
climate change	**journalism**	**racism**
crimes against humanity	**literary theory**	**renaissance art**
ethics	**middle east**	**romanticism**
existentialism	**medieval philosophy**	**socialism**

Dewey
A Beginner's Guide

David L. Hildebrand

ONEWORLD

OXFORD

A Oneworld Book

Published by Oneworld Publications 2008

Copyright © David L. Hildebrand 2008

All rights reserved
Copyright under Berne Convention
A CIP record for this title is available
from the British Library

ISBN 978-1-85168-580-6

Typeset by Jayvee, Trivandrum, India
Cover design by Simon McFadden
Printed and bound in the United States
of America by Thomson-Shore Inc.

Oneworld Publications
185 Banbury Road
Oxford OX2 7AR
England
www.oneworld-publications.com

Learn more about Oneworld. Join our mailing list to
find out about our latest titles and special offers at:

www.oneworld-publications.com

For Nicholas and Camilla

Contents

Preface   ix

Acknowledgments   xii

Abbreviations   xiv

Introduction   1

1 Experience: mind, body, and environment   8

2 Inquiry: knowledge, meaning, and action   40

3 Morality: character, conduct, and moral experience   63

4 Politics: selves, community, and democratic life   94

5 Education: imagination, communication, and participatory growth   124

6 Aesthetics: creation, appreciation, and consummatory experience   146

7 **Religion: religious experience,**   183
      community, and social hope

      Conclusion: philosophy as   207
      equipment for living

Notes   213

Bibliography   229

Further reading   235

Index   238

Preface

.

If the twenty-first century has a watchword, it is 'sustainability'. For whatever our anxious concern – be it environmental changes or energy politics, healthcare availability or economic indicators, war or education funding – the overriding philosophical question at stake is 'How can we find a *balance* which can sustain what we value?' Such language is telling. By framing contemporary goals with terms like *balance* and *sustainability*, our era distinguishes itself from earlier ones seeking the 'holy', 'good', 'profitable', or 'efficient'. While those values are still important, my point is that it is becoming ever more routine for us to describe our enterprises' *overarching* goal in language that is deeply functional and ecological. (We no longer ask 'Are we *there* yet?' so much as '*How* are we doing?') More and more, our philosophical questions imply that answers will be sought amid the processes and materials of life, not in a realm beyond our experience or in the distant future or past.

The attitude that goals and values should be sought *within* experience, among the events and objects of the natural world, forms the core of Dewey's philosophical vision. As he expresses it,

> [T]he process of growth, of improvement and progress, rather than the static outcome and result, becomes the significant thing . . . The end is no longer a terminus or limit to be reached. It is the active process of transforming the existent

> situation. Not perfection as a final goal, but *the ever-enduring*
> *process* of perfecting, maturing, refining is the aim in living.
>
> (MW12:181; emphasis mine)

Dewey's philosophy is one of change. He writes not just *about* change, but *for* a changing world. Readers may be surprised to find that this progressive viewpoint extends to every major area he considers. Dewey's approach is motivated, I believe, by his personal drive to ameliorate a burgeoning array of human problems with tools his philosophy could provide. Whether he is considering issues in education, politics, aesthetics, religion, or anything else, Dewey's moral commitment is for these human achievements to adapt, survive, and grow. For this reason, Dewey's philosophy stands out as a twenty-first-century philosophy of sustainability.

Purpose of the book

In the past two decades, Dewey scholarship has flourished in both quantity and quality. While Dewey's popularity remains small relative to, say, Nietzsche or Wittgenstein, it is increasingly easy to find dissertations, books, articles, seminars, conferences, and even professional societies devoted to studying Dewey's thought. Indeed, at the present time, the most prominent academic society for American philosophy (the Society for the Advancement of American Philosophy) has a president, past president, and incoming president who have all written extensively on Dewey. Given the range of material now available on Dewey, a word about where this book fits in the larger corpus of Dewey studies is in order.

This book's main purpose is to clearly communicate a detailed account of the widest possible range of Dewey's philosophical views. From the nature of man to the nature of God, I explain Dewey's views by an approach one might call 'taking the car apart, then putting it back together'. In other words, these pages explore what Dewey said rather than attempting to place him into the grand sweep of philosophical or intellectual history.

Put differently, there are several things this book is *not*. First, this is not an esoteric monograph offering a 'radically new interpretation' of Dewey. (If anything, this book reinforces my previous interpretation in *Beyond Realism and Antirealism: John Dewey and the Neopragmatists*.) Second, there are no attempts to correct other Dewey scholars; I pick no internecine fights here. Secondary sources are cited to advance an explanation or enliven a particular point's description. Third, this is not an intellectual biography of Dewey or a work of philosophical history; no attempts at career-long, developmental accounts of Dewey's thought on any particular topic are given. (Dewey's 'mature' views predominate in the text.) Nor are there any serious attempts to rank Dewey within philosophy generally or within 'pragmatism', the movement with which he is most closely associated. Historical context is frequently offered but this is done solely to amplify understanding of the matter at hand. Any of these alternative approaches are, of course, legitimate. I have not taken them because they would have dramatically diverted me from my purpose: to give the *most* detail of the *widest* range of Dewey's views. Readers whose critical appetites are whetted by mention of a particular topic or historical period should consult the list of further reading that rounds out this book.

Acknowledgments

Friendship and intellectual camaraderie are blessings by themselves; I am fortunate enough to have found them combined in several of the people who helped this book come about. Robert Talisse was instrumental in the inception of this project; his work on Dewey has both educated me and helped me guard against philosophical complacency. Conversations and correspondence with Michael Eldridge, James Campbell, Gregory Pappas, John Capps, Thomas Alexander, and Bill Myers helped me to clarify or correct issues that arose during the course of my research. Students in my Spring 2006 seminar on John Dewey at the University of Colorado Denver provided me with friendly and intellectually perspicuous feedback about my interpretations. The Society for the Advancement of American Philosophy and the Summer Institute in American Philosophy have continued to provide intellectual fellowship and expertise.

My graduate research assistants, Monique Bourdage and Louise Martorano, provided me with generous, timely, and critical assistance in editing the manuscript. They did so with efficiency and alacrity – despite both working and attending graduate school full-time. Financial support for this book was provided by various organs of the University of Colorado Denver: special thanks are due to Mark Tanzer and the Philosophy department, The Center for Faculty Development (in particular, Bob Damrauer and Ellen Stevens), and the Mentorship Program (especially Brenda J. Allen).

This book came about between the birth of my first child, Nicholas, and my second, Camilla. With the help of their loving caregiver, Cari Tritz, they graciously permitted me countless hours to go off and write. Finally, not a word here could have been written without the love, patience, and intellectual companionship provided by my wife, Margaret Woodhull. She deserves the best; while she's waiting, I'm lucky to have her.

Abbreviations

The following abbreviations are used for references to John Dewey's work. They come from the critical edition by Southern Illinois University Press, edited by Jo Ann Boydston. Citations give text abbreviation, followed by volume number and page number.

EW *John Dewey: The Early Works*, 5 vols (Carbondale: Southern Illinois University Press, 1969–72)

MW *John Dewey: The Middle Works*, 15 vols (Carbondale: Southern Illinois University Press, 1976–88)

LW *John Dewey: The Later Works*, 17 vols (Carbondale: Southern Illinois University Press, 1981–91)

Introduction

Philosophy is criticism; criticism of the influential beliefs that underlie culture; a criticism which traces the beliefs to their generating conditions as far as may be, which tracks them to their results, which considers the mutual compatibility of the elements of the total structure of beliefs. Such an examination terminates, whether so intended or not, in a projection of them into a new perspective which leads to new surveys of possibilities.

(LW6:19)

In many ways, John Dewey epitomizes what an intellectual life can be. An enormously productive scholar, teacher, family man, and prominent public intellectual, Dewey's ideas were keenly attended by both academic and lay audiences over the course of three generations. As a public figure, he lectured extensively at home and abroad, including travel to China, Turkey, Mexico, and the Soviet Union. While he did engage in the specialized dialectic of philosophers, Dewey also spoke to ordinary people about issues of broad moral significance such as economic alienation, war and peace, human freedom, race relations, women's suffrage, and educational goals and methods. Frequently, he did more than write or lecture; Dewey was founder and first president of the American Association of University Professors, first president of the League for Independent Political Action, and president of the American Psychological Association; he helped found the National Association for the Advancement of Colored People, and was deeply involved in the teachers' union movement in New York City.

As a scholar and writer, Dewey's oeuvre is extraordinary: forty books and approximately seven hundred articles in over one hundred and forty journals. Many of his most renowned works were published after he was sixty years old. He had an eminent career as a professional philosopher, and is universally considered (along with William James and Charles S. Peirce) as a primary founder of American pragmatism. Dewey also served as an early president of the American Philosophical Association and was invited to speak in philosophy's most prestigious lecture series.[1]

Dewey's biography is complex, but several facts are worth mentioning. Born in 1859, he grew up in a merchant-class family in New England, strongly influenced by a devoutly religious mother. After college, Dewey taught high school before taking up graduate studies at Johns Hopkins with Charles S. Peirce, George Sylvester Morris, and G.S. Hall – a pragmatist, Hegelian, and experimental psychologist, respectively. (Dewey's dissertation critiqued Kant's psychology and earned him a Ph.D. in 1884.) In retrospect, Dewey credited his graduate study of Hegelianism with liberating him from both personal and philosophical difficulties.[2] This early liberation initiated Dewey's lifelong enterprise of treating various experiences (bodily, psychical, imaginative, practical) as capable of integration into dynamic wholes. Though Dewey's work became increasingly less Hegelian, the basic intent (of framing phenomena in a synthetically organized way) remained influential throughout his career.

Dewey's family and his reputation as a philosopher and psychologist grew while he taught at various universities, including the University of Michigan.[3] In 1894 he landed two major positions at the University of Chicago, chairing departments in Philosophy (including psychology) and Pedagogy (including the directorship of the Laboratory School). In Chicago, Dewey became active in social and political causes, including Jane

Addams' Hull House. Dewey resigned his Chicago positions in 1904, over conflicts related to the Laboratory School, and soon accepted a position at Columbia University in New York City. Dewey spent the rest of his teaching career (1905 to 1930) at Columbia (including Teacher's College). Almost two decades after his wife died, Dewey married Roberta Lowitz Grant. John Dewey died of pneumonia in his home in New York City on 1 June 1952.

Dewey's popularity has surged over the past couple of decades. While some of this may be due to the rediscovery of his particular genius, several other contributing reasons seem likely.[4] One reason is that Dewey appeals to people as a thinker who is both intelligent *and* engaged. By keeping his scholarly work connected to practical affairs beyond the academy, Dewey ensured wider interest in, and test of, his ideas. Such public intellectuals are rare today, and renewed interest in Dewey may indicate a general yearning for more responsible and informed discussion of contemporary moral and political issues. Another explanation of Dewey's resurgence may derive from some important historical parallels. Dewey's early twentieth-century America was searching for guidance on many problems which concern people today: problems of unemployment, homelessness, and the lack of medical services for the poor; the indifference of the wealthy toward the poor and working poor; the balkanization of pluralistic societies into economically and culturally stratified suburbs; the isolation brought about by consumerism and hyper-individualism. As such problems have captured the attention of philosophers and political scientists, there has been increased interest in 'communitarian' moral and political philosophy. Insofar as Dewey is regarded as a philosopher deeply concerned with democracy, 'the public', and 'the Great Community', contemporary scholars are looking back to his work for insight.

Two keys to understanding Dewey

The chapters that follow will thoroughly acquaint readers with Dewey's philosophical ideas and methods. Here, I outline two beliefs fundamental to Dewey which will aid readers in their understanding of the occasionally complicated terrain that lies ahead.

Practical Starting Point: the first guiding belief concerns one's approach or stance toward the activity of philosophy.[5] For too long, philosophy has been largely concerned with logical demonstration based on certain premises – it has approached issues with a 'top down' rather than 'bottom up' method. The top-down method may be said to use a 'theoretical starting point' because it *already* assumes much about what *must* be discovered *prior* to any actual philosophical inquiry. For example, investigations into the nature of perception that start out with fairly definite presumptions about, say, 'subjects' and the 'objects' they are perceiving; or, investigations into moral questions that presume that, whatever particular answers are found, morality consists in one overarching and universal principle.

Why, Dewey asks, should each successive generation of philosophers accept these theoretical assumptions? Why should it be *assumed* that there is, for example, a single overarching principle of morality – or a dualism between subject and object in perception? Such predeterminations are unfounded; moreover, Dewey argues, they lead philosophical inquiry into insoluble problems and dead ends. They divert philosophical talent away from addressing practical problems.

Instead, Dewey urges a practical starting point, a bottom–up approach to philosophical inquiry. Drawing strongly upon William James's 'radical empiricism', Dewey proposes that philosophers avoid prejudicial frameworks and assumptions and accept experience as it is lived. Such an approach is self-consciously empirical, fallible, and social; employing it,

Dewey writes, can 'open the eyes and ears of the mind . . . [with sensitivity] to all the varied phases of life and history' (LW1:373). By recommending a more humble and mindful respect for experience, Dewey is not suggesting a surrender to irrationality; after all, it is *in* experience that one finds patterns of inquiry and logic useful for ordering and directing future events. Rather, he is suggesting that philosophy seek greater coherence with life as experienced *throughout* the day. Thus, this practical starting point is more than a strategy for doing philosophy; it is the profound and consequential acknowledgment that philosophy's inquiries are similar to many others: done by particular people, with particular perspectives, at a definite time and place, with consequences that must be considered. In other words, philosophy must be done as if it actually *matters*.

Melioristic Motive: the second guiding belief is the view that philosophical questions about knowledge and truth can never be completely walled off from efforts to create and preserve value. Dewey is an inveterate arguer whose works frequently begin with devastating critiques of traditional positions. But however diverse the subject matter, these critiques are frequently unified by Dewey's meliorism. Meliorism is the belief that *this* life is neither perfectly good nor bad; it can be improved only through human effort. Philosophy's motive for existing, then, is to make life better.

This is no blind faith, tossed off sentimentally by Dewey; it is a working hypothesis, drawn from experience. To accept the challenge implied by the melioristic hypothesis is to admit that the proper purpose of intellectual inquiry is to search for ways (ideas, practices) to improve *this* life rather than to look for absolute value or reality *per se*. If philosophy is more than intellectual recreation, it must somehow engage with 'the problems of men'. This is Dewey's touchstone.

Dewey's entreaties – that philosophy start from lived experience (practically), motivated by moral ends (meliorism) – are prescriptive but necessarily vague. They pose a challenge to professionalized philosophers, who tend to respond by demanding specifics. *Which* cherished philosophical problems should be abandoned – and *when*? *Where* should philosophical investigations be focused instead? *What happens* to the identity of philosophy once it abandons traditional problems? Dewey's general retort to such responses is 'look around'. Philosophy can discover new problems in the crucible of common life if its practitioners have the courage and emotional intelligence to trade certain answers for questions which aim to make life better.

Plan of the book

Chapter 1, 'Experience', takes up areas fundamental to Dewey's naturalism – what it means for things to exist in modes which might be labeled *physical*, *psychical*, and *semantic* (or meaningful). Issues covered here include Dewey's 'psychology' as well as his special account of how organism–environment transactions produce 'experience'. *Chapter 2*, 'Inquiry', explores Dewey's naturalistic reconstruction of epistemology (with its traditional components of knowledge, justification, and truth). Inquiry is a central feature of Dewey's instrumentalist philosophy, and plays a significant role in every other chapter in this book because each of them (morality, politics, education, art, and religion) constitutes a special inquiry of their own. *Chapter 3*, 'Morality', explains how Dewey uses transactional experience and experimental inquiry to revamp moral theory. The result, 'moral science', is presented as a way to address practical problems without becoming insensitive to the complexities and nuances of moral life. *Chapter 4*, 'Politics', focuses on Dewey's critique of liberalism and its account of the individual's relation to society. Dewey's emphasis on community-based, participatory democracy is also explored, along with its necessary, interdependent relation to liberal education. *Chapter 5*, 'Education', covers the area for which Dewey was most widely known. Here I explain why Dewey rejected many of his era's conventional restrictions on children, teachers, and curriculum and why he believes that fostering children's self-sustaining habits of creativity and cooperative inquiry should be the primary mission of a humane (and democratic) education. *Chapter 6*, 'Aesthetics', explores how Dewey's metaphysical views about experience apply to art objects, artistic production and appreciation, and communication in general. For Dewey, aesthetic experience describes a phase characteristic of *any* deeply meaningful experience – regardless of whether an artwork is involved. In this regard, aesthetics promises important clues for how ordinary life could be made more fulfilling. *Chapter 7*, 'Religion', looks at religious experience, concepts, and institutions through the eyes of a devoted naturalist and pragmatist. Dewey rejects transcendentalism in religion, and argues that life's tribulations are more effectively addressed by instrumental intelligence. Because religions have forged many communal bonds helpful to the social and moral good, Dewey argues that rather than renouncing religions wholesale it would be preferable to draw from religious experience those elements consistent with a secular, non-transcendental 'common faith' in intelligent inquiry. Finally, the *Conclusion*, 'Philosophy as Equipment for Living', argues that Dewey is worth reading today not only for his philosophical insights, but also for the uses his methods provide in a variety of fields outside philosophy. Three such fields (medicine, environmentalism, feminism) are sketched.

Each chapter is designed to stand on its own. While the book strives to offer a cumulative and integrated portrait of Dewey's thought, those interested in just a few specific topics (e.g., religion and art) can obtain informative and coherent content by selectively reading the pertinent chapters.

1

Experience: mind, body, and environment

Psychology is concerned with the life-career of individualized activities. . . .[Its] subject-matter is the behavior of the organism so far as that is characterized by changes taking place in an activity that is serial and continuous in reference to changes in an environment that persists although changing in detail.

(LW5:224)

After ignoring impulses for a long time in behalf of sensations, modern psychology now tends to start out with an inventory and description of instinctive activities. This is an undoubted improvement. But . . . till we know the specific environing conditions under which selection took place we really know nothing. And so we need to know about the social conditions which have educated original activities into definite and significant dispositions before we can discuss the psychological element in society. This is the true meaning of social psychology.

(MW14:66)

Introduction

To understand the world, we try to understand ourselves: how we perceive, feel, think, and act. We ask questions like, what is an emotion and what, if anything, is it about? How do habits form and why are some so difficult to change? What is consciousness? More grandly, we wonder about the relation between all of our mind's various functions and our sense of what life is all about. We wonder, in short, how psychological experiences can add up to the experience of a meaningful world.

Many today hope that psychology can resolve questions about life's meaning. We look to surgery, pills, and therapy to help 'correct' our brain functions, expecting that these procedures will answer our questions. Dewey, too, began his career with the expectation that psychology held the key to philosophy's big questions. As he developed his own psychological theories, Dewey came to two realizations: first, that psychology's accounts of human behavior were inadequate because they were built upon several old and misleading philosophical assumptions. Second, he came to see that grappling with the meanings of human existence required more than the discipline of psychology could ever provide. In his view, psychology was one, and only one, tool for understanding experience, but much about experience is comprehensible only through art, politics, ethics, and religion – all beyond the bounds of psychology. He came to see that philosophy as a discipline was morally bound to greater engagement with these arenas than scientific psychology.

This chapter is foundational to the rest of the book because it explains how Dewey's reconstruction of the psychological components of human behavior (instincts, perceptions, habits, acts, emotions, and conscious thought) lead to his development of the concept of experience – a concept that Dewey invokes in *every other area of his philosophy*. This notion of experience is crucial because it empowers Dewey to liberate the individual mind from subjective isolation so that it can be understood as it functions with and through the natural and social environments.

To understand Dewey's mature psychology and philosophy of experience, let us briefly consider several important philosophical and psychological influences near the start of Dewey's career. Philosophically, Dewey began as a Hegelian Idealist. His graduate study of Hegelianism in the 1880s with George Sylvester Morris offered Dewey hope that longstanding divisions between 'subject and object, matter and spirit, the divine and the human' could be overcome (LW5:153). Hegelianism inspired Dewey to believe that all kinds of human experience – bodily, psychical, imaginative, and practical – could be explained as integrated parts of whole, dynamic persons. Though Dewey eventually leaves Hegelianism behind (for experimentalism), his early study of Hegel inculcated in Dewey a fundamental bent toward interpreting phenomena in syntheti-cally organized ways. (As later chapters on morality, politics, education, etc., will show, this approach – overcoming dualisms and reaching new syntheses – remains central to Dewey's approach for the remainder of his career.) It was also during this period that Dewey ambitiously pursued studies in psychology. He had high hopes for this new discipline's ability to describe and explain experience; at this time he referred to psychology as the 'completed method of philosophy' (EW1:157). Though he later downgrades this lofty estimation of psychology's potential, it nevertheless remains for Dewey one of the most important ways that solid scientific fact can be put in conceptual connection with more freeform philosophical theories.

The period in which Dewey studied (and tried to recon-struct) psychology was a fertile one for the field, and a few words about the historical context should be helpful. During the late nineteenth century, psychology was dominated by two schools, introspectionism (or 'mentalism') and the newer physiological psychology (imported into America from Germany). Introspectionism arose out of the classical associationist psychol-ogy of eighteenth-century British empiricists such as John Locke and David Hume. The vocabulary used by these early figures varies somewhat, but in essence classical associationism accounts for intelligent behavior with two main components: (1) internally inspected − 'introspected' − entities, such as perceptual experiences (which can supposedly be discovered through mental self-examination) and (2) thoughts or ideas. Intelligent behavior, they argued, arises as the product of associative learning. In short, the mind takes its internal sensations (sometimes called 'impressions') along with their fainter copies (mental images) and through repeated associations with ideas (or thoughts), basic intelligence develops. These basic associative pairings (e.g., pairing of 'red' with a red-stimulus or internal image of red) are then further associated with other such discoveries, and the resulting web of interrelated concepts is what we commonly call 'knowledge'. Through complicated sets of such associations, animals and people become familiar with their environment and how to act in it; more sophisticated animals use association to discover the causal structure of the world.

The important link between the associationists' account and 'introspectionism' stems from the fact that the method of discovery (of the mind's components and their linkages) is one of introspection. This method had a tenacious hold on many in psychology; even when later psychologists such as Wilhelm Wundt (Leipzig) and E.B. Titchener (Cornell, NY) endeavored to explain mental phenomena with the ascendant physiological and experimental methods (e.g., by using dedicated laboratories), they nevertheless retained classical associationism's commitment to introspection as an indispensable part of the method for revealing mental life. In the early part of the twentieth century, introspectionism was further attacked by the ascendant behaviorist movement, which condemned its perpetuation of a mind–body dualism and for the lack of explicit, experimental, and verifiable standards.[1]

The other important movement during Dewey's formative period was physiological psychology. Dewey first studied it in graduate school with G. Stanley Hall, taking all of Hall's classes (including classes in theoretical, physiological, and experimental psychology); in addition, Dewey conducted experiments on attention in Hall's laboratory. Unlike the intuitive approach of introspectionism, its methods incorporated strict experimental controls. Furthermore, this approach to psychology brought with it an organic and holistic model of experience, which Dewey thought could overcome the dualisms that made older, associationist models too subjective and isolated for the evolutionary spirit of the times. Dewey writes,

> The influence of [evolutionary] biological science in general upon psychology has been very great . . . To biology is due the conception of organism . . . In psychology this conception has led to the recognition of mental life as an organic unitary process developing according to the laws of all life, and not a theatre for the exhibition of independent autonomous faculties, or a *rendezvous* in which isolated, atomic sensations and ideas may gather, hold external converse, and then forever part.
>
> (EW1:56)

Still, Dewey could not simply adopt physiological psychology as it was. While appreciating its more rigorous scientific approach, Dewey saw that physiological psychology still retained some of the modern period's more noxious epistemological elements that would have to be pruned away. In particular, it retained the view that experience was a patchwork of atomized 'sense data', which operated like a mechanical sequence of causes and effects. Dewey's Hegelian perspective allowed him to realize that such assumptions about experience would prevent psychology from ever developing accounts that made contact with the world in which we actually live: a world of experienced meanings. Addressing this wider world meant that a much wider arena than that considered by physiological psychology would have to be considered germane to investigation. For Dewey, this arena had to relate the individual's mental life to that of other individuals, and to the collective, social environment.

> The idea of environment is a necessity to the idea of organism, and with the conception of environment comes the impossibility of considering psychical life as an individual, isolated thing developing in a vacuum . . . I refer to the growth of those vast and as yet undefined topics of inquiry which may be vaguely designated as the social and historical sciences,–the sciences of the origin and development of the various spheres of man's activity.
>
> (EW1:56–7)

This critical point is simple, while also entailing an enormous undertaking. To understand experience, psychology must begin to account for how organisms function in environments. However, any single function can be related to multiple environments, some remote; psychology must expand its method so that it can incorporate data beyond immediate biological or mechanical actions. This would mean it must draw from those sciences charged with studying more complex contexts: anthropology, sociology, ethnology, and linguistics, for example. No longer allowed to wall itself off as a study of 'the mind', psychology could only progress by accepting into its studies those very facts already evident in every psychologist's daily, practical life: that individual mental life is necessarily filled with social dimensions (more on this in a while). In other words, if psychology meant to become *truly* empirical, its method would have to search farther and wider for more data. Let us turn now to Dewey's reconstruction of psychology.

Dewey's challenge was to develop a conception of experience which took account both of experimental limits and the pervasive influence of culture. His new approach would have to temper the excesses of the physiological approach (its atomistic materialism) while also tempering excesses in the Hegelian philosophies which first inspired him (especially the assumption of an Absolute reality which was essentially unified and perfect).[2] It was likely that William James's tour de force, *Principles of Psychology* (1890), showed Dewey how a unified consciousness and intelligent self could be explained without appealing to a transcendental Absolute. Infinite absolutes do not instruct us about what to do next; such practical guidance comes, rather, from 'study of the deficiencies, irregularities and possibilities of the actual situation' (MW14:199). Thus, content to leave deterministic materialism and quietistic idealism behind,

> Dewey's 'new psychology' would start with lived experience and attempt to understand it in terms of its organic movement and wholeness. Abstractions, in other words, were to be understood in terms of *it* rather than vice versa . . . By starting with experience as it is lived, the method of psychology can come to understand how the various phases or elements arise within it and so be understood in terms of their functional origins.
>
> (Alexander 1987, 19, 23)

This holistic or functionalist approach to psychology is powerfully represented in his 1896 critique of the reflex arc concept, which he wrote during his tenure at the University of Chicago, a period of deepening engagement with educational theory and practice. To understand Dewey's functionalism, it is best if we begin with his critique of the 'reflex arc' and then summarize how this critique amounted to a statement of his new psychology.

Toward functionalism and instrumentalism

A contemporary trend in psychology offered Dewey the opportunity to create a new synthesis from the opposition between physiological and introspective psychology. 'The Reflex Arc Concept in Psychology' (1896) stands today as a major step forward for his view of experience as well as a seminal contribution to the field of psychology.

At the time, growing numbers of psychologists looked toward the reflex arc concept to help explain human behavior in experimental and empirical ways. The hope was that this new model of behavior, built using pairings of cause (stimulus) and effect (response), could replace explanations which relied on 'psychic entities' or 'mental substance' and so rescue psychology from entities that were mysterious, unobservable, and untestable. The reflex arc model works as follows: a passive organism encounters an external stimulus; this engenders a sensory and motor response; in some cases, this is a conscious response. In a typical example, a child sees a candle flame (stimulus), reaches toward it (response), burns his hand (stimulus), and quickly wrenches his hand away (response). This model argues that these plainly observable elements are *the* basic stimuli and responses in the event; in time, all their connections could be satisfactorily described with mechanistic and physiological terms; no recourse to the unobservable was necessary.

Dewey criticizes the reflex arc framework for several inadequacies. First, it artificially separates events in order to make them discrete (and analyzable). Sensory stimulus, central response, and act are all separate events on this description. 'As a result', Dewey writes, 'the reflex arc is not a comprehensive, or organic unity, but a patchwork of disjointed parts, a mechanical conjunction of unallied processes' (EW5:97). Second, it misdescribes how we interact with our surroundings. It is simply untrue that organisms *passively* receive a stimulus and then become active responders. The nature of organisms is to *interact continuously* with their environment in a manner that is cumulative and mutually modifying. No child is a passive spectator when he first encounters a candle; he is already actively engaged with his environment – exploring the room, anticipating that he will find something, for example. The child's notice of the candlelight *modifies* these ongoing activities. 'The real beginning', Dewey writes, 'is with *the act* of seeing; it is looking, and not a sensation of light' (EW5:97). Third, this model too rigidly identifies events as *the* starting point (stimulus) or *the* ending point. Both stimulus and response are enmeshed in an ongoing matrix of sensory and motor activities. A stimulus comes from somewhere and a response leads elsewhere – to further coordination and integration of both sensory and motor responses. Depending on how the wider range of events are framed, a stimulus can be a response, and a response a stimulus.

In effect, Dewey is criticizing the metaphysical assumptions behind the reflex arc concept. But rather than trying to parse whether there is an underlying reality we may designate as *pure* 'stimulus' or 'response' we should see that problem as one of pragmatic consequences. We are seeking to discover 'what stimulus or sensation, what movement and response *mean*' and we are finding that 'they mean distinctions of flexible *function* only, not of fixed *existence*' (EW5:102; emphasis mine). We need not abandon terms like 'stimulus' and 'response', so long as we remember that they are attached to events based upon their function in a wider dynamic context, one that includes interests and aims.

Instead of the reflex arc model's patchwork of stimuli and various responses, Dewey suggests one that understands organism–environment interactions as 'sensori-motor coordinations', circuits in continual reconstitution and adjustment. Instead of starting with a narrow 'seeing' or sensory stimulus, he recommends we start from the *act*: a *seeing-for-reaching*. 'What precedes the "stimulus" ', Dewey writes, 'is a whole act, a sensori-motor co-ordination . . . [T]he "stimulus" emerges out of this co-ordination; it is born from it as its matrix; it represents as it were an escape from it' (EW5:100). The response that follows, too, is an act. It is not just a 'reaching' but a *reaching-guided-by-seeing*. These acts take place in and because of an *environment*, which contains the problems and surprises that spur us to grow.

As every non-specialist knows, once burned, the child never *sees* the candlelight the same way again. He is changed by the experience and therefore never experiences the exact same stimulus again. In fact, the disruptive and painful nature of the first burning event makes him pay special attention to future encounters with candlelight – it makes him treat it *as* a stimulus and investigate what *kind* of stimulus it is. A newfound unease makes him attend to how candles appear – the color of their flame, the reach of their heat. Separated by conscious reflection from the stream of experience, the candlelight-as-stimulus gains detail and nuance. Experience is transformed and there is growth.

Through his proposal of a coordinated circuit, Dewey sets the stage for several important developments in his later philosophy. First, on psychological and metaphysical grounds, he shows why neither nature nor experience are ultimately categorizable as 'stimulus' or 'response' and how psychology's reflex arc concept is merely disguising philosophy's old psychophysical dualism.[3] His coordinated circuit represents a new, more nuanced and holistic approach which can oppose physiological psychology's narrowly analytical method without thereby embracing its opposite, introspectionism. Second, Dewey's critique and reconstruction of the reflex arc in psychology has implications for later work in logic and the philosophy of science. The specific insistence that psychology's scientific method must be more attentive to function and context lays the groundwork for similar and universal claims for all the sciences. Scientific distinctions are *not* meaningful by reference to something essential or 'real' in a world beyond our experience; rather, their meaning can *only* be determined by relating them to specific situations, histories, and future experimental and practical consequences. Because human beings *make* meaning – rather than just discover it – it must be seen that even the most regal scientific and philosophical terms arise humbly: in a historical, socio-cultural matrix where organisms are trying to adapt, survive, and flourish. The final and perhaps most important consequence of Dewey's reconstruction of the reflex arc is that it provides an innovative way of understanding (and changing) how we learn. If experience is an ongoing-and-cumulative coordination, then learning, too, proceeds as a living rhythm – not by a series of truncated arcs, fits and starts. Learning is movement from an initial disequilibrium (confusion, doubt) toward equilibrium (satisfaction, knowledge). The learner is not an empty vessel or a wax tablet, 'impressed' by discrete and external stimuli, but an agent actively engaged with her environment and growing insofar as she *frames* and *uses* events in experience.

Dewey's functional critique and reconstruction of the reflex arc is simultaneously a new *paradigm* for interpreting psychological phenomena and a *warning* about the traditional logical methods used to describe and interpret such phenomena. The *paradigm* starts, as Alexander put it earlier, 'with the idea of the organism already dynamically involved with the world and aiming toward unified activity' (Alexander 1987, 129). The *warning* is against taking the *eventual* outcomes of analysis and then supposing that these outcomes were *already present* from the very beginning. With these points in mind, let us move on to examine a number of other psychological phenomena traditionally thought to exist in some self-complete fashion: instincts, impulses, perceptions, sensations, habits, emotions, consciousness, and mind, to name a few. The challenge for Dewey's reconstruction of these psychological phenomena is to both heed the warning and live up to the paradigm.

How do infants grow into complicated adults? What kind of explanation can we derive from the obvious presence of instincts and impulses in the young? Dewey's reconstruction of the concepts of instinct (or 'impulse' – he uses these terms interchangeably) starts by criticizing his contemporaries' methods of answering these difficult questions. Psychology, he complains, begins with a descriptive list of instinctive activities (e.g., the sex drive, egoism, altruism) and then attempts to explain complicated human conduct (e.g., courtship) by directly referring to these instincts as if they were unchanging, self-complete things ('native powers'). Such explanations are always inadequate, he argues, because impulses are actually *pliable*. If one observes a variety of individuals or cultures, it's clear that the basic instincts we share actually develop into so many different habits and customs. 'Any impulse', Dewey writes, 'may become organized into almost any disposition according to the way it interacts with surroundings. Fear may become abject cowardice, prudent caution, reverence for superiors or respect for equals' (MW14:69). Thus, the organization of instincts by environments is necessarily diverse, and this fact offers a strong clue that *no* primordial meaning for instincts should be sought by psychology. As with 'stimulus' in the previous discussion, the crucial aspect to determine about instincts are their *meaning*, and meaning can only be determined contextually – that is, by observing how instincts are built into personal habits and, more generally, how they are valued by the social and cultural contexts in which they function. Just as the word 'turbine' only has a meaning if one already knows both a specific language and set of activities, an instinct only means something *along with* its social context. Therefore, there is no psychology without social psychology. There is no 'pure, biological' account of instinct, impulse, or any other 'natural' power without some inquiry into environmental and social contexts.

For Dewey, then, an instinct/impulse must be understood transactionally, as an interactive phenomenon-in-environment. He likens them to pivots, which enable one to change direction or reform a habit. Sometimes these pivots channel activity down familiar paths, as an impulse for aggression becomes the habit of competition in sports. But sometimes a pivot leads to something new, overturning those customs which would color it, and so leading to innovation. For example, an impulsive outburst ('These meetings never accomplish anything!') might shatter the bovine complacency of a staff meeting and spark a revision in how the group deliberates. Regardless of whether an instinct perpetuates or revolutionizes custom, Dewey's point is that they should not be assigned a single, immediate, unchangeable meaning. As 'pivots', they must be understood transitively, in relation to their dynamic environment: a small child's 'anger' toward a bully is qualitatively different from the anger he displays toward the family cat. 'The notion that anger still remains a single force', Dewey writes, 'is a lazy mythology' (MW14:106).

The general lesson illustrated in Dewey's account of impulse and instinct is one of method. It is that strictly analytical methods – trying to build complex behavior out of simple elements – are inadequate for determining the meaning of psychological phenomena. We can now see how this lesson applies to traditional accounts of perception and sensation. In Dewey's day, it was typical for philosophers to describe perception as an event where (1) simple, external causes (2) completely pervade the mental state of (3) an empty, passive recipient mind. In many ways, this kind of model still permeates our commonsense notions about how perception works. Dewey argues that all three elements of the model misdescribe perception. They are rooted in an erroneous and radical separation of the perceiver from the world – what is called 'psychophysical dualism'. Now, let us see why each element of the model is mistaken.

First, regarding simple, external causes, the traditional picture starts with a self or mind that is fundamentally different and separate from its world. The world is 'out there' and the mind is 'in here'. Perception is the process that is supposed to explain how we come to know what is 'out there'. In perception, the story goes, the simple 'ideas' (or 'impressions' or 'perceptions') impinge upon the senses and make their way into our thoughts. Dewey's model rejects this 'inner/outer' model from the start. His is an *ecological* model – mind, body, and world are mutually created by their ongoing interaction. (A mind is like a friendship: it only *exists* through ongoing conversation and activity.) As an ecological model, it does not assume that perception starts with a radical gap between a subject and object (perceiver and perceived); therefore, it must also reject traditional accounts which, for example, describe a simple perception (like 'red' or 'sweet') impinging upon a waiting perceiver. Surely we have experiences involving red qualities; but the label 'perception' is simply a convenient shorthand for a more complicated process of interacting events. It is worth noting that just because the perceiver-side of the situation is active one should *not* infer that all events can now be defined *from* this side. A flash of light that catches me off guard is not *my* doing; nevertheless, its specific character *as this perception* depends upon how it is taken up and responded to by me, and that in turn depends on a long-term history of past experiences.

This redescription of perception along ecological/transactional lines has a metaphysical upshot, that is, it tells us something about Dewey's view of how reality is structured. By rejecting philosophies which describe perception's 'objective' causes and 'subjective' effects – identifying, for example, a lemon's tartness as a subjective perception *in* a perceiver – Dewey is proposing a new view of quality. Qualities cannot be simply identified or located this way; they are not 'in' anything because they arise out of our interaction with the world. A quality is a transactional event.[4] What is more, it is mistaken to think that perceptual experiences are involved with something as singular as 'red' or 'tart'. As a label, 'red' is simple; we typically do not see just red. The child sees most immediately a *red dress* – not an isolated color patch. Perhaps there is an occasion where she finds herself searching for the dress; in that case, a glimpse of 'red' might catch her eye, discriminating itself, so to speak. But in this situation, notice that red is discriminated because it is functioning *as a sign* that what is being sought may have been found. Too often, psychology and philosophy accept such signs as ontologically basic – fundamentally real – rather than seeing that they are abstractions which arose for pragmatic reasons.[5]

Second, Dewey rejects the idea that perception completely pervades (or takes hold of) one's mental states. Every perception we might single out to talk about exists, Dewey says, with an attendant 'fringe'. This fringe supplies a contrast, which imbues the focal perception – and indeed the entire situation – with its 'underlying qualitative character'. In a vivid perception (e.g., a bitter taste), *this bitterness* exists *as it exists* only given a slew of 'fringe' conditions: what I have just been eating, what I expected to taste, etc. Such fringes of feeling are indispensable guides to how we characterize our more prominent perceptions and even how to act.

Third, perception is never simply the mind's instantaneous, passive apprehension of stimulus. Perceiving is an activity undertaken by an organism *already* functioning with sensory-motor coordination. A new sight (sound, taste) is encountered by a living creature involved in the give-and-take of life; therefore, when it directs attention to this new portion of its sensory field, it acts not merely to receive, but to adjust. It reacts *selectively*. The process of perception, as adjustment, is thus never immediate; it evolves through interaction. While some perceptions happen quickly (blinding flash) and others take considerably longer (slow appreciation of a curry's spice), they always take *some* time. Perception is never naïve, never an encounter with 'raw' data; all seeing is seeing *as* – an adjustment set within larger acts of adjustment. If we think back to the case of the curious child and the candle, we find someone starting out with a variety of habits in place for coping with stimuli: habits of searching, screening, and selecting for focal engagement. The child may approach the candlelight *as potential amusement*, but respond to its burning heat *as disappointingly injurious*. Habits modify, and over time responses to a perception adjust, influencing the subsequent selection and interpretation of sensations.[6]

Acts, habits, and emotions

Having examined Dewey's criticisms and reconstructions of instinct and perception, let us move on to examine the somewhat 'thicker' psychological constituent, the act, along with two formations of the act, habit and emotion. Throughout this chapter, we have heard Dewey insist that psychological explanations of complex human experience cannot be built up analytically using simple parts – using instinct or perception, for example. The *act* is a more helpful unit for understanding complex human behaviors because it concerns the whole organism participating in a wider environment, which it inhabits (see MW14:105). Like instincts and perceptions, acts are transactional: we act *on* and *with* things. The environment with which we act both sets conditions and provides a stage for action: As I place a reassuring hand on the shoulder of another – my hand touches and is touched in the very same 'act'. In short, we can list three basic reasons for making acts fundamental to an analysis of meaningful human behavior. First, acts are inherently *selective* because they operate as a stimulus to liberate action and unify situations. Second, the selectivity of acts is manifest in experience as *interest*. Finally, it is the presence of both selectivity and interest that 'create the basis for an *organized context of meanings* and activities' (Alexander 1987, 133; emphasis mine).[7]

Like any other process of adaptation and coordination, acts unfold in time. As discussed previously, the earliest phase of the act is impulse (instinct). Impulse springs from need and gropes toward reintegration and satisfaction; it can function as the reorganizing 'pivot' of conduct, sometimes providing a needed opportunity for imagination, invention, and intelligent redirection (see MW14:117–18). The later phases or formations of the act include habits and emotions, to which I now turn.

Drawing upon various uses of 'habit' in the pragmatisms of William James and Charles S. Peirce, Dewey integrates habit into his philosophy much more broadly than earlier philosophers, such as David Hume, employing it to comprehend a wide range of human experiences: biological, ethical, political, and aesthetic.[8] Without habits, the large behavioral structures of our experience – walking, talking, cooking, conversing – would be impossible.

What is habit? Habits are not simple things; they are composed of acts. The process of a child learning to walk involves a thousand minor acts – grasping, rising, balancing, initiating movement, etc. For these to amount to something – the structured experience called walking – there must be a gradual and cumulative change in the act-series. That change comes about because the series of acts become so well associated that one leads naturally (or unconsciously) to the next. In short, when there is a cumulative linking of acts that structures experience, there is a 'habit'.

'Ah yes', one may object, 'but aren't habits automatic? Consider the habit of repeated overeating or smoking, which seem beyond control simply because there is no longer a space for willpower.' This objection is certainly part of our contemporary view of habit; that is, we think of habit as an 'automatic mechanism' because such conduct appears to be insulated from conscious intervention.

However, this view carries several connotations that Dewey takes pains to correct. First, it is mistaken to over-identify habits with repetitious acts. Habit, Dewey writes, 'is an acquired predisposition to *ways* or modes of response, not to particular acts' (MW14:32). Each new situation always slightly different, and so the exact same act is never repeated. What we acquire are 'tendencies' or 'dispositions'. Habits are also misconceived to be largely unchangeable. But unlike a machine's routine, our organic habits are plastic, capable of redirection and change. My habit to act in predictable ways (eating sweets when hungry) is subject to contingencies (a sharp toothache) and subsequent modification (restraint, substitution), typically beginning when conscious reflection on the habit is operative. Communication is the key to the evolution of habits.

Moving beyond our example, there is a third misconception, namely that habits are predominantly dormant – tools or reserves to call up on demand. Dewey views habits as not dormant but 'energetic and dominating ways of acting' that can determine what we do and who we are: 'All habits are demands for certain kinds of activity; and they constitute the self' (MW14:22, 21). One final misconception about habits is that they are individual possessions – '*my* bad habit of smoking', for example – held with the same subjective privacy we saw attributed earlier to sensations and feelings. Dewey argues that this likening of habits to property is wrongheaded. Unlike property, habits are dynamic functions which have the power to shape both the individual and the environment through their transactions: 'Habits enter into the *constitution* of the situation; they are in and of it, not, so far as it is concerned, something outside of it' (MW6:120). They are the ability of organisms to reconstruct their environment, not inner forces.[9]

Finally, like language, habits have an ineliminable social dimension. While it may be right for me to take personal responsibility for 'my' habits, they are not completely my inventions. Many 'individual' habits actually come about *through* the social environment created by family, friends, media, home, playground, etc. Once they exist, habits inform the cultural and natural sources that helped create them. For these reasons, it is better to conceive of habits as 'situational *structures* rather than individual reflexes, psychic associations, or repeated actions' (Alexander 1987, 142).

The importance of habits in Dewey cannot be underestimated. Habits connect the biological and the cultural, enabling us to do simple things like *walking* and sophisticated things like *interpreting* a particular action *as* walking. As we mature, we make sense of the world because of the habits we use to 'frame or establish a temporal *context*, a referential basis of interpretation and action' (Alexander 1987, 145). Without increased creativity and variety in our habits of interpretation, there can be no increasingly meaningful sense of life, no growth in wisdom.

Emotion is a complicated subject, and while I must treat it briefly here, it is an important component of Dewey's psychology, not least because his view of emotion (and feeling) is central to his accounts of mind and consciousness. Here again, Dewey bucked tradition. Philosophers, going back to ancient Greece, elevated cognition over emotion. Due to the importance of cognitive functions like clarification and discrimination (especially for aiding observation, understanding, and choice), philosophy developed an exaggerated respect for cognition as *the* way to access 'reality' and determine what is truly good. At the same time, they developed an exaggerated disrespect for emotion. (In fact, moderns such as Descartes and Spinoza go so far as to argue that emotion is merely a species of confused thought, which, once clarified, can reach the status of cognition.) Dewey sharply opposes the traditional denigration of emotion. He labors to redescribe the function and role of emotion in human experience. Emotion, he believes, is central to human experience and has an indispensable role to play in endeavors such as logic, ethics, art, and religion.

What is emotion? Recall that as our 'coordinated circuit' acts in the world, involvement takes two basic forms: habit and emotion. Habits are 'energy organized in certain channels' that develop as controlled responses to problematic situations. Emotion, in contrast, is not predominantly an organized or controlled response, but rather the organism's vibration *in sympathy with* the situation; it is 'a perturbation from clash or failure of habit' (MW14:54).[10] As with the other constituents of mental life, Dewey is reconstructing emotion along transactional lines and opposing the longstanding prejudice against the 'subjectivity' of emotions.

Dewey's view of emotion grew from his attempt to connect the accounts of Charles Darwin and William James. Darwin argued that internal emotional states give rise to organic expressions, which may in turn be subject to natural selection based on survival value. For example, I perceive something, feel sad, emote with tears, and garner sympathy which aids survival. James, on the other hand, thought it incorrect to consider emotion as a separate phase from its accompanying bodily expressions. What actually happens in emotion, James says, is that a perception excites a pre-organized bodily mechanism, and it is recognition of *that* change that is the experience of emotion: 'we feel sorry *because* we cry, angry *because* we strike' (James 1890, 450).

In 'The Theory of Emotion' (1895) Dewey mitigates the differences between James and Darwin, and emphasizes the integrated whole of both feeling and expression. *Being sad*, for Dewey, is not just *feeling sad* or *acting sad*. Being sad is my experience of *all* aspects of my condition as a purposive organism. In this way, Dewey gently corrects James's model's unfortunate reiteration of the traditional mind–body dualism, suggesting instead that to understand emotion we need to recognize that 'the mode of behavior is the primary thing' (EW4:174). Dewey's account of emotion, then, diverges sharply from those where a subject 'has' this incredibly private, subjective mental event called 'emotion'. For Dewey, emotion emerges from the fluid boundary connecting organism and event, 'called out by objects, physical and personal' as an intentional 'response to an objective situation' (LW1:292).[11] Frequently, that response is one that inhibits what one was previously undergoing.

To lighten this somewhat dense account, let me offer this example:

As I stride confidently across the street, my eye catches sight of a strange dog in my way. My predictable situation is suddenly precarious and the emotion seizing me indicates that my habit (striding quickly) must be inhibited so a readjustment (avoidance, perhaps) can follow.

Note that it is *the inhibition of habit* – rooted in my perplexity over how to adjust to this event – *that excites emotion*. Were I to encounter a familiar and friendly dog, I might pause and pet him, but that would not excite great emotion because my usual habits would lead frictionlessly to response. Again, in the case of a strange dog, it is the flood of *incompatible* responses (should I run? call for the owner? walk slowly?) that creates the tension that interrupts and inhibits habits, and thus is experienced as emotion.[12]

In Dewey's rendering, emotion arises within the field of action. There is no subject–object dualism, and no reason to devalue the reality of emotion. In contrast to many in the tradition, Dewey does not view emotion as an 'intrusion' into an otherwise harmonious and rational order, but as arising naturally 'in experience because experience is in a rhythmic alteration from stable to precarious and back' (Alexander 1987, 139).

The emergence of sentiency, mind, and consciousness

What does it mean to be a sentient being? What is mind or consciousness? How do these infamously mysterious mental abilities come to exist within Dewey's naturalistic model of psychology? So far, our discussion has been traveling up the behavioral ladder, toward greater cognitive sophistication. The foregoing accounts of impulse, perception, act, habit, and emotion now enable us to understand how sentiency, consciousness, and mind emerge organically from an environment of interacting organisms. In addition, we will also briefly consider how we reason and create aesthetically (since both are functions of conscious experience), and this will be built upon later in chapters two and six.

Consider an animal running through a maze whose progress is stopped by a dead end with two doors, red and green. The red door leads to a shock, the green door to food. After repeated lunges through both doors, the animal pauses a moment – he inhibits the habit of blind lunging. He notices the *color* of the doors; 'red' and 'green' are no longer mere physical stimuli. They become *noticed* qualities, and the creature noticing them has acquired 'sentience'.

What is happening in the above example? Consider this type of evolutionary step taking place over a much longer period. Creatures strive to achieve comfort and stability in their everyday life. When stable situations become precarious, comfort gives way to anxiety – and a struggle begins to reestablish balance by adjusting one's self, one's environment, or both. Of course there are various ways a creature can 'adjust' to a problem. Methods which are tried and true, or pre-organized responses, are often effective ways to adjust. But when problems are new, old responses may not work. In those cases, it becomes advantageous to *inhibit* pre-organized responses to events – to prevent an automatic response. Through inhibition, a 'pause' is implemented against the flow of immediate action, and a space is created. Within this space, a new qualitative experience emerges which Dewey calls 'sentiency' or 'feeling'.

To put it slightly differently, sentience (feeling) develops in just those creatures who, faced with obstacles, become divided within themselves – ambivalent – over *how* to respond. What happens is that in the ambivalent pause, 'there is a "moment"of hesitation; there are scruples, reservations, in complete overt action. . . . We have to "stop and think", and we do not stop unless there is interference. . . . [Our] division introduces mental confusion, but also, in need for redirection, opportunity for observation, recollection, anticipation' (LW1:237). Inhibition enables ambivalence, and ambivalence makes possible the consideration of alternatives. With practice, maturity in techniques of choosing alternatives is, for all intents and purposes, intelligence.

Let us return to the creature in the maze. By pausing and discovering how to experience the door colors in a new way, he develops a new (we could say 'higher') capacity; and suddenly a crude, physical situation has taken on complexity and meaning. Thus, Dewey writes, sentiency or ' "feeling" is in general a name for the newly actualized quality acquired by events previously occurring upon a physical level, when these events come into more extensive and delicate relationships of interaction' (LW1:204).[13] These newly extensive and delicate relationships are not *known*, then and there. Rather they provide the means for the development of intelligence when creatures develop the further ability to symbolize the relationships and manipulate the symbols, all for the purpose of more effectively managing future experience. In other words, were our maze dweller to become intelligent, he would move beyond the awareness that the doors have different colors with different consequences by transform- ing these meanings into ideas, perhaps naming items as 'red', 'green', 'shock', and 'food', and then interrelating all these words in a way that solves 'the problem of the maze'. Now *that* would be *smart*.

We are used to thinking of our 'mind' as we think of our 'body', that is, like a thing or substance that is separate and essentially different from everything else around it. Philosophers have traditionally categorized mind as a separate kind of substance, place, thing, or container. (This has led to various attempts to reduce the mind to the brain, or vice versa.)[14] Instead Dewey argues that these are not accurate ways of picturing mind. As with instinct, perception, emotion, and all the other mental abilities discussed so far, mind more closely resembles a range of dynamic processes – various ways we interact with the world. Think of how we use the word 'mind' to signify various functions: *memory* (I am re*mind*ed of something); *attention* (I keep you in *mind*, or *mind* my place in line); *purpose* (I have a goal in *mind*); *care* and *solicitude* (I *mind* my child, my step); paying *heed*, *obeying* (the driver *minds* the stop sign). In short, 'mind' comprises many activities: intellectual, affectional, volitional, and purposeful. Viewing them comprehensively, as a single psychological characterization, we see that,

> Mind is primarily a verb. It denotes all the ways in which we deal consciously and expressly with the situations in which we find ourselves. [In] its non-technical use, 'mind' denotes every mode and variety of interest in, and concern for, things: practical, intellectual, and emotional. It *never denotes anything self-contained, isolated* from the world of persons and things, but is *always* used with respect to *situations, events, objects, persons and groups.*

> (LW10:268, 267; emphasis mine)

How is mind an advance over sentience, for Dewey? How does mind emerge from those capacities? It is true that complex and active animals have a variety of different feelings. They are sentient in elaborate ways because they maintain a multitude of distinctive connections with their environment. But, Dewey argues, the reason we say certain animals cannot 'know' their feelings – that is, the difference between mere sentience and 'mentality' (or mindfulness) – derives from an animal's ability to recognize and use meanings and signs. Consider a bull charging a red flag. He is stimulated by the flag, but does not see the red quality *as a sign*. He cannot detach his charging from the stimulus 'red' the way a human driver can ignore a broken red light at an intersection. (Given what happens to bulls, he would treat the flag as a sign if he could!)

In other words, *mind* emerges once a merely sentient aware-ness of qualities can be 'taken up into a system of signs' through language (LW1:199). Language enables creatures to signify *what* is felt and how it might fit with a 'past' and 'future'. (Time, too, enlarges with language.) Language allows, in other words, the existence of objects *as* objects (as well as places, events, relations, etc.) because there is now a way to identify and differentiate them. *'Without language'*, Dewey writes, 'the qualities of organic action that are feelings are pains, pleasures, odors, colors, noises, tones, only potentially and proleptically. *With language* they are discriminated and identified. They are then "objectified"; they are immediate traits of things.' (LW1:198; emphasis mine.)[15]

Mind is not a spark of divinity, as ancients thought, nor an illusory ghost in the machine of material bodies. Rather, mind is at least the ability to adapt and adjust to problems using language, and even more, the ability to create, plan, and project one's vision of the future. Mind is 'an agency', Dewey writes, 'of novel reconstruction of a pre-existing order' (LW1:168). To further develop our understanding of mental agency, we should move ahead and understand how it makes consciousness a living reality.

Though he was greatly influenced by William James's metaphor of consciousness as a constantly moving 'stream of thought', Dewey came to believe that no fully adequate account of consciousness could ever be captured in words.[16] We speak indirectly about consciousness – calling it 'apparent' or 'conspicuous' or 'vivid' – without ever satisfactorily striking our target. The reason, in part, is that consciousness is evanescent; being neither thing, power, nor cause, we should not demand of language the impossible. Instead, we should recognize the limits of language and content ourselves to point to or evoke instances of consciousness.

Dewey points to and evokes consciousness in several creative ways. First, Dewey points at consciousness by contrasting it to minds-with-language. I summarize these contrasts in Figure 1 (derived from LW1:230).

I hope that Figure 1 evokes the reader's own associations with consciousness: that flash of emotion or idea that sparkles with vivid immediacy; a surprisingly lucid transition between moments. Dewey intended the contrasts to highlight how consciousness's bright moments are made possible *because* of their context; due, that is, to the persistent and pervasive system of meaning that is *mind*.

Mind is	Consciousness is
A whole system of meanings as embodied in organic life	Awareness or perception of meanings (of actual events in their meaning)
Contextual and persistent: a constant background	Focal and transitive
Structural and substantial: a constant foreground	A punctuated series of heres and nows
Enduring luminosity	Intermittent flashes of varying intensities
A continuous transmission of messages	The occasional interception and singling out of a message that makes it audible

Figure 1

Besides pointing out contrasts, Dewey also tries to evince the meaning of consciousness by engaging the reader in reflecting upon the experience of reading a book. Try it yourself: as you read this book, meanings appear and you are immediately conscious of them; as you forge ahead, they disappear. Those ideas before you at any one instant make sense because of mind ('an organized system of meanings of which we are not at any one time completely aware', LW1:231). Notice, though, that your mind does not supply sense the way a dictionary does. Rather, between the focal meaning ('consciousness') and the context of meanings ('mind') there is a spectrum or fringe that determines 'the habitual direction of our conscious thoughts and [supplies] the organs for their formation' (LW1:231). Much as your physical sense of balance controls walking, mind constantly adjusts and directs your interpretations of meanings before you. Your vivid consciousness of each successive idea is empowered to move smoothly ahead due to mind.

As with other mental elements, Dewey can only attempt to describe consciousness using a new vocabulary of dynamic, organic adaptation. Consciousness is thinking-in-flight, an ever-reconfiguring series of events that are qualitatively felt as they transform experience at its most urgent. If mind is the 'stock' of meanings on hand, then consciousness is the realizing and reconstructing of those meanings so that experience can be redirected, readapted, and reorganized. It is 'that phase of a system of meanings which at a given time is undergoing re-direction, transitive transformation' (LW1:233). Consciousness is the dramatic aspect of mental life, with mind providing the indispensable 'back-story' or narrative. No part of this narrative, moreover, is radically private; it is a social narrative, woven by communities present and past.[17]

This concludes our review of Dewey's more specifically 'psychological' accounts of human experience. With the foregoing psychology as our basis, we shift now to consider how his concept of 'experience' served his further philosophical goals.

Experience

Analysis of the concept of experience has an incredibly long provenance in the history of philosophy and occupied Dewey throughout his career. His explanations of experience are complicated and nuanced, and served Dewey in various ways for many different philosophical inquiries. Because a comprehensive rehearsal of experience lies beyond this chapter's compass, I aim instead to explain its core meanings for Dewey by showing how he rejects traditional assumptions attached to this term.

Historically, many philosophers have construed *experience* narrowly, as a sensation or perception privately had by a subject. Because an overriding goal for philosophy has been to achieve knowledge, philosophers have followed a strong inclination to view experience through the prism of this objective. This has lead some (for example, Plato, Descartes) to view experience as a remorseless flux, untrustworthy for the purpose of scientific or metaphysical knowledge. Others (for example, Locke, Hume) celebrate the sensory flux of experience, because it at least provides *something* observable and measurable. Despite the apparent opposition of the approaches, both schools generated a large number of intractable philosophical puzzles (e.g., whether we can assume there to be an external world, other minds, or free will). Dewey sees these puzzles as founded on a mistaken view of experience, and unproductive for helping solve practical problems.

In Dewey's view, an organism's experience cannot be reduced to the contents of consciousness. If philosophers could set aside their predetermined, theoretical objectives, they could appreciate that scrutiny of experience can reveal much more than sensation or intellectual thought. Beyond these contents of experience – which, no doubt, are present – it is clear that experience is 'double-barrelled', including not only *what* is experienced, but *how*. 'Like its congeners, life and history, [experience] includes *what* men do and suffer, *what* they strive for, love, believe and endure, and also *how* men act and are acted upon, the ways in which they do and suffer, desire and enjoy, see, believe, imagine – in short, processes of *experiencing*' (LW1:18). Just as a piece of music contains both notes and harmony, experience is both a process and a field. It is a 'field-process' (Alexander 1987, 128). The process is not random; it unfolds and has *order*. The field of action has *structure*. And it all transpires for a concrete individual with a particular perspective (that includes emotions, a culture, and a history).

The tradition is also mistaken in seeing experience as exclusively 'mine' or 'yours'. Of course, it is accurate to describe some experiences as predominantly private; but the tradition has so exaggerated this subjectivistic side of experiencing that the result has been to separate subjects from the physical and social world that sustains and even constitutes them. If we follow James and pay 'radically empirical' attention to experience, we find that while there are private aspects to experience (a secret thought one entertains about another), many other experiences are not private. After all, we are earnestly social beings. Indeed, if one considers the (previously described) symbolic advance creatures must take to evolve from sentience to cognition, it becomes clear that *mind itself is a social achievement* because the signs which make thought possible have meanings in virtue of social life. Dewey writes that the 'character of every-day experience . . . is saturated with the results of social intercourse and communication' because 'language . . . is . . . the instrument of social cooperation and mutual participation' (LW1:6).[18]

The traditional emphases of experience as both (a) privately owned and (b) the contents of consciousness have caused it to be identified with reflective thought, that is, knowing. Much experience, however, is *not* reflective; it is felt or had. Dewey describes these two kinds of experience at many points in his writings, and his names for these two kinds of experience vary. The first kind he calls: 'had', 'direct', 'immediate', 'undergone', and 'primary'. It is minimally regulated or reflected upon; it is felt, qualitative. The second kind he calls: 'known', 'indirect', 'mediated', 'reflective', and 'secondary'. It abstracts away from immediate feeling due to its abiding interest in relations and connections.[19]

The fact that there *are* two kinds or dimensions of experience is important, since the assumption of a merely one-sided kind of experience (reflective: the clear, distinct, and cognitive) makes any inquiry focusing on experience (psychology, epistemology, metaphysics) myopic and incomplete. The results of such inquiries are often puzzles, dead ends, and esoteric descriptions at odds with common sense. Given the primary focus of this chapter, psychology, what is important is that Dewey's approach to the psychology and phenomenology of experience insists that both 'had' and 'known' experiencing are equally valid objects of inquiry. In effect, he dares psychologists to stop treating reflective thought as the paradigm so that they might then reintegrate reflective experience into a more expansive and connected theory of experience, culture, and nature.

This chapter's focus on psychology has necessarily related experience to the creature's side of things. Nature (or environment) has been mentioned largely as the complement to organisms. It is important to realize, however, that experience and nature do not merely exist, side by side, however compatibly. Rather, experience and physical events exist on a continuum, and it is our own categorizing activity that sets some events apart as 'nature'.

> Experience emerges from interaction . . . There is . . . an inher-
> ent rhythm or shape to life as it oscillates between phases of
> stability and of instability . . . When sensation and conscious
> experience occur, they may be seen as a broadening and
> deepening of this character . . . Growth is the establishment of
> continuity . . . There is, in short, a dynamic rhythmic and
> growing nature to all interaction; experience exemplifies this in
> a heightened degree.
>
> (Alexander 1987, 127)

In short, our typical experiences – of feeling, habit, imagination
– do not simply arise, *deus ex machina*, in dumb and lifeless
creatures. Rather, these qualities emerge as they sum up the
accumulations of increasingly organized interactions.[20] In
Dewey's post-Darwinian and ecological account, 'nature' can
no longer be simply thought of as strictly 'external' to experiencing subjects. Nature is an affair of affairs, the dynamic and
changing arena of organismic change and adaptation.

Conclusion

The answers sought by philosophy and psychology are meaningful because they relate to tensions over how we are living –
and who we might become. We question what it means, for
example, to have a sexual orientation, a disposition toward
alcohol, or a high IQ because we are seeking insight into
ourselves and guidance for future action. In contrast to analytic
approaches that rely upon physically-based causes (for example,
neurological brain states) for explanations of conduct's meaning,
Dewey's theories of mind, body, and behavior *start* from an
expanded and meaningful standpoint, a practical starting
point. Human experience is what it is because it *already* consists
of shared meanings, produced with language in acts of social

participation. This does not mean psychology should not study the biological component of psychic experience, but it should be sanguine about the limits imposed by that approach. As Alexander puts it, 'an analysis of the body alone will not give us the mind' (Alexander 1987, 151).

Human experience, in other words, is tied up with meaning, and meaning is by its nature social and pragmatic. Thus, the human psychological phenomena most important to us cannot be satisfactorily expressed only with mechanisms, no matter how finely modeled. 'Personality, selfhood, subjectivity', Dewey writes, 'are eventual functions that emerge with complexly organized interactions, organic and social' (LW1:162). What psychology and indeed any philosophical theory must keep in mind is that every classification made is rooted in factors extrinsic to the thing or event studied itself. We study things for reasons, and those reasons are extrinsic to the thing itself. Every classification is an interpretation of one kind or another; what remains to be determined is how well an interpretation performs in satisfying the original requirements of the inquiry.

The upshot here is particularly troubling for those in psychology who press for it the tribute of 'hard science'. For the answers psychology offers can, by Dewey's lights, never be fixed; not only is it a changing discipline in a changing world, but the questions posed will come from different groups with different concerns – with different 'bodies of fact that are remote and extraneous' (LW1:256). With shift of need comes shift of interpretation. But instead of despairing that truth is a moving target never to be struck, we can reimagine psychology as a philosophy of experience, which can, with constant effort, become increasingly effective at addressing what is problematic about contemporary living.

2
Inquiry: knowledge, meaning, and action

Intelligence becomes ours in the degree in which we use it and
accept responsibility for consequences. It is not ours originally or
by production . . . Thoughts sprout and vegetate; ideas prolifer-
ate. They come from deep unconscious sources . . . Our active
body of habits appropriates it. The suggestion then becomes an
assertion. It no longer merely comes to us. It is accepted and
uttered by us. We act upon it and thereby assume, by implica-
tion, its consequences. The stuff of belief and proposition is not
originated by us. It comes to us from others, by education, tradition and the suggestion of the environment. Our intelligence is
bound up, so far as its materials are concerned, with the community life of which we are a part. We know what it communicates
to us, and know according to the habits it forms in us. Science is
an affair of civilization not of individual intellect.

(MW14:216)

The quest for certainty is a quest for a peace which is assured,
an object which is unqualified by risk and the shadow of fear
which action casts.

(LW4:7)

Introduction

What is knowledge? What is truth? Can creatures in a world of
sensation and appearance discover beliefs that are not just

opinion (temporary or mistaken) but real knowledge (permanent and certain)? Is knowledge even possible? Such questions are typical of 'epistemology' (the study of knowledge), and have long been identified by many with the aims of philosophy itself. As we will see, Dewey neither identifies philosophy with epistemology nor agrees with the deepest metaphysical assumptions that give life to traditional epistemology's 'big' questions.[1] Instead, he approaches issues of belief, knowledge, and truth from an evolutionary standpoint. Seen in this light, such concepts must be interpreted within the context of a dynamic, natural world where creatures struggle to adapt and thrive. To promote this dramatically different standpoint, Dewey finds himself obligated to critique traditional accounts of knowledge and truth, diagnose the reasons they came about, and then reconstruct them as his own proposal. His proposal for epistemology is called 'instrumentalism'.

This chapter, then, has three main parts: critique, diagnosis, and proposal. It starts by briefly examining Dewey's critique of three dominant epistemological schools: empiricism, rationalism, and Kantianism. Next it explains Dewey's diagnoses for the sources of those schools' errors. This chapter then explores Dewey's proposal for how knowing *emerges* as a kind of adaptive activity, along with several of knowing's most important patterns: doubt, belief, inquiry, and judgment. It concludes by summarizing the fate, in Dewey's hands, of two beloved and ancient concepts: knowledge and truth.

Critique and diagnosis: classical empiricism, rationalism, and Kant

Dewey's 'instrumentalism' (a name he abandoned toward the end of his career), responds to tensions between two historically dominant schools in epistemology (rationalism and classical empiricism), as well as to Immanuel Kant's attempt to supersede those approaches. To situate Dewey, here is a brief encapsulation of tensions between these approaches.

All sides agreed that we clearly *seem* to know things. Debates arose over the degree to which perceptions and/or concepts are responsible for knowledge. Classical empiricists stressed the role of sense experience. They worried that because the methods of their rival, rationalism, sought only to trace knowledge to thought itself – rather than relating it to particular sensory observations – it is unchecked (and uncheck*able*) by the evidence before our eyes. Such an approach ensures that epistemology remains cut off from actual experience – while at the same time preserving, uncritically, authoritative and dogmatic epistemologies of past philosophers. Part of empiricism's concern was for scientific progress. If science were to usefully advance, it needed to divorce itself from speculation and take perceptual encounters more seriously. Classical empiricist epistemology, then, insisted that knowledge originates only in sense experience; the mind starts out as a receptive, blank slate on which the physical world inscribes its replica, in the form of ideas. The association of ideas generates knowledge; with luck, mind becomes the mirror of nature.

Rationalism, for its part, refused to concede that sense experience could *ever* produce knowledge. Consider the character of sense experience: individual, fluid, and relative to a variety of externally produced circumstances. If philosophy is supposed to explain genuine knowledge – which is unchanging, self-evident, and certain – then clearly philosophy's methods must not draw upon a fluctuating, external world. It should rely on certain, inner concepts. Rationalist epistemology, then, argued that knowledge is abstract and deductively certain, an end in itself not tied to any practical purpose. Knowledge is produced by the mind, an immaterial entity with a capacity to reason and think that is innate and independent of its temporary housing, the material body.

In short, the views are at loggerheads. Empiricism maintains that an objective, external world writes its story elements in our minds; when we can express that story in an order that corresponds to the world, there is objective knowledge. Rationalism argues that knowledge is not an inner–outer correspondence but a coherence of inner concepts; this harmony is grasped not by the senses but by the introspective light of consciousness shining on its own conceptual landscape.

Into the chasm dividing empiricism and rationalism stepped Immanuel Kant. Kant argues that philosophy should rein in its ambition and stop pretending it can transcend the limits of experience. Philosophy's proper inquiry is to discover what can *possibly* be known in experience. Kant's account refuses to assign a predominant role to either perceptions or concepts; instead he argues that we have a permanent intellectual apparatus and set of categories that constrain how we can take up new sensory experiences. Speaking roughly, the mind does not make the world, nor does the world make the mind. There is freedom in how we think the world, but it is constrained and not absolute.

In Dewey's view, Kant fails to adequately address the problems of rationalism and empiricism. While Kant wisely criticizes the zealotry of the earlier schools' objectives, he unfortunately retains the schools' sharp distinction between intellect and nature by simply moving an absolute authority (of, say, Platonic Forms or God) into the universal structure of rational minds. He also retains the traditional assumption that knowledge must be *certain*, which results, Dewey argues, in a deeply inconsistent view of knowledge. Kant's empiricism states that one cannot appeal to things beyond possible experience as sources of knowledge and yet he also posits – without sufficient justification – an ideal realm of things-in-themselves that exists beyond possible experience. This 'noumenal' realm is central to Kant's project, for it makes possible free will, morality, and sensory appearances as well.

Kant's solution was unacceptable to Dewey for one other important reason. On Kant's account, the sensations which are necessary ingredients of knowledge are, initially, *inherently* inchoate. This sensory flux is never observed because it must first be formatted by mental categories to be experienced at all. But by what argument, Dewey objects, can we assume that sensation is initially like this? Dewey finds no satisfactory support for this assumption; instead, like William James, he chooses to start from the standpoint of 'radical empiricism'. On this view, experience *as we have it* is comprehensible, at least in part. It is also inherently relational; we do not begin with atomized bits of experience and then subsequently stitch them together. The relatedness of things is as present to direct experience as the objects themselves.

For Dewey, then, Kant fails to push far enough toward a philosophical perspective that can merge concept and perception, reason and nature, theory and practice. While Kant's active mental model was a clear improvement over the two previous passive ones, he unfortunately maintains their conviction that the mark of knowledge resides in an idea's faithful mirroring of realities beyond experience. For Kant, as for the others, the significance of ideas' power to predict, control, or guide future experiences remains irrelevant to knowledge.

For these reasons, Dewey came to believe that only a whole-hearted naturalism – an ecological conception of experience – could improve upon rationalism, classical empiricism, *and* Kantianism. That naturalism, outlined in the previous chapter, makes experience central to living (as well as knowing) by enlarging and activating it. Experience includes 'adaptive courses of action, habits, active functions, [and] connections of doing and undergoing' (MW12:131–32).[2]

Thus, the pragmatic or instrumental view of mind and knowledge begins by rejecting all three approaches to knowledge. Intelligence is no longer just a product of evolution, but stands now as an instrument or tool actively guiding evolutionary processes. As an epistemological theory, instrumentalism is completely at home within evolutionary naturalism; within this framework, the determination of knowledge is akin to how we judge the value of a hand or eye – by how well we are empowered to adapt and thrive in an environment: 'What measures [knowledge's] value, its correctness and truth, is the degree of its availability for conducting to a successful issue the activities of living beings' (MW4:180).

Dewey's efforts at resituating epistemology within a natural framework were often met by the non-comprehension or incredulity of peers, whose tradition-bound approaches required that knowledge be related to something fixed and non-natural. Thus, Dewey knew that if he wished to convince others that human meaning and intelligence emerge from the struggles and satisfactions shared by most other natural organisms, he would first have to help diagnose why there was such fervent resistance.[3]

One important source of resistance, according to Dewey, was an entrenched view of 'reality' and its corresponding view of knowledge. Definitions of 'knowledge' vary greatly, of course, but running through most of them is the central tenet that 'knowledge' is the result of a reflective activity which gives corporeal residents (of a changing world) access to a realm of ideas (which never changes). In essence, this view of knowledge makes it magical. Since knowledge is the spell that can take us beyond the world of sense and illusion, it must be more than illusion itself. Knowledge conveys our minds to the really real, and so it too must be really real. 'The commonest assumption of philosophies', Dewey writes,

> common even to philosophies very different from one another, is the assumption of the identity of objects of knowledge and ultimately real objects. The assumption is so deep that it is

usually not expressed; it is taken for granted as something so fundamental that it does not need to be stated.

(LW1:26–7)

This assumption about knowledge is grounded on a very peculiar metaphysical picture: a two-tiered reality. One tier is familiar to everyone: the mundane and bodily world of change; growth and decay, sensation and movement, etc. The opposing tier is also familiar: the 'divine' and ideational world of permanence; this is the realm of fixity and eternity, pure intellect and spirit – the realm of God. The problems that develop for philosophy, and for what Dewey refers to as the 'industry of epistemology', stemmed from the fact that these two tiers are *so* different that it becomes necessary to explain not what knowledge is or how to get it, but *how knowledge in general is even possible*. How could beings in a realm of *change* have ideas which are actually native to an eternal and *permanent* one? Or, rephrasing the problem in more modern language, 'How could a mind get beyond its own thoughts and feelings to know the objective world?'

So far we have seen that one's assumption of a two-tiered model of reality leads to the belief that knowledge itself has a special and ultimate metaphysical status. However, there is a second consequence of assuming the two-tiered model, and this too helps explain why Dewey's naturalist epistemology was resisted so vehemently.

Those who investigate the phenomenon of knowing with a deep-rooted belief in a two-tiered reality unconsciously start their inquiry from a standpoint that is deeply prejudiced toward what is permanent over what is changing. As they inquire, they are apt to commit what Dewey calls 'the philosophic fallacy', and it happens when one converts the discovery of an eventual function into an antecedent existence. For example, in examining how people think, one might notice that it is common for people to infer a general pattern from similar instances. The philosophic fallacy would do more than record that there is this function; instead, it would convert the function into an antecedently existing mental power – for example, a 'faculty' of induction – as if it had *always* been part of the mind's ultimate structure. I hope it is clear that characterizing discoveries in this way is, in effect, a subtle but unjustified imposition of one's metaphysical prejudice toward permanence. To discover that 'there is this activity of inference in such and such cases' simply cannot license conclusions about some *ultimate* inductive faculty of the mind.

A philosopher's habit of intellectual reflection, then, can remove her from the living and problematic situations that initially motivated inquiry. Over time, this habit of approaching inquiry from a purely theoretical starting point can become institutionalized; the result is a tradition of philosophers engaged in these practices and the construction – out of living processes of questioning – of ultimate metaphysical explanations of how things *really* are. The lamentable result, Dewey notes, 'is invariably some desiccation and atomizing of the world in which we live or of ourselves' (LW6:7).

Dewey proposed an alternative way of doing philosophy, which begins with a different approach to experience. Rather than starting out with intellectual or theoretical assumptions – and then committing the philosophic fallacy – Dewey adopts James's radically empirical (or practical) starting point.[4] Taking this fresh and unprejudiced attitude toward experience would free philosophy in several ways. For one, philosophy would finally be free to investigate, as natural phenomena, culture's imaginative (as well as reflective) artifacts: its 'magic, myth, politics, painting, and penitentiaries' (LW1:28). Philosophy would also be freed from fruitless quests to solve illusionary problems, such as how knowledge *in general* is possible or whether we can ever know 'the external world' or 'other minds'.

Let us consider just one such issue, 'the problem of knowledge in general'. When traditional philosophy attempts to answer this problem, it first must *deny* the fact that there actually *have been* many past successes at knowing specific things. Because it denies that there have been past cases of knowledge, it also neglects to conduct any useful empirical surveys as to *why* those successes worked. In lieu of this approach, Dewey suggests we be radically empirical about knowledge. 'Why not', Dewey writes, 'take the best authenticated cases of faithful reports which are available, compare them with the sufficiently numerous cases of reports ascertained to be unfaithful and doubtful, and see what we find' (MW13:60). In other words, approaching knowing as an empirical and scientific process creates no 'general' problem of knowledge! We find that there are 'specific instances of success and failure in inquiry' and we find that studying them helps us identify better 'ways of going about the business of inquiry' (MW10:23). The project of collecting, organizing, and systematically stating these findings about the conditions of inquiry amounts to 'logic', which is redefined as a general and 'important aid in proper guidance of further attempts at knowing' (MW10:23).[5]

The point is that some of traditional epistemology's most important 'problems' are not problematic at all. They have consumed philosophers' time and energy because their foundational metaphysical assumptions have remained unquestioned. By criticizing these underlying assumptions, Dewey hopes to show that epistemology's genuine problems are methodological, not metaphysical. The difficulties we encounter while trying to know things, Dewey writes, 'imply a difference between knowledge and error consequent upon right and wrong *methods of inquiry and testing*; *not a difference between experience and the world*' (MW10:23; emphasis mine). On Dewey's naturalistic account, knowing is something that occurs as we live, amid a range of other activities. The human capacity to reflect does not point beyond experience to something 'really real' but refers to 'the contextual situation in which thinking occurs' (LW1:61). The starting point of epistemology is not general wonder or the desire to penetrate illusion; the starting point 'is the actually *problematic*, and that the problematic phase resides in some actual and specifiable situation' (LW1:61).

Knowing as organic functioning

We come now to Dewey's proposal regarding how knowing arises in nature, and how we think. Dewey's epistemological naturalism starts from the fact that we are *in* and *of* this world, and that knowing is not a flash of divine insight but rather 'a connection of things which depend upon other and more primary connections between a self and things; [and] . . . which grows out of these more fundamental connections and . . . operates in their interests at specifiable crises' (MW6:119). Dewey's account of knowing must explain how it fits into a natural continuum (spanning brute physical existences, bodies, minds, and conscious experience) as well as how it operates. How, for example, do knowledge and intelligence *emerge* from the natural world?

Dewey's view explains the emergence of intelligence by describing how individual organisms behave in the two most basic contexts possible: stable and precarious environments. In the stable context, the individual is a contented member of its environment:

> There is the individual that belongs in a continuous system of connected events which reinforce its activities and which form a world in which it is at home, consistently at one with its own preferences, satisfying its requirements. Such an individual is in its world as a member, extending as far as the moving equilibrium of which it is a part lends support.
>
> (LW1:188)

In the second, precarious context, the individual is in conflict with its environment:

> Then there is the individual that finds a gap between its distinctive bias and the operations of the things through which alone its need can be satisfied; it is broken off, discrete, because it is at odds with its surroundings. It either surrenders, conforms, and for the sake of peace becomes a parasitical subordinate, indulges in egotistical solitude; or its activities set out to remake conditions in accord with desire.
>
> (LW1:188)

Knowing (and intelligence) *emerge* as functions that allow organisms actively to reconstruct precarious situations in ways that suit their imperatives. In that process, Dewey writes, 'intelligence is born . . . mind as individualized, initiating, adventuring, experimenting, dissolving [is also born]' (LW1:188).

Knowing does not develop for every species. It is a specific, signifying response (or function) that only develops given the prior development of more basic abilities (such as inhibition, feeling or sentiency, and anticipation). When an organism has *both* the need to address precarious circumstances *and* the ability to suspend overt action in anticipation of future possibilities, then the conditions are in place for signifying acts. Such acts treat the stimulus differently; rather than reacting immediately in one way or another, the stimulus is treated as a sign of something else. (As we saw in the child–candle example, the flame-stimulus can become a sign of something dangerous.) In contrast to the tradition, the creation of 'signs' or 'concepts' is neither a miraculous nor a purely subjective transformation of physical events. Rather, a brute stimulus becomes a sign-function when an organism considers that stimulus *in connection with* new and future possibilities. The stimulus is recast as a sign – as a function that signifies.

Signs are not transcendental but natural occurrences, without any essential nature.[6] Whether some actual event *is* a sign depends on functional and pragmatic factors, such as whether it can be employed as such in a particular situation. Does a wisp of smoke 'mean' fire? Only if it reliably *functions as a sign of fire in cases of actual trial*. In other words, a sign requires testing to evaluate its helpfulness as a function. This account is distinctively 'pragmatic' insofar as 'experiment or action enters to make the connection between the thing signifying and the thing signified so that inference may pass from hypothesis to knowledge' (MW13:53). *As a sign* smoke must do more than merely 'point' to fire; as a sign it fulfills some specific function within a larger situation – it directs me to be cautious, or soak the area with water, or yell hello to my barbecuing buddies, etc.

Like signifying, knowing is a kind of function; in particular, knowing is a certain *use* of signs. Given an organism's ability to take objective affairs (things and events) as signs, knowing is the ability to use signs as evidence for something (past or future), and then adjust its responses informed by these inferences. As beings gain expertise at using signs, they become better able to forecast the future, form reasonable expectations, and plan strategic responses (see MW10:15–16). Whether or not a being using signs should be called 'knowledgeable' ultimately depends on whether the uses bear practical fruit in future experience.

The foregoing paragraphs hopefully make clear how naturalism describes a framework in which knowing emerges functionally from organic environments. A naturalist framework provides an opportunity for epistemology to start examining *knowing* as a process that is practical and cooperative rather than explaining *knowledge* as the final (even divine) product of theoretical reflection.

Dewey's examination of knowing as a process, and the reconstruction of epistemology's central concepts and problems, has come to be called 'instrumentalism'. Its fundamental idea is that if knowing is a natural function, continuous with the rest of experience, then concepts and ideas are tools or instruments. This approach to knowing rejects traditional dualisms (action vs. thought, theory vs. practice), arguing that these dualisms are not *helpful*. The old theoretical division between action and thought should be replaced with practical distinction 'between blind, slavish, meaningless action and action that is free, significant, directed and responsible' (LW1:324). To understand how the function of knowing develops in a way that makes action 'free, significant, directed and responsible', we need to understand the way inquiry leads us, as C.S. Peirce might say, from doubt to belief.

Dewey's conviction that thinking has biological origins, moral significance, and real effects in the world comes directly from his pragmatist predecessors, in particular William James and Charles S. Peirce (with whom Dewey studied logic in graduate school).[7] Peirce's influential 1877 article 'The Fixation of Belief' argued that reflective inquiry (a term more expansive than the traditional 'reasoning') is born from demands placed upon organisms. The experience of those demands we call 'doubt' and the resolution of those demands we call 'belief'. Peirce writes,

> Doubt is an uneasy and dissatisfied state from which we struggle to free ourselves and pass into the state of belief; while the latter is a calm and satisfactory state which we do not wish to avoid, or to change to a belief in anything else . . . The irritation of doubt causes a struggle to attain a state of belief. I shall term this struggle inquiry, though it must be admitted that this is sometimes not a very apt designation.[8]

Thus, Peirce sets the drive to know – which he calls the 'fixation of belief' – into an explanatory framework that is natural and biological. *This*, he states forthrightly, is where epistemology *must start*, not from the standpoints that radically doubt everything possible (Descartes) or that begin with distinct realms of ideas and substance (Locke). Philosophy must start with life as it finds it.

Still, while all feel the sting of doubt, there are, Peirce and Dewey realize, *many* ways people can (and do) deal with the anxiety of uncertainty and doubt. There are many ways to 'fix belief', and some are better than others. Some responses just avoid a problematic issue (change the subject) or obstinately cling to what they already believe. Others decide the issue by simple appeal to an authoritative text or figure. Still others invent fantastic means to deal with the problem – imagining logical or factual scenarios (like winning the lottery) that dissolve, at least temporarily, subjective feelings of anxiety. However, Peirce says, there is still one other method for allaying doubt and fixing belief. While it may be more arduous than the others, in the long run it leads more effectively to satisfactory solutions for both immediate and long-term problems. This method cannot promise guaranteed or perfect solutions. It cannot promise comfort. Its virtue rests in the fact that those who use it to confront problems do so by developing beliefs aligned with *facts* and not just with wishes. Peirce calls it the 'method of science', while Dewey calls it, among other things, 'reflection', 'reflective thinking', 'method of inquiry', or just 'inquiry'.

The pattern of inquiry What does it mean to think reflectively? How is this useful method called inquiry supposed to work? An answer can begin by looking briefly at what Dewey called 'the pattern of inquiry'. This pattern is composed of phases or stages observable in our experience.[9] To keep the discussion simple, here is a five-phase breakdown.

Phase 1: *An indeterminate situation in which a difficulty is felt – 'Something's wrong . . .'* Inquiry that may become reflective typically does not begin that way; rather it begins by having a feeling that something is wrong (for example, a strange noise wakes me up in the middle of the night and I feel a vague doubt that something is amiss). We should not try to dismiss the doubtful quality as *just* a subjective feeling – it is the *entire situation* which is doubtful, unsettled, or disturbed. '*We* are doubtful', Dewey writes, 'because the situation is inherently doubtful' (LW12:109). If this characterization sounds odd, please recall that Dewey is describing events in a transactional *system* involving both organism and environment. If such interrelational systems truly exist, then we should no longer follow older epistemologies by quarantining doubt exclusively in a subjective doub*ter*.[10]

This first, felt phase is indispensable, and no inquiry could ever get going without it. The feeling of this phase is unique, it has a single pervasive quality: *this* doubtfulness. This quality is necessary for helping us decide how forcefully to respond to it, and once we are inquiring the quality helps regulate further thinking insofar as it forms the background of further inquiry. If we get lost during inquiry we can remind ourselves of how we felt initially.[11]

Phase 2: *The institution of a problem; its location and definition* – '*The problem seems to be . . .*' Beyond the initial feeling of a doubtful or uncertain situation, a problem must be described in definite terms. But problems do not preexist inquiry as an exam problem might await students who have not yet arrived at school. Rather, the indeterminate situation *becomes problematic* as we subject it to inquiry and judge that it is 'a problem' (see LW12:111). In addition to judging *that* it is a problem, we judge *how* it is – we define it. Whether we define the problem adequately is crucial to whether it can be resolved in a satisfactory manner. 'The way in which the problem is conceived', Dewey writes, 'decides what specific suggestions are entertained and which are dismissed; what data are selected and which rejected; it is the criterion for relevancy and irrelevancy of hypotheses and conceptual structures' (LW12:112).

Revisiting this phase of inquiry is typical, even after further inquiry has taken place. This is because identifying the precise character of a problem is crucial and therefore requires a great deal of experimentation and ingenuity. Indeed, often what is first thought to be *the* problem changes and early characterizations are revised or amended. (Ironically, the character of a problem usually becomes fully definite only after a satisfactory solution is in sight.)

Phase 3: *Hypothesis of a possible solution* – '*Maybe what I should do is . . .*' After provisionally defining the problem, inquiry proceeds by hypotheses that go beyond what is immediately felt and observed to something absent – a possible solution. Hypothesis utilizes both the perceptual facts and theoretical ideas making up the situation by putting them into conceptual play with one another. In this imaginative process, past facts are used to make forecasts about the consequences of executing various operations under observed conditions (see LW 12:113).

Skilled hypothesizers pay unusual attention to detail and proceed cautiously; when more information is needed, a hypothesis is embraced only tentatively – as a 'working' hypothesis. Sometimes, creating a hypothesis adequate to the task requires revisiting earlier phases of inquiry to make more observations or reconsider the ideas defining the contours of the problem-so-far. This phase of inquiry is quite risky, without definite rules; patience, courage, and artistry are all very important virtues for creators of successful hypotheses. Like any other creative skill, though, it can be cultivated.

Phase 4: *Reasoning out the bearings of the suggestion* – '*Doing that would mean . . .*' In the fourth phase of inquiry, which Dewey calls 'reasoning', the meanings of ideas central to the hypothesis are analyzed and an estimate of possible consequences is made. Since words can have multiple meanings (depending on audience, context, and practical implications), a phase which traces out possible meanings and their relations can help uncover meanings and consequences, perhaps undesirable ones, which are not immediately apparent. For example, imagine an inquiry about immigration which formulated its key hypothesis in language that described border crossings as 'invasions'. Here the phases of reasoning could help cast light on the meanings implied by 'invasions'. Illuminating those meanings, in turn, could reveal unforeseen consequences provoked by using these meanings – such as vigilantism. Thus, the connection between the way the hypothesis is worded and the possible events would demonstrate that the language of the initial hypothesis requires revision.

Meaning analysis, then, performs a quality check on hypotheses. Hypotheses which seem plausible may not survive, while others which seem implausible at first can gain new vigor on deeper inspection. (One can imagine how implausible the hypothesis of vaccination must have seemed at first!) Either way, this phase moves inquiry ahead because it can winnow the list of hypotheses down to those which stand the best chance of resolving the indeterminate or problematic situation.

Phase 5: *Active experimental or observational testing of the hypothesis – 'Let's try this and see what happens . . .'* The final phase of inquiry engages in the actual testing and evaluation of hypotheses not eliminated in earlier phases. Depending on the nature of the problem, confirmation of a hypothesis may come through simple observation; often, more complicated experimentation is needed. What is crucial to underline here is the Peircean point that only meanings *tested in action* (either observation or experiment) can justify a conclusion of inquiry.[12] Theory must be validated in practice. As a theory of meaning, this notion that ideas or concepts are made meaningful by action or test is 'pragmatism'.

This, then, is the five-phase pattern of inquiry. In sum, inquiry is an active method of responding to problems that involves feeling, abstract analysis, and practical experimentation.

The measure of whether inquiry is successful is the creation of a determinate situation out of one which was indeterminate. Again, inquiry is not a purely logical process – feeling is a useful and orienting presence throughout each phase.

Three caveats about inquiry are worth mentioning. First, inquiry need not begin with unexpected problems; in fact, the growth of knowledge often requires that we stir up scenarios to help us hypothesize about future problems. Such acts of planned anticipation greatly improve the quality of eventual response.[13] Second, the pattern of inquiry Dewey describes is a schematic model; most actual inquiries consist of patterns with less than discrete phases, and with an order that moves forward and back between, say, definition and hypothesis. Movement between phases is dynamic, and what happens at one phase can affect the overall pattern for that inquiry. Third, Dewey does not argue that this pattern of inquiry describes how people *always* think but how they *would* think if they imitated the most exemplary cases of inquiry, such as those of empirical science. Dewey wants to highlight for educators and others the real benefits made possible by science's experimental attitude and its forward-looking belief that 'ideas are statements not of what is or what has been but of acts to be performed' (LW4:112). By explicating the patterns of thought most effective in producing reliable scientific knowledge, Dewey hoped that more general lessons could be drawn from those methods and used by those looking to solve moral, political, and social problems.

No discussion of inquiry would be complete without a brief mention of judgment, for 'the heart of a good habit of thought lies in the power to pass judgments *pertinently* and *discriminatingly*' (LW8:211). While we typically think of judgment as the *final* phase of reflection – the 'verdict' that sums up the facts and orders that actions be taken – for Dewey judgment is a function involved in *every* phase of inquiry, with *both* facts and ideas.

> Judging is the act of selecting and weighing the bearing of facts and suggestions *as they present themselves*, as well as of deciding whether the alleged facts are really facts and whether the idea used is a sound idea or merely a fancy. . . . [A] person of sound judgment is one who . . . is a good judge of relative values; he can estimate, appraise, evaluate, with tact and discernment.
>
> (LW8:210)

Judging is no mere act of synthesis, but operates at multiple points in inquiry, in both analytic and synthetic ways. Consider a cook with 'good judgment'. He monitors the occasion of the meal (*judging* the problematic situation) as he chooses ingredients and tools (*judging* facts) and orchestrates these to prepare the meal (*judging* methods or ideas). Were we to formalize this aspect of judgment, we could see three important 'judgment moments' in inquiry: (1) judgment about how to 'take' the initial problematic situation; (2) judgments about how to sift, define, and elaborate the facts and ideas proffered as relevant; and (3) judgment in its usual sense, the issuing of a final decision that satisfies the initial inquiry while also providing a rule or principle for future inquiries.

No judgment, Dewey says, is ever *absolutely* right or wrong, *per se*. This is because each judgment is situated within a specific inquiry and outcomes are always modified by the specific purposes, stakes, and personal perspectives in play. For example, my judgment to give away a loaf of bread to someone who is hungry is affected by whether I am giving it to a mendicant at my door or to someone with whom I am sharing a lifeboat on the open sea. Moreover, the judgment is made not from a completely neutral standpoint but by *me* – with my habits of understanding and whatever store of previous meanings and experiences I have had. Judgment is never perfectly final, neutral or mechanical; it is provisional, perspectival and organic.[14]

Knowledge and truth

At last we come to the terms 'knowledge' and 'truth'. The reason they arrive so late in our discussion is that Dewey believed both were misleading terms whose importance had been vastly overinflated by philosophy. First, let us consider knowledge. If we accept Dewey's account of the dynamic ways that our biological and cultural environments create and shape our inquiries, it becomes easy to see why the traditional emphasis on knowledge – i.e., an abstract possession of wise and skilled persons – must be dropped. 'Knowledge, as an abstract term', Dewey warns, 'is a name for the product of competent inquiries. Apart from this relation, its meaning is so empty that any content or filling may be arbitrarily poured in' (LW12:16). In short, if one wants to understand the *product*, knowledge, one must go to the *process*, inquiry. That is what we have done above.

The denial of the importance of knowledge is, ultimately, a denial of the picture in which mind is a substance separable from the rest of nature. It is an affirmation of a picture that describes the mind's activities as strategic moves made by organisms to the pressures of living affairs. Contrary to some fears, Dewey's redescription does not depreciate knowing. Indeed, Dewey is explicitly about the mediating role knowing can play at moments of individual and societal conflict. 'The life of all thought', Dewey writes, 'is to effect a junction at some point of the new and the old, of deep-sunk customs and unconscious dispositions, that are brought to the light of attention by some conflict with newly emerging directions of activity' (LW3:6).

The study of how we think and of inquiry has enormous value for human beings, whether it is called 'epistemology' or not. But the scope of what we must take into consideration as relevant to epistemology and logic must expand far beyond the semantic and symbolic, to the biological and cultural aspects of life.

> Logic is a social discipline . . . [E]very inquiry grows out of a background of culture and takes effect in greater or less modification of the conditions out of which it arises. Merely physical contacts with physical surroundings occur. But in every inter-action that involves intelligent direction, the physical environment is part of a more inclusive social or cultural environment.
>
> (LW12:27)

What of truth? Like knowledge, Dewey finds the term 'truth' a misleading term, one that smacks of finality, certainty, and correspondence with real reality. Thus, it is of little use for Dewey's inquiry into human inquiry and judgment. That being said, he does give accounts of truth. This should not be taken as proof he thought truth existed in a traditional sense. Given his rejection of 'a reality beyond ours', such efforts should be seen as dialectical; that is, Dewey defines 'truth' mainly because his interlocutors refused to consider his theory of inquiry sympa-thetically *until* they had heard his stand about the nature of truth. Here is one of Dewey's (reluctant) definitions of truth:

> The 'truth' [of any present proposition] is, by the definition, subject to the outcome of continued inquiries; *its* 'truth', if the word must be used, is provisional; as *near* the truth as inquiry has *as yet* come, a matter determined *not* by a guess at some future belief but by the care and pains with which inquiry has been conducted up to the present time.
>
> (LW14:56–7)

Notice how Dewey's definition directs attention back upon the *process* of inquiry, the *event* of truth-making. Truth is a label characterizing what *inquiry* has come up with – in *that* situation, for *those* purposes. But since new problems crop up all the time, we should never expect to be finally confident about the certainty of any belief inquiry has produced. 'The attainment of settled beliefs', Dewey writes, 'is a progressive matter; there is no belief so settled as not to be exposed to further inquiry' (LW12:16). If we need to honor a statement by calling it 'true' or 'knowledge', let us follow science in thinking that we honor it because it is settled enough to be a *resource* for future inquiries. To say it is *true* that 'Fresh bread, when eaten, provides nourishment' is to announce that this belief can be used reliably as a conceptual ingredient in future inquiries. It is *not* a statement about the way the world *really* is.

There is a function to 'truth' that needs to be preserved; we need to identify which assertions have proved useful or reliable. For these reasons, Dewey begins to use 'warrant' or 'warranted assertibility' to capture the element in his theory closest to traditional truth (or 'knowledge' in its honorific sense of true-belief). Saying that a statement or proposition 'warrants assertion' is useful but not misleading, as it indicates that inquiries which rely on it can proceed with confidence.

Conclusion

For too long, philosophers have presented themselves as gatekeepers of knowledge, truth, and reality. Epistemology has become an industry of self-appointed experts solving puzzles they have produced themselves. These roles, Dewey believes, are priestly, undemocratic, and false. Paying attention to one's experience – indeed, one's everyday life and needs – reveals that knowing copes with a world neither completely within us nor without us. In this world – our *life* – we confront obstacles, formulate problems, devise solutions, and act experimentally. Knowing and living must be connected; Dewey does this first by explaining the natural roots of inquiry, and then by detailing how inquiry can work (over a diverse range of situations) to make life better.

Dewey hopes that instrumentalism (and pragmatism) can benefit many areas of life. In 'What Pragmatism Means by Practical', he points out that 'it lies in the nature of pragmatism that it should be applied as widely as possible; and to things as diverse as controversies, beliefs, truths, ideas, and objects' (MW4:101). If pragmatism is to be an honest philosophy, it must live by its own rules and become, Dewey writes, 'not a contemplative survey of existence nor an analysis of what is past and done with, but an outlook upon future possibilities with reference to attaining the better and averting the worse. Philosophy must take, with good grace, its own medicine' (MW10:37–8). Philosophy and pragmatism 'take their own medicine' as long as they present themselves as keenly aware that their own concepts and conclusions are provisional, capable of revision or rejection. Whether Dewey exemplifies this attitude must be left, for now, to the reader.

3

Morality: character, conduct, and moral experience

Introduction: moral experience and critique of traditional ethics

For many in the Western tradition, the primary ethical question has been 'Why be moral? Why should one do something that is not in one's interest?'[1] The question is based on the belief that morality is not something anyone *wants* to embrace – one must be persuaded it is *in one's interest* to be moral, and that morality, at its core, is a constraint on what one would *really* like to do. The assumption behind the central importance of this question – and the reaction mentioned above to it – is that morality is something imposed by an external source, be it a transcendental authority (God, Nature, Reason, etc.) or supra-individual custom (society, religion, cultural traditions, etc.). Moral *experience*, as understood by this framework, is something radically distinct from everyday experiences of domestic and industrial relations; moreover, there is implied a special moral *realm* which, while not as obviously extra-mundane as the realm called 'spiritual', is nevertheless seen as deserving the specialized study of moral theorists.

For Dewey, morality is not like this. Looking at everyday life, one sees how moral concerns permeate much of experience and require nearly constant deliberation and choice of action, whether issues are minute or momentous. To take 'Why be moral?' as the *central* question of ethics struck Dewey as absurd, and he responds with an alternative that critiques traditional assumptions and reconstructs ethics in a way that emphasizes the integral connections between human beings, nature, and society. No man is an island, the poet says; for Dewey this means more than 'no man is self-sufficient'. It means that each person's identity exists only in virtue of social interaction. Just as one is a 'fullback' in soccer only through existing relations to other positions (and the rules), humans are moral individuals in-and-through their interactions with groups. Economists speak of 'interest satisfaction' as if human conduct could be understood by aggregating the preferences of numerous atomic individuals. But no 'interest' is never meaningful in such strict isolation; interests (needs, desires) are meaningful only as understood within the social and historical contexts that help form them.

These examples help introduce a central Deweyan point: any moral theory that assumes a model of experience that views interaction as *accidental* – as something happening to already-formed individuals – is superficial. For Dewey, experience is the complex interplay and transaction of one-as-participant-and-product of the world; it is inadequate for moral theories to depict moral agents as inert atoms, pushed around by the gravity of custom; nor is it appropriate to vest in each agent a moral universe unto herself. Traditional theoretical choices (objective realism *or* subjective idealism) falsify and obscure moral experience's complexity. In part tradition errs by assuming an inadequate model of human nature and conduct; in part, it errs by seeking a moral theory aspiring to the rigor of Newtonian physics. But such approaches are too abstract, spectatorial, and fixated on certainty to be of use to real people with problems. As Gregory Pappas put it,

> Dewey's concern with ethics arose out of his perception that individuals and institutions had not been able to find viable alternatives to the moral absolutism offered by custom and

authority, on the one side, and the subjectivistic views supported by moral philosophers on the other. He thought that such ethical theories, as well as the economic and political institutions that depend upon and perpetuate them, have tended to encourage habits and attitudes that impoverish moral life.

(Pappas in Hickman 1998, 101–2)

Dewey offers both a redescription of moral experience and a reconstruction of ethical theory based on this new understanding of our living moral realities. 'If moral theory is *in* and *for* our moral life', Pappas writes of Dewey, 'then one cannot determine what an adequate ethical theory will be without considering what kind of moral theory works better within our actual moral lives' (Pappas in Hickman 1998, 104). Dewey demonstrates that, contrary to traditional assumptions, philosophy should not attempt to reconcile the diametrical opposition between interest and morality assumed by 'Why be moral?' Instead, philosophy should critique past theories' mistaken descriptions (of moral experience, ends) and prescriptions (about how to live) to equip individuals and communities with more constructive methods for addressing problems.

To understand Dewey's ethics, begin with the dramatic statement: 'moral life is tragic'. If moral theory begins from the practical starting point of everyday life, what is found? First and foremost that living consistently involves us in situations both precarious and stable. Prosperity is suddenly shattered by adversity and a struggle to adjust ensues. Stability may be more or less recovered, but even this lasts a relatively short while. For those living in hope of constant harmony, the above picture is, at best, a compromise, and at worst, tragic (blamable perhaps on our expulsion from the Garden of Eden). Moreover, traditional ethics typically rejects this practical starting point altogether. Rather than accept, as a basis for theorizing, the genuinely precarious and conflictual nature of human life, political and ethical theories have sought certainty instead. This pursuit of certainty has required the invention of a separate realm for ethical concepts. 'Moral philosophers', Pappas writes,

> have consistently sought to prove that there exist, independently of the 'phenomenal' changes that occur in the world, special moral precepts that are universal, fixed, certain, and unchanging. But in Dewey's view, change, conflict, contingency, uncertainty, and struggle are at the very heart of moral experience.

> (Pappas in Hickman 1998, 107)

The first key, then, to understanding Dewey's ethics is 'moral experience'. Moral experience, as defined in Dewey's and Tufts' 1908 book *Ethics*, 'is . . . that kind of conduct in which there are ends so discrepant, so incompatible, as to require selection of one and rejection of the other' (MW5:194). In contrast to cases where one knows, automatically, what to do, for Dewey 'only *deliberate* action, conduct into which *reflective* choice enters, is *distinctively moral*, for only then does there enter the question of *better* and *worse*' (MW14:193, emphasis mine). The gravity of the choice, it is worth noting, does *not* help discriminate 'moral' from 'non-moral'. A momentous decision (for example, to kill another person), given the right circumstances, may raise *no* moral issues while a more trivial decision (to privilege an older child over their siblings) may be rife with moral implications. In other words, the custom of identifying 'moral' choices with 'weighty' ones must be surrendered. For Dewey, the difference between a moral and non-moral experience derives from the agent's need to perceive and select from incompatible alternatives.

Dewey's approach will strike many as counterintuitive. After all, it requires that one reject the deeply ingrained notion that experiences concerning weighty issues (like life and death) are always 'moral'. It also requires that we stop identifying the moral with choices affecting motives, consequences, or aspects of character. Such elements may need to be considered, but what characterizes morality, *per se*, is the existence of a *situation* saturated by conflicting elements which *demands* that engaged agents determine *reflectively* what to value and what ends to pursue.

> It is *incompatibility of ends* which necessitates consideration of the true worth of a given end; and *such consideration* it is which *brings the experience into the moral sphere*. Conduct as moral may thus be defined as activity called forth and directed by ideas of value or worth, where the values concerned are so mutually incompatible as to require consideration and selection before an overt action is entered upon.
>
> (MW5:194, emphasis mine)

A moral situation obtains when one is unable to choose between ends. There may be several causes for the indecision. Perhaps the values of the various ends have, until now, been equal in the agent's view; or perhaps the present juxtaposition of options is so unusual that the agent has never considered them as competitors. Then again, the agent may see that one of the choices entails profound changes in their future character and they are ambivalent about taking that path. Regardless of what best explains any particular case, the difficulties inherent in moral situations help draw attention to another central feature of moral experience: the role of habit.

When a choice stops one cold, at least a pause in physical action is necessary. Like other creatures in a problematic situation, some way forward is needed to cope with the problem, but no immediate solutions present themselves. There is a dearth of habits. Habits are not simple 'hardwired' instructions but sets of functions that embody previously chosen ends; habits are largely responsible for the continuity of conduct. 'Habit' covers not only rudimentary behavioral phenomena such as walking, but many complex skills involved in mating, food-gathering, conversation, and play. Some reach far back into the history of our species and are so automatic we call them 'instinct', while others trace back only into the history of one's nation, family, or individual development.

Most of the time, habits quickly tell us what to do: sniff the mushroom, nod politely, duck the flying object. In such cases, pragmatically, there is no question about which end to pursue and habits smoothly carry us forward. What makes an experience especially 'moral' is that *habits necessary to resolve the problem are missing* (or undeveloped), yet one is aware that a choice for the better *must* be made. In Dewey's view, traditional emphases on 'reason' over 'habit' (a 'mind/body' prejudice, essentially) overlook what is truly crucial to ethical theorizing, namely recognition that what demands discrimination is 'not between reason and habit but between routine, unintelligent habit, and intelligent habit or art' (MW14:55). Rather than addressing problems with the general question, 'What action should one take?', ethics should instead ask 'What *habit* is appropriate for addressing problems of this type, how can it be developed, and how can it be incorporated as a stable feature of conduct?'

Being ethical requires that one knows what to do, and how to keep doing it. Accomplishing this first requires that one criticize approaches that rely upon singular and certain ('magic bullet') answers to moral dilemmas. Regular reliance on such answers rigidifies habit, and makes it less adaptable and successful. (Accepting Dewey's description of moral experience can help resist such reliances.) Being ethical also requires that one understand what moral inquiry is and then engage in it. Such inquiry has both scientific and artistic qualities. Like science, moral inquiry must be broadly empirical, experimental, and hypothetical; like the arts, it must use techniques that are imaginative and dramatic so that deliberation can assist with the widest possible range of morally problematic cases.

One of Dewey's most compact criticisms of traditional ethics is 'Three Independent Factors in Morals' (1930). Consider again the primordial question for much of the ethical tradition: Why be moral? If this is the *central* challenge for ethics, then the answer (if found) should provide an answer that can 'clarify' the conflictual nature of moral problems in a way that is absolute, objective, and certain. A number of ethical systems have been developed to eliminate this uncertainty. One influential approach makes character (or virtue) central; morality, then, is a system of praise and blame organized around the development of a healthy character living a meaningful life. Aristotle is the most famous Western proponent of virtue theory. A second approach makes consequences (or desire) paramount; an action's moral worth is estimated by relating it to the amount of pleasure created for the maximum number of persons. John Stuart Mill and Jeremy Bentham are the most famous proponents of this utilitarian approach. A third approach takes rights (or duty) as central to morality; since a moral agent is a rational being, the morality of any choice is determined not by looking at consequences or character, but by evaluating whether the choice itself was an exclusively rational expression of the agent. Immanuel Kant is the most famous proponent of this deontological ethics.[2]

While these theories diverge at many places, and stand in sharp opposition to one another on fundamental points, Dewey believes that they share several devastating flaws. First, all dismiss the reality of the *uncertainty* that is a part of any moral situation. To them, conflict is mere appearance awaiting philosophy to bring reality (and goodness) as a solution:

> Whatever may be the differences which separate moral theories, all postulate one single principle as an explanation of moral life.

> Under such conditions, it is not possible to have either uncertainty or conflict: morally speaking, the conflict is only specious and apparent. Conflict is, in effect, between good and evil, justice and injustice, duty and caprice, virtue and vice, and is not an inherent part of the good, the obligatory, the virtuous.
>
> (LW5:280)

According to the tradition, moral uncertainty about, say, whether to prolong someone's life on a respirator is no different than, say, the perceptual uncertainty of a stick submerged in water. Is the stick straight or bent? If the stick is part of a world independent of thoughts about it, the stick can only be straight *or* bent – it *is* only one of them, regardless of how much perceptual ambiguity the perceiver *feels*. The same holds, traditionalists reason, about morally ambiguous cases. There must be some *moral way the world is* – some single, determinate reality that is independent of moral agents. Though *we* are morally ambivalent about active euthanasia, we can at least be sure *it* is right or wrong.

Why do philosophers think of reality this way? Dewey argues that the main impetus to *presume* a reality that transcends ordinary experience derives from an age-old 'quest for certainty'. That quest spawned centuries of attempts to demystify reality with grandiose theories covering *all* cases one could encounter. Moral philosophy has taken up this quest insofar as it has sought a single cause or overarching explanatory principle for conduct. Such an ambition is irresponsible in at least two important ways.

First, it is *intellectually irresponsible* to search for such theories once experience provides sufficient evidence to conclude that more than one factor is likely to be at work in moral experience. This prejudice (to produce a single explanation) tends to set theoretical camps against one another. Since all share the presumption that there should be only *one* explanatory principle ('right duty' *or* 'good consequences' *or* 'virtuous character', etc.), cooperation among philosophers is mooted at the very start of concrete moral inquiry. This shared prejudice (against a practical and fallible approach) prevents philosophers from developing multicausal (and empirically sensitive) explanations, which may be the *only* form a solution can take. For these reasons, Dewey writes, we must reject traditional ethical theories 'which identify morals with the purification of motives, edifying character, pursuing remote and elusive perfection, obeying supernatural command, [or] acknowledging the authority of duty' (MW14:194).

Second, monocausal explanations are *irresponsible in practice* because they are typically unable to address morally complex issues (such as war or economic justice) and so they waste precious opportunities to alleviate human misery. One reason for these theories' impotence is their predilection to assume that *their* principles are decisive – even before a single, concrete case of moral inquiry is before them. As a result, excessive attention is paid to one idea or factor ('duty', 'consequences', etc.) of a complex situation while the remaining situational details are neglected. The result is a lack of serious, empirical scrutiny and the disconnection of ethics from everyday life. Of the attention paid to such ideas, Dewey writes,

> Such notions have a dual bad effect. First they get in the way of observation of conditions and consequences. They divert thought into side issues. Secondly, while they confer a morbid exaggerated quality upon things which are viewed under the aspect of morality, they release the larger part of the acts of life from serious, that is moral, survey. Anxious solicitude for the few acts which are deemed moral is accompanied by edicts of exemption and baths of immunity for most acts. A moral moratorium prevails for everyday affairs.

> (MW14:194)

Given the magnitude of humanity's problems, we can neither afford to 'divert thought into side issues' nor enact 'a moral moratorium . . . for everyday affairs'. In fact, the practical cost of irresponsible and ineffective moral theories is, itself, moral. By wasting time and energy on overambitious or myopic ethical fantasies, philosophers ignore practical problems and deprive actual people of the aid or relief they deserve.

The larger point of this discussion about monocausal explanations is about inquiry. Moral progress, for Dewey, really comes down to *process* – the degree to which we habitually inquire in nuanced and scrupulous ways:

> [M]oral progress and the sharpening of character depend on the ability to make delicate distinctions, to perceive aspects of good and of evil not previously noticed, to take into account the fact that doubt and the need for choice impinge at every turn. Moral decline is on a par with the loss of that ability to make delicate distinctions, with the blunting and hardening of the capacity of discrimination.
>
> (LW5:280)

This little paragraph nicely encapsulates pragmatism's existentialist and instrumentalist dimensions. To exist as a moral being is to be aware that *choice is an ever-present obligation*; in order to fulfill this obligation in a way that propels us toward growth (or authenticity), we must hone the ability to *devise distinctions that make a difference* to future practice. Both objectives, in turn, imply that the reconstruction of ethical theory must turn away from traditional theory and toward the resources of contemporary science.

Reconstructing ethics

So far we have seen that, for Dewey, the reconstruction of ethical theorizing begins with a practical, radically empirical, starting point. Taking this approach is an acknowledgment that the concrete necessities of situated moral experiences are *more* relevant *to theory* than most of the abstract principles inherited from past systems. It helps reveal major blind spots of traditional theories, including (1) their denigration of the inherently uncertain character of moral problems; (2) their disregard of the complexities of moral experience; and (3) their exaggerated confidence that philosophy could address living moral issues with overarching and monocausal explanations. With these fundamentals out of the way, Dewey's positive proposals for ethical theory can now be discussed.

What should ethical theory be and do? According to Dewey, ethical theory must be 'more than a remote exercise in conceptual analysis' or 'a mere mode of preaching and exhortation'. It is not theory's job to 'provide a ready-made solution to large moral perplexities'. Rather, theory should 'enlighten and guide choice and action by revealing alternatives . . . [including] what is entailed when we choose one alternative rather than another'. While theory does not make personal and reflective choices for us, it serves as 'an instrument for rendering deliberation more effective and hence choice more intelligent' (foregoing quotations from LW7:316).[3] Moral theories are, then, similar to all other theories – they are functions within a larger problem-solving act, moral inquiry.

Moral problems are addressed, then, by moral inquiry, which includes the functional phases mentioned above, deliberation and choice. Like other types of inquiry, moral inquiry exhibits regular patterns, and some can be made explicit. 'There are three predominant stages in Dewey's model of moral inquiry. First, the agent finds herself in a morally problematic situation. Second, the agent engages in a process of moral deliberation. Finally, she arrives at a judgment that results in a choice' (Pappas in Hickman 1998, 108). This account, so far, seems to express a commonsense schema of a problem; there is awareness of moral tension, the consequences at stake, and one's duty to safeguard important principles and values.

Deweyan moral inquiry becomes interesting when parallels with scientific inquiry are highlighted. As in science, moral inquiry is *predominantly hypothetical and prospective*. While respecting the capacity of past experiences to *inform* present choices, the *worship* of past experience is avoided; precedent can never be treated as a template for action. Previously chosen values are not talismans but clues that must be worked into an ongoing decision process. For example, when I choose from a restaurant menu I often recall my previous meal at that restaurant. Memory assists my decision *not* because it forces a repetition of past choices, but because it provides *data* (about what is valuable) that can be factored in. This example is obviously non-moral, but it helps reinforce Dewey's point that the general hypothetical approach (commonly found in everyday life, science, and technological innovation) is *also* appropriate to moral inquiry.

Because moral inquiry is hypothetical, it is disposed to treat every problematic situation (and resulting solution) as unique. And while a hypothetical stance does not demand that morality be reinvented for every case – sometimes old rules survive intact because of their virtuosic usefulness – it does release moral inquirers from blind obeisance to old formulas, laws, and classifications that no longer relate to present conditions.

> *A moral law*, like a law in physics, is not something to swear by and stick to at all hazards; it *is a formula of the way to respond when specified conditions present themselves*. Its soundness and pertinence are tested by what happens when it is acted upon. Its claim or authority rests finally upon the imperativeness of *the situation* that has to be dealt with, *not* upon its own *intrinsic nature* – as any tool achieves dignity in the measure of needs served by it.
>
> (LW4:222, emphasis mine)

All past moral solutions – laws, rules, prescriptions – are provisional, and their survival depends upon how they perform in future inquiries addressing new problems. A rule considered 'authoritative' ('Refrain at all costs from harming innocent persons') has *acquired* this authority because it has proved so adequate in mediating experience that, on reflection, we have singled it out for praise and incorporated it as a habit.

Ethics makes progress, then, by emphasizing the hypothetical approach of moral inquiry. As we have seen, this approach insists that moral rules and laws possess, at best, a provisional status, not an absolute one. The hypothetical approach also encourages a greater tolerance toward *persons* with diverse points of view – those with whom we already disagree and those with new, seemingly radical, ideas. Writing in 1949 about interfaith understanding, Dewey says

> Genuine toleration does not mean merely putting up with what we dislike, nor does it mean indifference . . . It includes active sympathy with the struggles and trials of those of other faiths than ours and a desire to cooperate with them in the give-and-take process of search for more light . . . There may be, there will be differences on many points. But we may learn to make these differences a means of learning, understanding that mere identity means cessation of power of growth.
>
> (LW15:183)

Dewey's writings on education (see chapter 5) are particularly eloquent on the pedagogical steps needed to create tolerance (which he enlarges to the pedagogical ambition of a 'total attitude'). What is noteworthy here is that Dewey's hypothesis-based tolerance is valuable not only because it exhorts compassion, but because tolerant conduct enables cooperation that, over time, yields more satisfactory intellectual and ethical results.

Dewey believes that ethics can do more than borrow from scientific method, and become scientific itself. Why would this be necessary? First, Dewey observes that the complexity and stakes of contemporary moral choices are becoming increasingly complex and momentous. Average people, facing such choices, should be able to appropriate and use the same powerful logical tools which have helped science and industry master the physical forces of nature. Second, Dewey notes that the scientific approach has the enviable advantage of keeping the burden of proof on any critic whose proposals brought only provisional justification. This scientific habit would help not only by preventing rash ethical judgments (with little or no evidence) but would also incorporate into moral judgment the disposition to revise conclusions when new conditions complicate previously accepted solutions.

Understood as a science, then, ethics 'is concerned with collecting, describing, explaining and classifying the facts of experience in which judgments of right and wrong are actually embodied or to which they apply' (MW3:41). Considering that morality's compass is so broad, moral theory has to do more than borrow from the physical sciences' *methods* of inquiry; it needs to utilize the *content* of scientific discoveries, too. In other words, since moral inquiry focuses on moral *situations* (rather than the rules, duties, or calculative procedures or moral agents) the range and quantity of empirical data necessary to construct a rich characterization of such situations is far greater than ever before. Examples of relevant scientific research might begin with 'biology, physiology, hygiene and medicine, psychology and psychiatry, as well as statistics, sociology, economics, and politics' (LW7:179).

Thus, the enterprise Dewey calls 'a genuinely reflective morals' would be an inquiry with a range of data extraordinarily broad when compared with traditional ethics. And while it would draw from the content of many scientific disciplines (psychology, biology, etc.) it would *also* incorporate the lessons of social custom, jurisprudence, and biographical texts.[4] Finally, genuinely reflective moral theory would continue to reread philosophy's great moral systems, not because some new system can be pieced together out of them – or because they can be reconciled – but because the wealth of this variety of thoughtful moral positions (with, of course, objections, counterexamples, and implications) may cast light on present problems. By studying philosophers such as Plato, Hume, and Kant (to name just three) we are rewarded by their ability to 'reveal the complexity of moral situations . . . [so as] to bring to light some phase of [our] moral life demanding reflective attention, and which, save for it, might have remained hidden' (LW7:180).

We have been talking about Dewey's theory of moral inquiry in some fairly abstract ways – the structure of moral inquiry, its basic methodology, and the various intellectual resources useful for its reconstruction. Before leaving the topic of moral inquiry, let us revisit the perspective of someone stuck in a moral jam, for part of Dewey's explanation (of how pragmatist moral inquiry can assist people in jams) is an expansive account of deliberation, including a phase called 'dramatic rehearsal'.

Moral inquiry, recall, is a reflective response – intervening with analysis and imaginative deliberation – when action is frustrated. Deliberation in ethics has traditionally meant a mechanical calculation of future pains or pleasures, advantages and disadvantages. Dewey expands the meaning of deliberation; it includes traditional forecasting, but also much more. Deliberation may also proceed by dialogue, visualization, imagining of motor responses, and imagining how others might react to a deed done. Some deliberation uses 'dramatic rehearsal' to illuminate the emotional color and weight of various possibilities.

> Deliberation is a process of active, suppressed, rehearsal; of imaginative dramatic performance of various deeds carrying to their appropriate issues the various tendencies which we feel stirring within us . . . We give way, in our mind, to some impulse; we try, in our mind, some plan. Following its career through various steps, we find ourselves in imagination in the presence of the consequences that would follow; and as we then like and approve, or dislike and disapprove, these consequences, we find the original impulse or plan good or bad. Deliberation is dramatic and active, not mathematical and impersonal.
>
> (MW5:292, 293)

Obviously, one benefit to such rehearsal is that no great commitment in physical action is made; various hypotheses about what is best to do can be tested imaginatively without provoking irrevocable consequences. Just as important, though, as the avoidance of consequences is the way dramatic rehearsal serves to make us more self-conscious of what we already think is valuable. This happens because by trying out various courses of action in imagination, we not only map out logical possibilities, we also evoke and make explicit *our* reaction; we test how we would feel if we did an action – what sort of person we would become. And while deliberation connotes a solitary act, much deliberation is actually social, 'not only in the sense that we must take consequences for others into consideration but also in the sense that conversation with others provides the means for reflection' (Fesmire 2003, 82).

Dewey's expanded notion of deliberation (as dramatic rehearsal) finds connections with his writing on education. As early as 1893 Dewey was advising high-school ethics teachers to focus students' earliest training on picturing the details of proposed moral dilemmas rather than focusing on 'the' solution to them. His argument was that the training of flexible and creative student imaginations would be of much greater use in actual moral quandaries than the memorization of rules or principles. The argument still seems a powerful one.

By this point in our discussion, some readers are likely to be harboring an impatient question: 'Yes, yes, morality involves inquiry, and inquiry involves deliberation. That's easy to accept. But isn't morality about the nature of the *values and goals* a person should strive for? Shouldn't theory tell us whether values are discovered or constructed, and even which specific values are *good*?' As we start to consider Dewey's theory of moral value, consider that philosophical moral theory was born, in part, from peoples' need to think and act outside rigid moral codes and values (or ends) sustained by *custom*. As situations developed that could not be addressed by these customary guides, a crisis arose for moral agents and society. On one hand, unreflectively obedient conduct no longer worked; on the other hand, the instinct to hew to past practice was so intense that acting outside customary morality seemed akin to either moral rebellion or anarchy. In short, when custom fails, the way is obscure. What ends should be pursued? What is good, after all? One result of such crises is a renewed appeal to 'traditional' or 'eternal' moral truths; another result is sensualism – shallow, reactive choices for what gratifies immediately. Neither strategy has been particularly effective in creating the adjustments required.

In lieu of these approaches, Dewey promotes the capacity of pragmatic moral inquiry to sort out the nature of a problem and its possible solutions. Inquiry also has the ability to reconsider and reconstruct even the moral values and ends at stake, questioning the purposes people use to direct their conduct, and why such purposes are good (LW7:184). Moral inquiry not only discovers morality, it *makes* it.

Since moral values are not absolute, they must occasionally be constructed or modified. Of course, in any particular moral situation one may *find* that things already possess value. In such cases one has an immediate experience of something 'good', say, or 'bad'. If I witness a bystander being assaulted – without warning, by a stranger, for no apparent reason – I typically do *not* need to construct any values regarding harm to innocents. The facts before me are plain, and I perceive the 'wrongness' of the event as immediately as I perceive the 'blueness' of the victim's coat. But the fact that I can quickly interpret this event's morality does *not* mean there was not some *previous* occasion where others had to work out what was happening and decide what value should attach to it. I am simply the beneficiary of their inquiry, and I don't need to reconstruct the value at stake before me because the object or person I'm judging as valuable already possesses 'a certain *force* within a situation temporally developing toward a determinate result' (MW8:29). What is important, from the standpoint of Deweyan ethics, is that we do not read too much into the immediacy with which values are sometimes appreciated; the *experience* of a good or value should not be confused with an *endorsement* of it.[5] Dewey writes, 'To say that something is enjoyed is to make a statement about a fact, something already in existence; it is not to judge the value of that fact . . . But to call an object a value is to assert that it satisfies or fulfills certain conditions' (LW4:207–8).

The difference between immediate experience and reflective endorsement as set out by Dewey is the difference between '*valuing*' (or '*prizing*') something and '*evaluating*' (or '*appraising*') it. *Valuing* is immediate – value is felt as present in experience. *Evaluating* (also called 'valuation' by Dewey) is mediate or reflective – value is indeterminate and inquiry must endeavor to clarify the situation. Anyone who diets knows that these two are easily distinguished since 'the fact that something is desired only raises the question of its desirability; it does not settle it' (LW4:208). I love carbohydrates – and I *value* this cream donut before me. But this fact about the situation does not settle whether I should eat the donut, given other considerations, such as my health. My course of action requires *evaluation*, and that requires inquiry.

Dewey's distinction between values felt (prized) and values considered (appraised) replaces the is/ought (descriptive/normative) distinction, which was traditionally used to demarcate moral from non-moral questions. For Dewey, 'is' and 'ought' differ not categorically but by the degree to which someone regards 'some desires and interests as shortsighted, "blind," and others, in contrast, as enlightened, farsighted' (LW13:214). There is no immediate intuition of is and ought, no instant sizing up of the 'objective values' to be safeguarded in a situation. Is and ought, shortsighted and farsighted, can be distinguished only by intelligently considering how a desire or interest affect further consequences. They are the eventual products of operations of inquiry. 'In short', Dewey writes, 'a truly moral (or right) act is one which is intelligent in an emphatic and peculiar sense; it is a reasonable act. It is not merely one which is thought of, and thought of as good, at the moment of action, but one which will continue to be thought of as "good" in the most alert and persistent reflection' (MW5:278–9).

Much effort in moral theory has been spent searching out what is really and unqualifiedly good or valuable. Traditional theory harbors a major divide between those who believe that 'the ends can sometimes justify the means' and those who maintain that some means are strictly immoral, no matter how good the final end. One influential school, so-called teleological ethics, refuses to judge absolutely that a particular act (means) is right or wrong. One cannot judge means in isolation from whether they might, in fact, contribute to ends (consequences) good enough to justify them. One may tell a white lie (a means or instrumental good) to one's grandmother about her awful cooking to preserve a warm and loving relationship (an end or intrinsic good). An opposing school, so-called deontological ethics, argues that right and wrong can and should be determined *without* reference to possible consequences. What the teleologist is willing to call a 'mere' means (or instrumental good) may on its face conflict with what the deontologist believes is our rational duty (e.g., not to lie). Morality, for deontologists, requires that conduct conform to principle, not consequences, and so good acts cannot violate our duty to principle. Sorry grandma.

Dewey believes that this conflict (between teleological and deontological ethics) does not exhaust the possible ways moral experience can be framed. We can avoid the dilemma by avoiding the fundamental assumption made by both schools – that moral judgments must be made on a basis that is monocausal. Deweyan ethics refuses to base all moral judgments upon *either* 'consequences' or 'duty' (means or ends, good or right) and instead considers them as multiple, contributing factors in moral experience (along with virtue or character).[6] In complex situations, such factors are often interrelated and interdependent. And in living moral practice, there is no categorical difference between a means and an end. 'Means and ends are two names for the same reality', Dewey writes. 'The terms denote not a division in reality but a distinction in judgment . . . "End" is a name for a series of acts taken collectively – like the term army. "Means" is a name for the same series taken distributively – like this soldier, that officer.' (LW14:28.)

The distinctions made between means and ends are functional ones. If I seek to accomplish some end (playing Bach's *Goldberg Variations*), that end functions by organizing and directing the means-process; once I choose my means (learning to read music for example), those means become, temporarily, ends as well. They are ends-in-view. This way of treating means as temporary ends is actually quite pragmatic: 'Until one takes intermediate acts seriously enough to treat them as ends', Dewey writes, 'one wastes one's time in any effort at change of habits' (LW14:28). In short, *what counts as a 'means' and an 'end'* (or 'cause' and 'effect') *depends on where one draws the boundaries of the situation*. Nothing can be called, absolutely, a 'means' or 'end' because, Dewey writes, 'the distinction between ends and means is temporal and relational' (LW13:229).

Dewey's point about means and ends is perhaps best illustrated in his philosophy of education; in contrast to traditional views, he believes that children are not 'incomplete' adults (mere means), empty vessels that need to be filled as efficiently as possible. Pedagogy must start with the understanding that the child has a point of view, too (is an end). While any lesson surely functions as a means (say, of learning the alphabet) it is also what-the-child-does: an end-in-view. The pedagogic burden shifts, then, toward answering empirical questions such as, what makes *this* particular means–ends significant (not trivial), humanizing (not alienating)? The difference will depend, in part, upon whether the lesson *and* the child are seen as ends, and not mere means.

By rejecting the notion – in education, morality, and everywhere else – of absolute ends-in-themselves, Dewey insists that theorists take a practical starting point. For ethics, this means surrendering the idea that key ethical concepts (value, good, right, virtue, etc.) have *any* anchor in a fixed and final reality, transcendent of human experience. To judge some act or event good or bad does not attribute to it the metaphysical character of 'goodness' or 'badness'. It makes a practical judgment about *doing* something, sooner or later. Because moral judgments do not pretend to be metaphysical reports, we are relieved of deciding whether moral values are 'really' in an agent's mind, a Platonic Form, or in an 'objective' and material world. For the practical ethicists, inquiries shift away from such metaphysical inquiries toward empirical ones concerning how to discover, make, and sustain value for struggling creatures in a changing world.

Adaptation never happens wholesale; each problem inhabits a situation that is uniquely new. And confronting the new requires choosing what to do, what to value or disvalue. As we tackle these challenges – experimentally and hypothetically – it is of little use to inquire into whether things or events 'really' have value, or whether value 'really' can be created. Some things will be experienced as valuable, non-reflectively; they will present themselves as 'obviously valued'. But such valuings will always be situated in a context, and contexts change. No matter how stable the context, no matter how forceful, universal, and enduring a value, it is still illegitimate to infer that this value is, therefore, eternal and unqualified – and thus immune to reconsideration (inquiry) at some future moment. Experience and inquiry are ongoing processes, and if one assumes a pragmatic and hypothetical stance, absolute values simply have no place.

Though his philosophy rejects absolute perspectives, values, and criteria in morality, Dewey did not shrink from holding moral views and values. Some moral stands were philosophical, and some were political; at times, they exposed Dewey to serious personal and professional risks. Dewey's moral theory cannot be equated to a set of prescriptive commandments or timeless values, therefore some claim that it represents one more token of moral relativism, even nihilism. But Dewey can reply that if critics require a moral criterion which is central to his ethics, he will point to *growth*. Whether one is judging the worth of an action or the direction of a person's character, the measure for that judgment must be taken *not* by looking to static outcomes, results, or final goals but to the *process* – whether there is growth. In morals, Dewey writes,

> The *end* is . . . the active process of transforming the existent situation. Not perfection as a final goal, but *the ever-enduring process of perfecting, maturing, refining is the aim in living.* Honesty, industry, temperance, justice, like health, wealth and learning, are not goods to be possessed as they would be if they expressed

fixed ends to be attained. They are directions of change in the quality of experience. Growth itself is the only moral 'end'.

(MW12:181, emphasis mine)

Critics such as John Patrick Diggins and Kenneth Burke have questioned the standard by which these processes (of *perfecting, maturing, refining*) are to be judged. Is it possible to believe that a separate standard exists for every individual?[7] Dewey thought that radically individualistic standards did not exist – that there was something *like* a human nature to measure whether a change should be considered 'growth'. Dewey's view, however, retains an important qualification: while we can identify central, recurring features of 'human nature' we do so *without* insisting that these features are *unalterable*. As an empiricist and a naturalist, Dewey can admit that scientific evidence shows that some human characteristics have barely changed since 'man became man' and are unlikely to change 'as long as man is on the earth' (LW13:286). Regardless of which exact traits comprise the most adequate portrait of human nature (a question which must itself be nested in a specific inquiry), the point is that their justification is empirical not speculative. Their purpose in ethics is pragmatic: to provide moral inquirers with a criterion for moral judgment:

> No individual or group will be judged by whether they come up to or fall short of some fixed result, but by the direction in which they are moving. The bad man is the man who no matter how good he has been is beginning to deteriorate, to grow less good. The good man is the man who no matter how morally unworthy he has been is moving to become better.
>
> (MW12:180–1)

Dewey's ethics must issue judgments, of course, if it is to help make life better. Since these judgments are fallible, they must be accepted with caution, and so must any standard of human nature on which they are based. Dewey's belief was that a cautious and fallible approach would enable moral inquiry to move ahead far less arrogantly than those based upon absolute systems. 'Such a [process-based] conception', Dewey writes, 'makes one severe in judging himself and humane in judging others. It excludes that arrogance which always accompanies judgment based on degree of approximation to fixed ends' (MW12:180–1).

Is Dewey a relativist – does he believe that moral principles and values can have no stability beyond that awarded to them by a person or group, no matter how arbitrary or capricious? Is he a subjectivist – does he hold that all moral positions come to no more than reports about that which the speaker approves or disapproves, or about the speaker's feelings? Critics such as C.I. Lewis and George Santayana took Dewey's rejection of absolute ethical standpoints as evidence for such judgments. Dewey's starting point in moral theory – the radically empirical approach emphasizing the experienced character of moral situations – lead both men to conclude that by placing narrow, self-interested experience above the more abstract and disinterested pursuit of moral ideas, Dewey neglects doing a serious inquiry into morality *at all*.[8]

One fast rejoinder to the force behind such criticisms is that even the most carefully crafted absolutist moral system can be ignored by actual people. Kant's answer, for example, to the question 'Why be moral?' may be rationally convincing and yet practically impotent.

If, following Dewey's advice, one renounces theoretical starting points in ethics and looks instead toward everyday experience, one can find all the authority that a moral theory could want – or need – for answering the question 'Why be moral?'

> [I]n an empirical sense the answer is simple. The authority is that of life. Why employ language, cultivate literature, acquire

and develop science, sustain industry, and submit to the refinements of art? To ask these questions is equivalent to asking: Why live? And the only answer is that if one is going to live one must live a life of which these things form the substance. The only question having sense which can be asked is how we are going to use and be used by these things, not whether we are going to use them.

(MW14:57)

Dewey's point, which we are now rehearsing, is that the activity of moral theorizing emerges from the actual affairs of life. Done this way, ethics does not presume to explain what lies *behind* or *before* your life. 'The choice', Dewey says, 'is not between a moral authority outside custom and one within it. It is between adopting more or less intelligent and significant customs' (MW14:58).

Further responses to charges that Dewey's pragmatism is relativistic or subjectivistic can be answered by taking a second look at the assumptions on which they are based. Individual relativism rests on the assumption that the self is essentially atomistic, while social or cultural relativism rests on the atomism of communities. As chapter 4 will explain, Dewey believes there is good evidence that neither the individual self nor the social group are atomistic in the ways assumed. But even if they were, Dewey could still point out that the conception of experience informing his ethics is not one which assumes that experience must always align with our fancies. Like physical forces that drag us to the ground, moral experience confronts us; in its face we are not little gods, but creatures struggling with a world not entirely of our own making nor under our absolute control. Therefore, doing ethics from a practical starting point means, in part, nipping in the bud those epistemological fantasies that give rise to 'the problem of relativism' or 'the problem of subjectivism'. Doing ethics requires that one observe the phenomenon of growth in one's own life so one might use their observations to help shape the development of moral criteria.

The moral self

To conclude this chapter, we take up Dewey's conception of the self in morality – the self that inquires, deliberates, chooses, acts, and ultimately grows or deteriorates. As the chapter on experience explained, the self is ineliminably social in many ways. While many needs and desires arise within the individual organism, their satisfaction (and eventual sophistication into novel forms) takes place by virtue of a social medium: we utilize socially mediated concepts to understand ourselves and communicate; we evaluate our actions against a social tableaux. Relationships literally make me 'who I am'. They are not merely 'added on' to my identity.[9] 'Who one is', in other words, depends on the kinds of activities and relationships which are *ongoing*, and the mode of this whole process is largely social. These facts about moral life help guide Dewey's reconstruction of moral theory because they form a new idea of what theory can assume a moral agent is: a *feeling* agent as well as a *rational* one; a socially constituted being as well as an individual center of consciousness and biography. Let us look at several of the most important ways in which Dewey develops and deploys a reconstructed notion of the self in moral theory.

The development of a self takes place within culture. The 'socialization' process is, then, *not* the subjugation of an individual's 'natural' or 'true' self to 'external' or 'unnatural' forces. Rather, it is a necessary part of how the social self is built. This cumulative process involves many activities, but permeating most of them is language, which is one of our earliest ways of forming relationships. Beyond language, membership in any number of activities contributes to and constitutes who we are as individuals:

> Cooperation, in all kinds of enterprises, interchange of services and goods, participation in social arts, associations for various purposes, institutions of blood, family, government, and religion, all add enormously to the individual's power. On the other hand, as he enters into these relations and becomes a 'member' of all these bodies he inevitably undergoes a transform-ation in his interests. Psychologically the process is one of building up a 'social' self. Imitation and suggestion, sympathy and affection, common purpose and common interest, are the aids in building such a self.
>
> (MW5: 16)

The notion of 'building up' a self seems strange to many; selfhood is supposed to be the basic property or underlying structure of an individual. Sure, one thinks, the self may undergo social and biographical happenstances but it is not *fundamentally* constructed by them! However, this 'property' model of the self is wrong. As Jennifer Welchman puts it, for Dewey

> personality or selfhood is not a property of human beings, like their natural endowments. It is instead a complex set of functions that these natural endowments may be used to perform. One *becomes* a person as one learns to perform the functions constitutive of personality, in accordance with the social rules for their performance.
>
> (Welchman 1995, 165)

Over time, we become so acclimated to our cultural environ-ment that we stop noticing the degree to which actions, reactions, and conceptual frameworks originate from social causes. This, however, does not make them less integral to personality. 'Apart from the social medium', Dewey writes, 'the individual would never "know himself"; he would never become acquainted with his own needs and capacities' (MW5:388).

The construction-by-social-function of the self may also be framed in terms of habit. Impulses may be biologically first, but they are given a social shape by habit. And while some habits are formed primarily in accord with an individual's private experience, most derive from the social world. Such social habits, also called 'customs', are enacted in concert with others and enable individuals to interpret their experience as individuals. Those particular organizations of habits that prove themselves to be relatively stable, successful, and enduring become nominalized as 'my self'. 'Habits constitute the self', Dewey writes, and 'character is the interpenetration of habits' (MW14:29).

Appreciating how important social environments are for the actual formation of the self should make it clear why the stakes of a moral dilemma go so far beyond utilitarian consequences or rational duty. By choosing what to do, I choose who to become; this is choice's 'double relation' to the self. Every deliberate choice, Dewey writes, 'reveals the existing self and it forms the future self. That which is chosen is that which is found congenial to the desires and habits of the self as it already exists' (LW7:287). A range of alternative selves is presented in our deliberation as possibilities, as we dramatically give 'all sides of character a chance to play their part in the final choice' (LW7:287). (One can easily see the ancient Greek chorus as a theatrical device to make this common psychological function explicit in art.)

So, while it may sound overly existential and melodramatic to say 'all choices are life-determining', this is an accurate representation of Dewey's view. The choice of what to do is ultimately the choice to be the 'sort of person who chose and did that action', whether the action is momentous or not. To give his theory a bit more color, imagine the following:

You are riding alone in an elevator toward the bottom floor of a building. Just as you approach the third floor, you hear a commotion outside the elevator. Shouts of 'Stop them!' and 'Get that money back!' ring out; as the elevators doors quickly open, six bank robbers rush in, and the doors close again. For whatever reason, your presence is not noticed. At the bottom, the elevator doors open to a dark and empty parking garage; the leader quickly disburses packets of money to his gang, and they all flee the garage. Stunned, you find yourself suddenly alone with a forgotten packet of cash worth $150,000. Nearby, your car sits waiting for you. Stunned by it all, you stand wondering, 'What should I do?'

This scene illustrates a number of foregoing points about Dewey's ethics. There is the paralysis of choice and action that characterizes moral experience and prompts moral inquiry. The inquirer must deliberate about what ought to be done, and this will likely involve playing out, mentally, multiple possible sequences. I have made the example dramatic to illustrate how choice can significantly remake the substance of one's identity. But, as Dewey points out, choices change us in this way whether they are momentous or not.

A common and fundamental moral question is 'What is a good character?' Because the people and their environments are so diverse and changeable, Dewey's ethics cannot offer a single template or portrait of 'the good character' to imitate. But, guided by the criterion of growth, it can describe what makes character strong or weak. Character, recall, is 'the interpenetration of habits'. To understand a person's character, we can investigate how well their habits are working to unify elements of the various situations life is dealing them (MW14:29). In people with 'strong characters', habits support and embody one another; they are *integrated*. In contrast, Dewey writes, 'a weak, unstable, vacillating character is one in which different habits alternate with one another rather than embody one another. The strength, solidity of a habit is not its own possession but is due to reinforcement by the force of other habits, which it absorbs into itself' (MW14:30).

The ideal type of character, then, has an integrated set of *functional virtues*: coherent dispositions that are both enduring yet adaptable to changes in the environment and to one's evolving identity (Welchman 1995, 162). If it becomes incumbent upon us to *judge* someone's character, Dewey's account obliges us to look at their acts not in light of *what they are* but rather *which direction their character is moving*.

> [S]ome acts tend to narrow the self, to introduce friction into it, to weaken its power, and in various ways to disintegrate it, while other acts tend to expand, invigorate, harmonize, and in general organize the self. The angry act, for example . . . is bad, because it brings division, friction, weakness into the self; [the expansive, invigorating act is] 'good', because it unifies the self and gives power.
>
> (EW4:244)

The arms dealer makes the world a more violent place in part by selling guns, and in part by becoming the kind of person willing to profit by the perpetuation of violence and war. His actions have bad consequences, but his character, too, can be denounced. Judged by his tendencies, he is marked by a deteriorating character, one whose actions and habits are increasingly in conflict with one another, or one whose conduct diminishes flexible interaction with others.

Ultimately, then, moral judgments apply not only to an action's consequences, but to character as well. Character leads to consequences, but those consequences also shape character in the process. Moral theories which disregard the transactional relationship of character and consequences, and focus on one or the other, operate half-blindly and with inferior efficacy.

Conclusion

Dewey's moral theory follows a similar approach to his others, combining sharp critiques of outmoded views with constructive proposals that should replace them. In part, he criticizes ethical systems (made up of fixed rules, absolute values, natural virtue, and utilitarian consequences) because these systems are driven by the overarching imperative of certainty (comprehensiveness, ultimacy, monocausality). This imperative, Dewey believes, actually renders theory less effective at resolving moral inquiry, and so in the end these moral systems fail – morally.

Because ethical systems are also driven by assumptions about human beings, Dewey criticizes a variety of these assumptions. He proposes, instead, that human individuals should *not* be considered as fundamentally separate, either from nature or other persons; a person subsists and flourishes in virtue of environment, natural and social. 'Conduct', Dewey writes, 'is always shared; this is the difference between it and a physiological process. It is not an ethical "ought" that conduct *should* be social. It *is* social, whether bad or good' (MW14:16).

Once one accepts that human sociality and interaction are neither accidental nor ad hoc, it becomes necessary to link questions about individual ethics to those concerning the best social structures for human flourishing. Such structures include political, educational, aesthetic, and religious institutions. As we will see, Dewey investigates the ethical impact of them all.

4

Politics: selves, community, and democratic life

Introduction

Enormous changes in American life took place during Dewey's lifetime. He was witness to enormous growth in population, scientific, industrial, and educational establishments, the Civil War, two World Wars, and a worldwide economic depression. America's landscape, traditionally dominated by rural spaces and agriculture, transformed into one that was increasingly industrial and urban. These changes indicated to Dewey that the way philosophers – and indeed, all Americans – conceived of politics would have to change as well. It may have been adequate for early Americans to regard democracy as a relatively self-perpetuating structure of governance, but these changes demanded a new approach to political theory and practice. Dewey's 'Creative Democracy: The Task Before Us' discusses the demands on theory informed by these extraordinary historical developments:

> At the present time, the frontier is moral, not physical. The period of free lands that seemed boundless in extent has vanished. Unused resources are now human rather than material . . . [W]e now have to re-create by deliberate and determined endeavor the kind of democracy which in its origin one

hundred and fifty years ago was largely the product of a fortunate combination of men and circumstances.

(LW14: 225)

The ongoing creation of American democracy could not rest upon government institutions or procedures. Now, more than ever, democracy had to become the *conscious* project of Americans' imaginations, deliberately undertaken, utilizing all of the physical and intellectual tools of scientific inquiry. Following the scientific spirit, as Dewey understood it, democracy would be conducted hypothetically – as an experiment tested in practice and revised on the fly. This proposal, Dewey knew, meant the reexamination of many cherished and bedrock assumptions.

Approaching questions of political life and philosophy from a practical starting point led Dewey to penetrating analyses of democracy's pillars: education, the economy, the media, and the tool most meant to analyze these, the social sciences. He responds with ambitious critiques and reconstructions of democracy's most important concepts: individual, community (and public), freedom, equality, and rights, and he publishes his analyses and exhortations in both scholarly and public forums.[1] We consider these responses below.

Dewey's functionalist political philosophy can be understood, at least in part, as a response to his intellectual and social milieu. About his early life in Vermont, he writes,

There was embodied in the spirit of the people the conviction that governments were like the houses we live in, made to contribute to human welfare, and that those who lived in them were as free to change and extend the one as they were the other when developing needs of the human family called for such alterations and modifications.

(LW5:194)

In stark contrast to his own formative experiences of political life, the political theory he read struck him as remote and intellectual. This basic discovery informs all Dewey's critiques and proposals.

Traditionally, political philosophy investigates a host of topics. It seeks the fundamental nature and function of human beings, government, and the state, and the definitions of relevant concepts such as justice, liberty, equality, property, rights, and law. It raises questions about legitimation, that is, by what authority the foregoing concepts – and government itself – can be put into actual practice.[2] Political philosophy investigates the different structures possible for government, and which freedoms and rights government should protect. It has paid special attention to certain issues central to the way society functions, such as property (and capital) and punishment, among others.

While it is impossible to detail Dewey's differences from all the major historical figures, much can be inferred if Dewey's practical approach is borne in mind. That approach entails that Dewey will not accept a priori objects or criteria as ingredients in inquiry. In political philosophy this means Dewey cannot accept, for example, political theories which rely upon claims of a human 'essence' or nature (for example, that humans are 'noble savages' or that 'man is a wolf to man'); or claims regarding inevitable historical destinies (economic, rational, etc.); or assumptions concerning rights, which are 'inherent' or 'inalienable'. It means, too, that Dewey is unlikely to support a political philosophy that binds various parts to a single, monocausal explanation (such as utility, duty, or virtue). We saw a similar resistance in Dewey's ethics.

Of course ideals like 'justice' and 'equality' play a powerful role in human life. Their nature is best understood, Dewey believes, not by attributing them to eternal and supramundane entities but by empirically investigating what exactly their roles are in experience, and then comparing those findings with their accepted intellectual connotations. This contrasts with most traditional approaches, as Alan Ryan explains:

> Dewey wanted to get away from Aristotle, and talk of man as a 'political animal', with all that suggested about some kind of instinctual drive toward political association; he wanted to get away from theories of the social contract, and he wanted to get away from utilitarian theories about the need to organize ourselves to maximize the general welfare . . . [For Dewey] the state is not the march of God on earth, nor is it a utility-maximizing machine; it is a collection of officials whose individual tasks vary enormously but whose raison d'être is to enable the infinitely various private projects of the citizenry to flourish alongside and in interaction with one another.
>
> (Ryan 1995, 218)

Ideals are important, Dewey believes, but they are important because they can function as tools. Once political philosophers remove ideals from their dynamic and human environment (e.g., elevating them as 'the Good' or 'Justice') they become idols – inert to the analysis and improvement of pressing problems, they close inquiry rather than enlarge it.

This difference over how to see ideals – and more generally, whether to employ or reject monocausal explanations – constitutes a significant way in which Dewey differs from traditional political philosophers like Aristotle, Hobbes, Rousseau, Mill, Hegel, or Marx. In Dewey's view, philosophy is responsible not only for interpretation and reconstruction of key concepts, but for explanations of how *we* have come to occupy *our* present situation. By resisting the traditional temptations to explain politics as 'monocausal individualism', laissez-faire, or 'monocausal collectivism of either a Marxist or Fascist kind', we remain open to more complex explanations of political experience; for Dewey this amounts to 'a multicausal, culturally and historically sensitive recipe for a liberal-democratic society built on a socialized economy' (foregoing quotations Ryan 1995, 327).

As explained in chapter 3, Dewey resists monocausal explanations because of a deeper commitment to the process by which he thought common problems were most effectively addressed: social inquiry. Social inquiry does not differ fundamentally from inquiry as described in earlier chapters. James Campbell gives a helpful description of how inquiry expands in the context of problematic situations that are social and political in scope and character:

> In our reasonably well functioning social system something happens and doubts and conflicts arise. Recognition of this trouble results in the development of a self-conscious public and the formulation of the problem. In its attempts to address the problem, the public then proceeds in some organized fashion through a process of social inquiry, hypothesizing and testing. The results of this inquiry, some proposed institutional change involving new laws or modified regulations, are then hypothetically introduced and socially evaluated. And, if all goes well, this hypothetical solution is adopted and works as a solution to the problem.
>
> (Campbell 1995, 148)

Philosophers could play a variety of more vigorous roles in these ongoing public inquiries than they do at present. For example, new problems alter existing social relations, and concepts once indispensable to addressing similar problems need to be analyzed and reconstructed. For example, what does 'privacy' mean today in Britain, where they have installed over four million cameras to monitor public and private spaces?[3] How have terms like 'freedom' or 'human rights' shifted in meaning, given their heavy deployment by speechwriters and ideologues in support of imperial adventures? What is 'war' in an age of increasingly asymmetrical conflicts involving non-state actors and private contractors?

Widespread confusion about meanings of key concepts in a time of dramatic societal change often cannot be clarified without radically reevaluating current meanings and assumptions. This is a philosophical task. 'Any significant problem', Dewey writes, 'involves conditions that for the moment contradict each other. Solution comes only by getting away from the meaning of terms that is already fixed upon and coming to see the conditions from another point of view, and hence in a fresh light' (MW2:273). While philosophers are certainly not the only ones able to reevaluate meaning, they are especially able to provide 'fresh light' due to a studied acquaintance with their culture's philosophical and historical background. Philosophy could assist actual social inquiries by interpreting, clarifying, and reformulating key terms for the public. Non-philosophers could then use philosophy's proposals by testing their practicality as solutions. Such tests would involve implementation (of some kind) by institutions, both governmental and non-governmental. Outcomes would vary; in some cases philosophical ideas might even engender the creation of new institutions; other times, there might simply be a modification of laws, bylaws, objectives, resources, or methods.

Dewey and liberalism

Dewey's political philosophy may be largely, if not exhaustively, described as a reconstruction of classical liberalism. Since philosophers and political scientists take the project of defining historical 'liberalism' as an enterprise unto itself, here follows a very short (hopefully benign) summary to provide readers with a contrast to Dewey's more radical version.

Early versions of liberalism (J.S. Mill, Immanuel Kant, John Locke, Thomas Hobbes, and Adam Smith) may be understood as having (1) a conception of human nature and (2) a political theory based on that nature.[4] Essential to human nature, liberals argued, was rational agency. While there is diversity of opinion regarding the definition of rationality, most agree that rationality is a feature ontologically distinct from human physicality. This liberal account of rationality, then, was grounded in a psycho-physical dualism (humans were hybrids: both physical-emotional and mental-rational). Moreover, it assumed that there was a normative hierarchy to this dualism: the mental-rational capacities were superior because they (not the physical-emotional ones) enable human beings to choose actions, means, ends, and values. It was also widely assumed that the human capacity for reason was a trait possessed equally by all and this conviction undergirded the liberal belief in the inherent and ultimate value of *every* human being.

Rationality therefore became a property of individuals, not groups. While individuals may form associations, such cooperative arrangements did not affect what traditional liberals understood to be fundamental for human flourishing. What is defined as human need, interest, desire, capacity, or norm does not rely, in theory, on the existence of social formations. This view – that human nature can be adequately described on the basis of individuals alone – is sometimes called 'abstract' or 'atomic' individualism. Insofar as atomic individualism informed classic liberal theory, humans were understood to be naturally egoistic, aggressive maximizers of their individual standing.

Liberal political theory is built upon the foregoing metaphysical assumptions about human nature which set the parameters for what would count as its basic political and moral values, problems, and methods for addressing those problems.[5] Because liberal theory divides over the *exact* nature of rationality, some liberals stress the value of individual autonomy and freedom from coercion when making judgments; others stress the value of each individual's pursuit of self-interest or fulfillment as they define it. As Jaggar notes, though, an important universal belief prevails:

> Whether autonomy or self-fulfillment is the primary emphasis, *liberalism's belief in the ultimate worth of the individual is expressed in political egalitarianism*: if all individuals have intrinsic and ultimate value, then their dignity must be reflected in political institutions that do not subordinate any individual to the will or judgment of another . . . *[T]he good society should allow each individual the maximum freedom from interference by others.*
>
> (Jaggar 1983, 33, emphasis mine)

Given these elements, the basic problem for liberal theory is how to 'devise social institutions that will protect each individual's right to a fair share of the available resources while simultaneously allowing him or her the maximum opportunity for autonomy and self-fulfillment' (Jaggar 1983, 33). Because humans are 'by nature' free and equal individuals, liberals argue that any constraint requires justification (for example, by a social contract); in other words, individual freedom is normatively fundamental and those wishing to restrain individuals must provide a justification. This fundamental liberal view of human nature and government function has helped legitimate government acting as the guarantor and protector of private property, free speech, commerce and contract, travel, worship, and education, to name just a few.

Contemporary liberalism, influenced in part by John Dewey, retains these early concerns while modifying some of its preoccupations, particularly in the economic sphere. As Ryan explains, early liberal theorists emphasize limits on government's interference with economic interests. However, as modern economies developed, liberal theorists began to notice that an individual's exercise of her formal and legal rights could be dramatically affected by the presence or absence of personal wealth. It came to be widely believed that liberal theory needed to reformulate its conception of the state in order to take issues of economic distribution (and their effects upon basic liberties) into account.[6]

As Dewey canvassed the national and international scene, he became skeptical that classical liberalism (which he called 'degenerate' and 'delusive') succeeded in preserving and promoting the values for which it supposedly stood. In Dewey's view, American attitudes toward government had evolved over time. Early Americans' fight for freedom from England was against 'a fairly gross and obvious form of oppression . . . of arbitrary political power exercised from a distant centre' (LW11:247). The high costs of that initial separation inculcated in Americans a deep suspicion of governmental power as 'the chief enemy of liberty' and identified, practically, the preservation of individual freedom 'with jealous fear of and opposition to any and every extension of governmental action' (LW11:247, 248).

In response, Dewey argues that Americans should now shed their understandably wary views of government and endeavor, intellectually *and* practically, to enact a government more thoroughly *by and for* the people. He declares in *Liberalism and Social Action* that a new liberal attitude was needed to guide the rapid pace of societal change.

> [Social] changes that are revolutionary in effect are in process in every phase of life. Transformations in the family, the church, the school, in science and art, in economic and political relations, are occurring so swiftly that imagination is baffled in attempt to lay hold of them . . . [Such change] has to be so controlled that it will move to some end in accordance with the principles of life, since life itself is development. Liberalism is

committed to an end that is at once enduring and flexible: the liberation of individuals so that realization of their capacities may be the law of their life.

(LW11:41)

In contrast to traditional liberalism, Dewey's call is for a liberalism reconfigured in light of recent historical developments. Because these developments had been so dramatic, Dewey believes that traditional liberal notions (such as 'individual', 'freedom') need to be modified or expunged to suit new times. If liberalism was to survive, it had to evolve into a theory flexible enough to mediate existent social changes, and this meant renouncing its ahistorical starting point. An engaged and contemporary liberalism would, in Richard Rorty's phrase, be 'putting politics first and tailoring a philosophy to suit',[7] redirecting energy away from old metaphysical disputes about human nature toward empirical inquiries about, for example: (a) the real, detailed causes of inequality and oppression so that it might (b) hypothesize effective (and peaceful) reconstructions of relevant societal institutions. 'Humane liberalism', Dewey writes, 'must cease to deal with symptoms and go to the causes of which inequalities and oppressions are but the symptoms . . . [L]iberalism must become radical in the sense that, instead of using social power to ameliorate the evil consequences of the existing system, it shall use social power to change the system' (LW11:287).

Dewey believes that a truly renascent liberalism should be understood not by its affinity with any particular political program or agenda, but with the method of intelligence.

The office of intelligence in every problem that either a person or a community meets is to effect a working connection between old habits, customs, institutions, beliefs, and new conditions. *What I have called the mediating function of liberalism is all one with the work of intelligence.* This fact is the root, whether it be consciously realized or not, of the emphasis placed by liberalism upon the role of freed intelligence as the method of directing social action.

(LW11:37, emphasis mine)

Deweyan liberalism, then, looks to the kind of intelligence which can mediate the old with the new; it is the type of free inquiry, expression, and discussion that the Bill of Rights intended to protect. This type of intelligence becomes the basis for liberalism when it can be deployed in cooperative inquiry and measured by effective action. As an ideal, this functional and flexible 'freed intelligence' is meant to replace classical liberalism's usual ideals (Nature, Providence, evolution, Manifest Destiny, etc.); those earlier ideals are absolutes, and are non-negotiable; they are *immune* to inquiry. Their inclusion in inquiry can distort results and render them less testable, less revisable – in a word, less intelligent.[8]

Not everyone, however, thought Dewey's expectations for human intelligence were reasonable. Reinhold Niebuhr and Joseph Wood Krutch both argue that Dewey's liberalism is too optimistic about human beings' ability to raise reason about narrow interest. Krutch argues that 'man's ingenuity has outrun his intelligence' and is now 'not good enough to manage the more complicated and closely integrated world which he is . . . [now] powerful enough to destroy' (Krutch 1962, 25). Niebuhr, arguing along similar lines, suggests that Dewey glosses over the fact that the human struggle between reason and desire is permanent; therefore, any liberalism premised upon its eradication is implausible.[9]

In Dewey's response to Niebuhr and Krutch, two points are most important. First, Dewey's account of intelligence does not presume that human intelligence could be 'perfected', but that human practices could exemplify *more* intelligence. Dewey hoped for the piecemeal betterment of human life, not its wholesale redemption, and he based this hope on the very real progress he himself had helped create in education. Second, outside formal education, Dewey had faith not that average people could become Aristotle or Newton, but that they nevertheless could integrate the best aspects of the scientific method into cooperative practices aimed at improving social relations.

The physical sciences, particularly, have demonstrated how effectively *community* inquiry can solve problems by making observations, gathering data, formulating hypotheses, and experimentally validating theories. Despite philosophical arguments about a fact/value dichotomy supposedly dividing 'hard' and 'soft' science, in actual practice physical scientists are no more exempt from culture (and values) than the 'softer' social and political sciences; they too must forge consensus about which problems are *important* and which norms *should* regulate scientific procedure. There are, Dewey recognizes, obstacles faced by the social sciences, which the physical sciences lack.[10] But these obstacles do not present any principled reason that social and political sciences cannot appropriate and apply much of physical science's experimental methods to the problems of human governance. 'Every measure of policy', Dewey writes, 'put into operation is, logically, and should be actually, of the nature of an experiment' (LW12:502)[11]

Long ago, physical science ceased to assume that correct solutions were already known and the only thing needed was facts to prove them. Progress in social policy waits upon a similar epiphany. Dewey believes that once social policy matters are rendered into forms amenable to empirical inquiry and experimental test, this will open the way to more corroborative and effective methods of inquiry.

Individuals, old and new

We have seen that Dewey believes that the reconstruction of liberalism depends on a frank acknowledgment that changing times demand an experimental and hypothetical approach. Taking just such an approach, Dewey was led to critique a central basis of traditional liberalism: the view that the human individual is essentially atomistic and prior, logically, to social or political relations with others. In the traditional (classical) view, each person is ready-made, as it were; they are entitled to whatever rights they possess independent of any relation they might have with any social or political organization. Indeed, on this view of the individual, there is a natural opposition between individuals and organized society, and consequently the primary right of individuals is to pursue private interests, unmolested by state interference.

Dewey argues that while these early conceptions of individuality might have served a purpose in the eighteenth and early nineteenth centuries (promoting 'invention, initiative, and individual vigor'), they are now preventing progress toward 'the formation of a new individuality integrated within itself and with a liberated function in the society wherein it exists' (LW11:250, LW5:86). In addition, for economic reasons mentioned earlier, older conceptions of individuality were now effectively *denying* the very rights liberalism supposedly guaranteed. By insisting upon a minimal role for government, classical liberalism had, in effect, elevated the 'wants and endeavors of private individuals seeking personal gain to the place of supreme authority in social life' (LW11:136). The irony, Dewey continues, is that this 'new philosophy, in the very act of asserting that it stood completely and loyally for the principle of individual freedom, was really engaged in justifying the activities of a new form of concentrated power – the economic, which . . . has consistently and persistently denied effective freedom to the economically underpowered and underprivileged' (LW11:136).

Dewey's rejection of the classical conception of the individual created for him the task of reconstructing notions based upon it. Liberty, freedom, and rights were especially important. Dewey will not, as he does in most other areas of his philosophy, objectify these terms; they are not to be understood as representatives of eternal Nature (or Human Nature). They are to be understood as conceptual tools functioning in the concrete situations that make up the political sphere.

For example, 'Liberty in the concrete signifies release from the impact of *particular* oppressive forces' relative to other forces at a given time and place (LW11:35). One is never concerned for one's liberty *in general*, but always for the liberty to speak at *this* protest, to assemble with *these* striking workers, to carry a gun through *that* neighborhood. 'Freedom', in practice, also breaks up 'into a number of specific, concrete abilities to act in particular ways. These are termed *rights*' (MW5:394).

A 'right', for Dewey, differs radically from traditional accounts. It is no longer a *possession* of individuals, that trait justifying why individuals should be free from state interference. Like art, language, and the self, rights are 'social in origin and intent' and are expressed in particular, concrete situations (MW5:394).

> A right is never a claim to a wholesale, indefinite activity, but to a defined activity; to one carried on, that is, under certain conditions . . . The individual is free; yes, that is his right. But he is free to act only according to certain regular and established conditions. That is the obligation imposed upon him. He has a right to use public roads, but he is obliged to turn in a certain way. He has a right to use his property, but he is obliged to pay taxes, to pay debts, not to harm others in its use, and so on.
>
> (MW5:394)

Rights are not essences (embedded in human nature) or abstract forms (transcending human actions, guiding them); rather, a right is 'a cluster of fundamental yet processive, social powers' (Campbell 1995, 168). This means that questions about which rights and liberties are important cannot be determined abstractly. What will turn out to be *most* important will be a situational determination, not a metaphysical one. As such, it will depend on many concrete factors: historical moment, political and economic circumstances, existing institutions, the specific persons and groups involved, and so on.

If one accepts Dewey's argument that 'rights' and 'liberties' are types of social power, the kind of question which is important for political philosophy to ask changes. For example, instead of the question, 'Why must the individual be left alone?', the question becomes, 'What present conditions need to be attenuated or removed so that individuals can flourish and grow?' This latter question is a relative one – that is, its formulation requires an attuned answer by those who inherit the society existing today. The answer Dewey gave to this question, for his time, was premised on his observation that the individual had become 'lost'.

In 'The Lost Individual', Dewey looks at what had become of American life, and the effect on those around him. The tenor and pace of life for many individuals was marked, Dewey thought, by 'unrest, impatience, irritation, and hurry' and people exhibited a 'feverish love of anything as long as it is a change which is distracting, impatience, unsettlement, nervous discontentment, and desire for excitement' (LW5:68). Such behavior, Dewey believes, demands serious explanation, for 'only an acute maladjustment between individuals and the social conditions under which they live can account for such widespread pathological phenomena' (LW5:68). What were these conditions of life?

For one, individuals had been 'submerged' beneath economic goals in a civilization that Dewey calls 'outwardly corporate', where 'our prevailing mentality, our "ideology", is . . . that of the "business mind" [whose] . . . prevailing standards of value [are] those derived from pecuniary success and economic prosperity' (LW5:66, 69). In such a culture, Dewey notes,

> the loyalties which once held individuals, which gave them support, direction and unity of outlook on life, have well-nigh disappeared. In consequence, individuals are confused and bewildered. It would be difficult to find in history an epoch as lacking in solid and assured objects of belief and approved ends of action as is the present.
>
> (LW5:66)

Psychologically, individuals need 'stable objects' to ally themselves with and invest their imagination. An individual gains stability through, for example: career, social and religious associations, long-term friendships, creative projects, etc. But for a multitude of reasons, modern life has made such objectives harder to reach. Dewey singles out constant economic insecurity as one of the most important contributors to the instability of individuality. Writing shortly after the 1929 crash of the American stock market, Dewey noted that

> The most marked trait of present life, economically speaking, is insecurity . . . Insecurity cuts deeper and extends more widely than bare unemployment. Fear of loss of work, dread of the oncoming of old age, create anxiety and eat into self-respect in a way that impairs personal dignity. Where fears abound, courageous and robust individuality is undermined.
>
> (LW5:66–7)

It seems unquestionable that the economic factors Dewey mentions as undermining of individuality (mechanization, regimentation, the idealization of blind economic forces) are as influential today as ever before. Like Karl Marx and others, Dewey worries that when workers become appendages to business technologies, their individuality is made both less stable and less meaningful. The technologies of mass production and consumption have produced, Dewey believes, 'everywhere a hardness, a tightness, a clamping down of the lid, a regimentation and standardization, a devotion to efficiency and prosperity of a mechanical and quantitative sort' (LW3:134). But devotion of this sort promotes a false sense of unity in the social and economic orders, which can fall apart without much stress. (In contrast, real unity, perhaps best exemplified in Dewey's aesthetic theory, is not tight but flexible, not mechanical but improvisatory. A serious philosophical renewal of individualism would have to make this clear.)

Interestingly, the aforementioned effects afflict not only the working (or 'proletarian') classes, but what is now called the 'middle' or 'upper' classes.[12] The problem for all, Ryan notes, is that 'capitalism evacuates the meaning of work from the activity of capitalists and workers alike. [For Dewey] that makes it morally intolerable and psychologically unsatisfying' (Ryan 1995, 317). For those objecting to government intervention in the 'free market', Dewey can point to widespread economic and existential misery to press his case. Any system which fails to provide even elementary security for millions of people is obviously not protecting their liberty. For if the *actual exercise* of liberty first requires conditions of relative security, a truly liberal government has to address the conditions contributing to the 'lost' state of its individuals – economically, politically, and existentially.

Dewey's criticisms of industrial work-life complement his critiques of education. He worries that our 'epoch of combination, consolidation, concentration' permeates both spheres; workers and students are being conditioned toward narrow and competitive goals (LW6:97). At school and later at work, people are trained in activities that exclude the organic place of 'personal judgment and initiative', and a truly renascent liberalism would insist on reconstructing the institutions involved so that their aims increased 'on the part of every worker [or student] his sense of the meaning of the activities that he is carrying on, so that more of his own ideas, thinking, will go into it' (LW5:137, 240).

So much is premised (laws, institutions, pedagogies, economies) upon the traditional conception of the individual (as atomic, asocial, ahistorical, and so on) that Dewey believes it is necessary to reconstruct the concept. Unless this is done, none of the social and political forces currently damaging individuals can change in a way that reflects people's experience. What 'new' individualism does Dewey propose? How should we think about the relation between individuals and their society?

First of all, individuals are not prior to social groups; each exists *in and through* their transaction with them. 'Assured and integrated individuality is the product of definite social relationships and publicly acknowledged functions' (LW5:67). This proposition does not deny the existence of private experiences, nor does it suggest that all aspects of individuality can be explained as ultimately social phenomena. There is something unique and original that cannot be eliminated about being an individual. 'Every *new* idea', Dewey writes, 'every conception of things differing from that authorized by current belief, must have its origin in an individual' (MW9:305). He echoes and amplifies this point in *Individualism, Old and New*: 'Individuality is inexpugnable because it is a manner of distinctive sensitivity, selection, choice, response and utilization of conditions. For this reason, if for no other, it is impossible to develop integrated individuality by any all-embracing system or program' (LW5:121). One becomes an individual by virtue of social engagements with communities. My style and talent *as* an individual musician happens *through* these performances, *before* these crowds, *with* these musicians. 'Only in social groups', Dewey writes, 'does a person have a chance to develop individuality' (MW15:176).

This philosophical reconstruction of 'individual' erases sharp lines between self/society and self/other, preferring to understand these elements as dynamic, ongoing events. Becoming a person is a project that may still seem 'up to me', but my responsibility for this project no longer sets me apart from the social context in which I act. In fact, my actions in the context serve both to create who I become *and*, to a degree, what the context becomes:

> To gain an integrated individuality, each of us needs to cultivate his own garden. But there is no fence about this garden: it is no sharply marked-off enclosure. Our garden is the world, in the angle at which it touches our own manner of being. By accepting the corporate and industrial world in which we live, and by thus fulfilling the pre-condition for interaction with it, we, who are also parts of the moving present, create ourselves as we create an unknown future.
>
> (LW5:122–3)

By moving beyond traditional liberalism's asocial and ahistorical individual, Dewey is placing a *greater* burden on the individual, for now there is a responsibility to choose not only for one's self, but for the environment defining and creating that self. (Becoming an American individual, for example requires not only the self's choice of reaction *to* American consumerism, but a choice about whether to sustain or change consumerism.)

The problems and questions faced by individuals now and then are no doubt different. The question of Dewey's day was 'Can a material, industrial civilization be converted into a distinctive agency for liberating the minds and refining the emotions of all who take part in it?' (LW5:100). Our question must, in its particulars, differ. But we have no doubt inherited his general concern for creating stable selves. In that sense, the stakes are just as high.

Community and public

Besides reconstructing the idea of the individual, Dewey also proposed a reconstructed notion of community. Psychologically, human individuals develop through their communicative relations with communities. This fact raises interesting questions for political philosophy. For example, What *kind* of community encourages the individual to thrive? What qualities make a community hospitable to individual health? What kind of institutions and procedures are best able to further individual and communal growth?

The word 'community' has both descriptive and normative senses, and Dewey uses it in both ways to advance his arguments at various points. In political philosophy, the normative sense is the most important, and so Dewey's philosophical project requires that he redescribe the general ideals, activities, and modes of communication most appropriate to a *healthy* and *growing* communal life. In Dewey's use, 'community' is more fundamental than 'government' or 'state' because communities preserve and create human values. Governments and states are merely the machinery (or technology) responsible for implementing communities' values. This 'subordination of the state to the [free and self-governing] community' is, Dewey says, the 'great contribution of American life to the world's history' (LW5:193). Whatever cohesion states and governments possess comes ultimately from the intimacy of their relationships to the communities they serve. 'We [Americans] are held together by non-political bonds, and the political forms are stretched and legal institutions patched in an *ad hoc* and improvised manner to do the work they have to do' (LW2:306).

Several features define a community: as a precondition they must have (1) an *interactive* or *associative* nature; they must hold (2) *shared values,* which arise out of (3) *shared action.* In 'The

Search for the Great Community' (1927), Dewey defines community in a way that brings these elements together:

> Wherever there is conjoint activity whose consequences are appreciated as good by all singular persons who take part in it, and where the realization of the good is such as to effect an energetic desire and effort to sustain it in being just because it is a good shared by all, there is in so far a community.
>
> (LW2:328)

Regardless of who the particular individuals are in a community – male, female, white, black, old, young, etc. – *genuine* community has 'a central core of common felt values which operate as significant values for the community' (Campbell 1995, 175). *Having* common values (as well as common aims, beliefs, aspirations, and knowledge) is not a passive affair; it requires a range of ongoing activities, particularly communication. Only with communication can community sustain itself.

Thus community not only provides the environment in which we create and sustain *value* (through association and communication), it also provides the conditions for *knowledge*. Inquiry is an activity engaged in by cooperative groups, and the quality of those groups' relationships will critically affect the products of their inquiries. This means a narcissistic or neurotic culture cannot become wise.

Like community, 'public' has a very special meaning for Dewey. Unlike the everyday phrases such as 'the public', meant to refer indiscriminately to 'the masses' or population at large, public has a connotation for Dewey that closely connects to inquiry and social action. For Dewey, a public forms in the following way. In the course of daily life, problems are encountered that cannot be solved easily or by individuals alone. In some cases, the consequences are 'direct', felt within one's private group or association; in other cases the consequences are 'indirect', and have an impact outside one's group. When consequences are 'indirect, extensive, enduring, and serious', such that a socially problematic situation can be said to exist, then, all the conditions necessary for the formation of a *public* exist (LW2:314). Perceiving that the implications of the problem are important and far-reaching, the next logical step is often to organize a governmental or institutional response. Through communication, the public arranges for representatives of its interests (officials) to manage it – by prevention or regulation – in a way that remains responsive to the public's final control. Insofar as these publicly charged officials are systemically related to one another, they form a government. Together, the public and its government form a state.

As he did in so many other areas, Dewey is urging that we conceive of the public and the state by starting, empirically, with human behavior and practice. So, while we may habitually think of the 'public' as singular; on Dewey's account, there can be many 'publics'. For example: a group of neighbors concerned about the impending actions of a commercial developer; workers in the airline industry worried about layoffs; students at a public college anticipating a steep rise in academic fees. These publics, large or small, arise (or fade) contingent upon the way a variety of common needs are manifested in concrete situations (i.e., in various groups, at various times and places). This means that 'no two publics will have precisely the same membership . . . and any given public will have members from other publics' (Gouinlock in LW2:xxvi).

Since the state is built upon the fluctuating needs and specific requirements of its publics, it must not be objectified as something permanent; the state is a functional, if enduring, response to problematic situations. As Gouinlock puts it, for Dewey,

> The form of governing institutions would not be conceived as eternal and immutable, but would change in order to perform

particular functions in particular circumstances. Thus the state under some conditions might have much to do, and under others rather little. The state is not an all-inclusive entity (as it is according to Hegelians), incorporating the entire life of the community. The state is only one of the associations in which one participates.

(Gouinlock in LW2:xxvi–xxvii)

It is worth remembering how Dewey distinguishes 'public' and 'community'. *Publics* are problem-driven, meaning they are subject to dissolution once focal concerns are addressed. *Communities*, because their bonds are not tied to problems, are not dissolved by the satisfactions of inquiry. A 'public', in Dewey's sense, is a term with much stronger political connotations than 'community'. A community – for example, of guitar-makers or coin collectors – may find itself with a problem and so *become* a public, but their existence as a community is not due to their problems.

Perhaps Dewey's most interesting contribution to dialogue about the nature of public and state is his call for the development of 'self-conscious' publics. The self-awareness of this public (both of its own interests and the forces frustrating them) makes it especially effective when dealing with problems. Dewey thought such a public was painfully absent from American life. Looking around at the multiplying distractions of technology, entertainment, and the stresses of work, Dewey called the publics of his day 'inchoate'. They were, that is, politically and morally impotent to effect conditions and enrich experience. What is more, the development of a mass news and entertainment media had done little to help.[13]

The members of an inchoate public have too many ways of enjoyment, as well as of work, to give much thought to organization into an effective public . . . At present, many consequences are felt rather than perceived; they are suffered, but they cannot be said to be known, for they are not . . . referred to their origins. It goes . . . without saying that agencies are not established which canalize the streams of social action and thereby regulate them. Hence the publics are amorphous and unarticulated.

(LW2:321, 317)

Understanding, the human ability to formulate and share meanings, is a social affair. A public that is inchoate cannot solve problems because that requires knowledge, and knowledge requires inquiry involving *cooperative* communication. Inchoate publics, made up of self-isolating individuals, cannot produce understanding because their impulses and wants cannot be translated into purposes and desires with a commonly understood meaning. For example, an individual who is both for 'low taxes' and 'safe drinking water' will simply not understand why achieving both will require *increasing* the tax burden on corporate polluters. For 'without an adequate public to help us, we do not understand the meaning of the constant stream of events. We can neither comprehend the importance of the facts we uncover nor place the consequences of our actions in understandable future orders' (Campbell 1995, 176).

In contrast, individuals who are part of a truly self-conscious public take *as part of their identity as ordinary citizens* the habits of communal inquiry: the ability to interpret shared facts in social contexts, to cooperatively investigate problems, to make socially acceptable comparisons and evaluations, and even conduct wholesale reappraisals of common goals and values. Though such habits cannot just be pulled off a shelf, Dewey thought the call for a self-conscious public could not be separated from the instrument of its creation, a democratic education. This will be taken up in chapter 5.

Various critics of Dewey's complained that his call for a self-conscious public was unrealistic. People are too apathetic, morally flawed, or uneducated to be the kind of vigorous inquirers that Dewey envisaged.[14] In response to Dewey's participatory model, critics such as Walter Lippmann argued that democracy would be better off ignoring much of the public in favor of disinterested experts who would be charged with making decisions in the public's best interests.

The role of the expert and the capacity of a democratic populace formed the core of a complicated debate between Dewey and Walter Lippmann during the 1920s and 1930s. In books such as *Public Opinion* (1922) and *The Phantom Public* (1925), Lippmann maintained that public affairs were beyond the capacity of the average person; burdened by work and family, diverted by entertainment and non–political activities, there was insufficient time or ability for most citizens to even gain the faintest notion of what the 'public interest' was – let alone bring it into existence. The better route, Lippmann thought, was for experts to manage public affairs. The public's role would simply be to punish the experts whenever their management became self-interested or malignant.

Dewey's vigorous response to Lippmann, most fully expressed in *The Public and its Problems*, clarified his conviction that democracy *requires* the interested and active participation of citizens, empowered by direct and open communication. Lippmann's proposal underestimated the very real concern that elite experts would likely become remote from the public they served; Lippmann also failed to acknowledge a sense in which democracy *could be more* than the blunt will of an uninformed majority. The character of the majority, in other words, was not a fixed and inferior thing, and an educational system oriented toward democratic education could make people better suited to act as citizens.

> Democracy demands a more thoroughgoing education than the education of officials, administrators and directors of industry.

Because this fundamental general education is at once so necessary and so difficult of achievement, the enterprise of democracy is so challenging. To sidetrack it to the task of enlightenment of administrators and executives is to miss something of its range and its challenge.

(LW13:344)

According to Dewey, Lippmann was selling the people and promise of democracy short. Yes, a large society needs experts; but the proper role for a democracy's experts is to facilitate the gathering and interpretation of complicated facts (about health, housing, city planning, national defense, and so on) so that *public* conversation and debate can put those facts in the service of values.[15] The question of value priorities must be left to the public. Such public oversight and regulation of moral issues would apply not only to government, but to business as well, where meaningful work was rapidly disappearing as a result of the myopic and antidemocratic value choices by owners and managers.

Democracy

The last piece of Dewey's political philosophy to consider is also the most comprehensive, which is his conception of democracy. Democracy may be viewed narrowly, as a form of political machinery or system of government or, more broadly, as a social and moral idea. While many continue to identify democracy with its mechanisms – recurring elections, universal suffrage, political parties, trial by one's peers, politicians' accountability to the public, and so on – these mechanisms do not express the soul of democracy for Dewey: 'A democracy is more than a form of government; it is primarily a mode of associated living, of conjoint communicated experience' (MW9:93). This way of life entails far more than minimal protection or survival; more than a majority banding together to protect life and property from tyranny. It is 'wider and fuller' than even ideas about the ideal state because it ultimately relates back to the kinds of moral and intellectual virtues a citizenry can exemplify in their everyday practices.[16] It is because democracy is such a comprehensive concept for Dewey that he spends so much time criticizing and reconstructing the ideas (individuality, community, the public) and institutions (education, religion, the arts, industry), which he considered its indispensable elements.

While Dewey was writing political philosophy, democracies around the world were, at best, stable. This may in part be due to the historical circumstances; still, there are reasons to think that democracy is inherently precarious. First, democracy requires that the majority of the population be continuously educated for cooperative inquiry; second, it requires that those charged with communicating public information (for example, the news media) remain unbowed by the profits that can be gained through entertainment or propaganda; finally, it requires that citizens who become self-conscious democratic agents realize that their agency cannot simply be passed down, like a keepsake, to their children. Their children, to be agents themselves, must enact and vivify their own milieu with whatever resources they have.

> [E]very generation has to accomplish democracy over again for itself; that its very nature, its essence, is something that cannot be handed on from one person or one generation to another, but has to be worked out in terms of needs, problems and conditions of the social life of which, as the years go by, we are a part, a social life that is changing with extreme rapidity from year to year.
>
> (LW13:299)

Granted, the renewal of democracy, as Dewey describes it, places a great burden on human beings. That being said, he argues that this is the cost of continued growth and sustainable moral conduct. Participation is central to democracy because it is only through participation (particularly in inquiry) that we can discover more comprehensive viewpoints, which can help us bridge the gaps created by our more intractable conflicts (MW9:336). Democracy, in other words, arranges life to optimize meaningful growth. It is 'but a name for the fact that human nature is developed only when its elements take part in directing things which are common, things for the sake of which men and women form groups − families, industrial companies, governments, churches, scientific associations and so on' (MW12:199−200).

One of Dewey's recent critics, Robert Talisse, has pointed out that Dewey's use of the word 'growth' is not unproblematic: after all, who defines 'growth'? Which ideals determine the criteria for 'growth'? What is more, in societies that are pluralistic − that contain groups with radically disparate values and worldviews − how can democracy work cooperatively toward the reconstruction of societal institutions in a way everyone can agree with?[17] Talisse takes this to be a serious problem for Dewey, because if Dewey's justification of democratic ideals and growth rests upon his particular account of experience and intelligence, then any group who rejects his account of experience and intelligence would be oppressed by the Deweyan democracy based upon it. Schools, government agencies, companies, etc., would not represent the way of life of anti-Deweyan communities, and would instead be their antagonizers.

Though this challenge is too complicated for a full reply here, Dewey might respond by noting that his democratic proposal never promised to eliminate *all* social conflict; conflict is endemic to human life. Deweyan democracy's advantage lies in its potential to divert conflicts away from violence toward argument and social inquiry that can make the 'widest possible contribution to the interests of all − or at least of the great majority' (LW11:56). The task for Deweyan democrats is to 'bring these conflicts out into the open where their special claims can be seen and appraised, where they can be discussed and judged in the light of more inclusive interests than are represented by either of them separately' (LW11:56).

Talisse would probably argue that this response fails to allay his concern because it has not spelled out how it will be decided *whose* 'inclusive interests' will decide any given conflict. To this Dewey can only reiterate that his commitment to the perspective and situation-bound nature of inquiry prevents him from giving the kind of prescriptive definitions requested.[18] Dewey's proposal is offered as a way of improving, in the long run, the functioning of American society as he found it. It is not a recipe for resolving *every possible* social conflict. In the long run, education is crucial because it trains citizens not in the creation of perfect prescriptive solutions but in 'the *habit* of amicable cooperation' (LW14:228; emphasis mine). The education of such habits, it is worth adding, may someday even *produce* bonds and sympathies among the most bitter antagonists so that they may see how shared concerns pull them to higher, common ground.

Conclusion

Ultimately, for Dewey, democracy requires reconception of what it means to be an individual, a community, a public; it requires the reconstruction of those cultural institutions responsible for shaping character in ways that nurture and grow the richest forms of human experience. All of these objectives rest upon a conviction which cannot itself be justified: that the source for our aims, methods, and values must come from experience itself, and not from some external authority outside the experience.

Democracy is the faith that the process of experience is more important than any special result attained, so that special results achieved are of ultimate value only as they are used to enrich and order the ongoing process. Since the process of experience is capable of being educative, *faith in democracy is all one with faith in experience and education.* All ends and values that are cut off from the ongoing process become arrests, fixations. They strive to fixate what has been gained instead of using it to open the road and point the way to new and better experiences.

(LW14:229, emphasis mine)

This is a faith both in one's fellows (their common sense, their educability, their willingness to cooperate) and in the answers and satisfactions that can emerge in the process of experience. While democracy offers no guarantees of eventual and perfect results, many of its fruits can already be enumerated and its potential for new experiments lie open to inspection and invite earnest trial.

5

Education: imagination, communication, and participatory growth

Introduction

Education is absolutely central to Dewey's thought, both as a human enterprise and a philosophical subject matter. Whether philosophers recognized it or not, he believed education was 'the supreme human interest in which . . . other problems, cosmological, moral, logical, come to a head' (LW5:156). Moreover, it was the area which represented his best attempts to 'sum up' and 'most fully expound' his philosophical position.[1] As pedagogue, Dewey wrote educational materials: lesson plans, schedules, syllabi, lectures, etc. As philosopher, he articulated a profound new vision of how learning occurs, how teaching should reflect and respond to learning, and how the school should be organized to optimize this process of growth.

Dewey's comment that his writings on education 'summed up' his *entire* philosophical position expresses his conviction that any adequate educational philosophy must look deeply not only at the processes of learning but at the experiential contexts which make learning – and democracy – possible. For Dewey, this meant that philosophy of education had to be informed by relevant theories, especially those in psychology, morality, politics, and inquiry. Dewey attempts this in *Democracy and Education* by, 'connect[ing] the growth of democracy with the development of the experimental method in the sciences, evolutionary ideas in the biological sciences, and the industrial reorganization, and [the book] is concerned to point out the changes in subject matter and method of education indicated by these developments' (MW9:3).

What is education and who is it for? Dewey answers this most concisely in 'My Pedagogic Creed' (1897) by listing and explaining five main areas of his educational philosophy: (1) the purpose and nature of education; (2) the function of schools; (3) how subject matters should be conceived and arranged; (4) what methods of instruction are appropriate; and (5) the role education plays in social progress. In brief, education's purpose is to prepare us to survive and, hopefully, flourish in a future that is by nature uncertain. This is best provided by enabling each child to take full command of her own powers, rather than merely fashioning her to fulfill society's current needs.

It is important to understand, at the outset, that Dewey sees education as a *primarily* social process, not an individual achievement. This is because individuals are, in large part, constituted by social experience. Education, of course, is concerned with both individual psychology and social structures, but these must be understood as organically related, interdependent factors. No child's interests, words, or deeds exist in a vacuum; it is through the reception and response they receive in society that they gain meaning. The school must provide a socially interactive atmosphere for education to succeed. At the same time, social factors do not have a self-sufficient meaning either. Their meaning depends on the perspective of the child being educated. For this reason, education must heed the child's instincts, habits, and powers as important clues as to the meaning social factors (agents, circumstances) have for that child. Education which overemphasizes either factor – the child or the social forces – becomes either haphazard or coercive.

Schools are primarily social institutions that must be considered valuable for their own sake. While schools equip children with information and training useful for the future, the school and its teachers are part of the child's present community; they shape the context of his experiences. These informational and existential facts must, in the school, function together to deepen and extend those values and capacities most pertinent to a given environment. Schools can do this, in part, by representing community life to the child through activities simplified for the child's understanding but nevertheless continuous with his experience. By seeing how school subjects and activities have a larger significance, the child gains insight into why their participation in learning portends their own social significance.

Dewey's philosophy of education arrived during a period of considerable pedagogical debate. In the 1890s a heated battle between educational 'traditionalists' and 'romantics' was ongoing, and Dewey satisfied neither group.[2] *Traditionalists* (also called 'old education' by Dewey) pressed for a 'curriculum-centered' education under the leadership of William Torrey Harris, who saw children as blank slates on whom teachers must write the lessons of civilization. Subject matter ('content') was of supreme importance, best taught with step-by-step discipline. The child's role was to remain docile and receptive to the wisdom being poured into her. *Romantics* (also referred to as 'new education', and 'progressive education' by Dewey), urged a 'child-centered' approach. Advocates such as G. Stanley Hall argued that the child's natural impulses were the proper starting points of education. Children are active and creative beings, and education must ensure that their unfettered growth take precedence over all else – including content instruction which, while necessary, was of subordinate importance.

Neither group much respected the methods and values of the other. Traditionalists saw themselves as authoritative conveyors of centuries-old wisdom, whereas their opponents had foolishly relinquished this authority for the immature desires of children; as a consequence, the romantics had developed a pedagogy of chaos, anarchy, and ineffectiveness. Romantics, for their part, saw their pedagogy as loyal to children's spontaneity and joy; traditionalists, in their view, were suppressing children's unique spirits with a pedagogy both mechanistic and depersonalizing.

Dewey criticizes both educational philosophies. Traditionalists subordinate children to the curriculum because they mistakenly see education as 'formation from without'. Their overemphasis on curriculum creates their mistaken ideal of a learner who is docile, receptive, and obedient. When traditionalists compare *actual* children with their ideal, children seem impulsive, self-centered, narrow, confused, and uncertain; their boredom or inattention to the curriculum is construed as a *moral* failing. Consequently, traditionalists' solution to the problem of connecting the curriculum with the living interests and activities of the child becomes 'discipline', and so numerous punishments and rewards (extrinsic to learning) are institutionalized as part of pedagogy.

Dewey also criticizes romantic (or 'child-centered') educators. This approach (with which Dewey is frequently confused) overestimates the degree to which education is 'development from within', and afflicts its pedagogy with excessive reliance on the child's present interests and purposes. While agreeing that these interests and purposes are crucial ingredients for educational practice, Dewey insists that it is up to teachers to actively direct them toward fruitful expression in history, science, art, and so on. Child-centered schools, Dewey warns, must be careful not to craft their identity on the mere rejection of traditional methods, as this makes them more liable to new dogmatisms. Every new method proposed for education must examine, radically and self-critically, both underlying principles and present conditions. Only by doing this can educational content (curricula and disciplinary boundaries) and agents (students, teachers, and administrators) be assured of practical connection with present experience.

In contrast to these two schools, Dewey proposes that regular change is the one fact educators can predict with certainty – and the one, stable guide on which a new pedagogy can be constructed for children.

> The open mind is the mark of those who have . . . learned the eagerness to go on learning and the ability to make this desire a reality. The one precious thing that can be acquired in school or anywhere else is just this constant desire and ability . . . There will be almost a revolution in school education when study and learning are treated not as acquisition of what others know but as development of capital to be invested in eager alertness in observing and judging the conditions under which one lives. Yet until this happens, we shall be ill-prepared to deal with a world whose outstanding trait is change.
>
> (LW17:463)

Traditional schooling's reliance on rote memorization and restrictive discipline renders the mind passive, closed, and backward looking.[3] An open mind is not passively open (like a door), but *actively* open (like being 'open' to new ideas or experiences). The condition of being critically and actively open is the heart of Dewey's pedagogy. We will return to this shortly.

When Dewey arrived in Chicago in 1894 to chair the Philosophy department, he had mostly taught college. He increasingly believed that a truly participatory democracy could only emerge from a population adequately schooled for such activities; public education therefore had to be adapted. Dewey planned to accomplish these aims by teaching and researching pedagogy alongside his philosophical and administrative duties, and he convinced the trustees and President of the university to create a separate academic department of pedagogy for him to direct. The opportunity proved an exceptional one, both professionally and personally.

The practical manifestation of Dewey's proposals and the position afforded him by the university was the Laboratory School of the University of Chicago. With the assistance of President Harper, Dewey and his wife Alice founded the school (which opened in January 1896). It provided a real site for Dewey to test his theories about learning and the formation of democratic communities. As part of a larger campaign for educational reform in Chicago, Dewey's Laboratory School became nearly synonymous with progressive education. Dewey, however, was cautious not to over-identify his educational philosophy with 'progressive education'. While this label was reasonably descriptive of many parents' solution to the problems of traditional education (over-regimentation, excessive discipline, etc.) it glossed over Dewey's unique strategies for non-traditional learning.[4]

Dewey's philosophy of education

Dewey's seminal critique of the reflex arc concept in psychology (see chapter 1), argued that psychologists had been misdescribing human experience as a series of fits and starts, rather than as a continuous circuit of activity.[5] As a special case of human psychological interaction, learning also does not occur in fits and starts; learning is a progressive and cumulative process in which the dissatisfaction of doubt alternates with the satisfaction that attends problem solving. Children, no matter how young, are never passive recipients of sensation; they are actively engaged agents in life's ongoing dramas. Educators who grasp this fact must surrender the picture of children as blank slates awaiting inscriptions and grasp that 'the question of education is the question of taking hold of [children's] activities, of giving them direction' (MW1:25).

However not everyone saw Dewey's view of education as benign. Traditionalist critics like Mortimer Adler blasted Deweyan education for failing to *impose* values on students – thus leaving civilization value-less and vulnerable to fascist forces.[6] But Dewey could not accept Adler's premise that values are *only* acquired from external sources. Any child begins school, Dewey argues, with four basic impulses, 'to communicate, to construct, to inquire, and to express in finer form', and the educator who properly appreciates the psychological nature of these impulses will see them as 'the natural resources, the uninvested capital, upon the exercise of which depends the active growth of the child' (MW1:30). None of these resources are devoid of values, but for educators to make use of these resources they had to take a *personal* approach – knowing the children as individuals, understanding how *their* interests and habits derive from *their* homes and neighborhoods.

Teaching active learners is no simple matter. Teachers must both know their subject matter *and* also be able to integrate it into their students' individual and cultural experiences. Unlike traditionalist teachers, who can use punishment or humiliation to motivate children through fear, and unlike romantics who can look to the child's whims to shape the lesson, Deweyan teachers have to reconceive the whole learning environment. They have to match the present interests and activities of these pupils with preexisting curricular goals (for instance, of history or chemistry) by identifying specific problematic situations capable of integrating the two. This problem-centered approach demands a lot from teachers; it requires not only they be trained in the subject matters, but also in child psychology and a variety of pedagogical techniques for creating experiences which weave child, problem, and curriculum together. About teaching at the Laboratory School, two colleagues wrote:

> Like Alice, [the teacher] must step with her children behind the looking glass and in this imaginative land she must see all things with their eyes and limited by their experience; but, in time of need, she must be able to recover her trained vision and from the realistic point of view of an adult supply the guide posts of knowledge and the skills of method.[7]

This was a tall order, and while some might argue that Dewey achieved it in Chicago, it is more debatable that it provided a model that has endured elsewhere in the country. Some, like Alan Ryan, doubt that it *can* be accomplished, given its requirements: small and well-equipped classes, curricula resistant to external metrics ('accountability' as it is called today), and extraordinarily versatile teachers able to teach various subjects while still having time to regularly revise methods (Ryan 1995, 147). While this is an important criticism, it is based on empirical claims about present possibilities, which cannot be debated here.

For many, education's purpose is simple: training for work. Dewey rejects this aim as too narrow − and also too classist. Central to education, Dewey believes, are 'occupations' not 'vocations'. 'Vocational' (or 'pre-professional') training aggravates social class differences; some in society are provided with a limited set of skills and information to do particular jobs, while others receive a more generous and humanizing 'liberal education'. Such educational 'tracking' might work for utopian fantasies (as described, for example, in Plato's *Republic* or Huxley's *Brave New World*) but it contravened Dewey's hope for a more democratic America.

Instead, education should train for 'occupations': 'a mode of activity on the part of the child which reproduces, or runs parallel to, some form of work carried on in social life' (MW1:92).

In Dewey's school these activities included carpentry, cooking, sewing, and textile work. Children, some as young as four years old, were divided into age groups to pursue various projects: cultivate and process farm crops like cotton and wheat, study local history and geography, construct a replica of a colonial American home, conduct experiments in anatomy or political economy. (A project done in the same spirit today might still involve cooking, though it might also involve the creation and editing of a movie.)

The point of taking the occupational approach was this: engaging the child's interest lays down a motivational foundation for more abstract curricular lessons to be introduced later. For example, a child who has started cooking a meal has an emotional investment in the activity as a whole. If an obstacle is presented that can be overcome by consulting a book, it becomes immediately obvious why reading is important. The conventional problem of 'getting children to read' is overcome, gradually and naturally, at an early age.

Occupational projects also introduced children to the experimental method of inquiry. Faced with 'problematic situations' of their own making, children realize that overcoming obstacles requires observation and hypothesis-formation. Trial and failure of hypotheses leads naturally to developing analytical methods (to determine what went wrong) and inquiry into how proposed solutions should be revised. Such firsthand involvement with inquiry is central to education because it truly frees the mind of the child by impressing on him the need to 'take an active share in the personal building up of his own problems and to participate in methods of solving them' (MW3:237).

Finally, unlike vocational training, occupation-education is not tied to narrow objectives. Each successive project in which children engage illustrates more diverse interrelationships and more general lessons. While a specific gardening project initially requires one to furrow the soil, questions introduced later (e.g., about optimizing plant health) raise more general questions of biology, chemistry, and meteorology. Cooking the garden's products would necessitate specific lessons about food preparation; but again, that process is utilized as a fulcrum for discussing more general topics (such as how kitchen work could be divided among many people – 'fairness').

In brief, then, occupation-centered methods propose that education proceed, as Raymond Boisvert puts it, in widening concentric circles (Boisvert 1998, 103). Dewey outlines this approach in 'The University Elementary School' (MW1:318): (1) *Start with interests.* Courses of study that start from students' interests, activities, and contexts are better able to engage students in learning. Subject-matter and methods must call the whole child into activity at each subsequent educational level. (2) *Employ cumulative sequences.* Subject-matters should progress naturally, year to year. Each new year should begin with a review, not a repetition, of the preceding year's problems and materials. A review presents previous materials as prospective of what is to come. (3) *Introduce specialization gradually.* To engage students at the level of experience, studies should not seem remote or disconnected from ordinary life. For this reason, specialized topics and concepts should be introduced *within* problematic contexts as useful tools applicable to that context. (4) *Introduce abstract concepts and symbols when appropriate.*[8] Later stages of study introduce students to more abstract thinking, formal methods, and increased facility with symbols (words, numbers, formulas). Textbooks are more extensively used than at previous stages. Unlike traditional schools that often frustrate students by prematurely forcing their involvement with abstract tools, Deweyan schools help students anticipate the use of abstract methods through gradual and practical exposure.

The social atmosphere of the school is as important as any lesson taught there. Schools must create a culture of communication and cooperative activity. Unfortunately, in Dewey's view, schools are largely institutions that lack 'a social atmosphere and motive for learning' because they assume there is an 'antithesis between purely individualistic methods of learning and social action' (MW9:310). By creating an atmosphere based on this false opposition (between individual and community), schools are controlling education in a way that is destructive to learning. Imagine a classroom of students who must all read the same books, recite the same lessons; each day, tasks and results are the same. In such regimented environments there 'is no opportunity for each child to work out something specifically his own, which he may contribute to the common stock, while he, in turn, participates in the productions of others . . . The social spirit is not cultivated – in fact . . . it gradually atrophies for lack of use' (EW.5:64). Something tragic is done to the personality in such an environment since, as discussed in the chapters on morality and politics, the self is naturally social and flourishes through interaction and cooperation with others. By creating environments at odds with social needs, schools contribute to the creation of children who tend toward solipsism and the anxious expectation that others are more likely to be competitors than partners in social inquiry.

Control is, of course, necessary to education; but there are other approaches to control besides the external imposition of power typical of traditional schools. When a spirit of cooperation and participation pervade an activity – such as in a family or on a baseball team – there is order, not because one person or authority is imposing it, but because of the 'moving spirit of the whole group'. Dewey adds, 'The control is social, but individuals are parts of a community, not outside of it' (LW13:33).

In Deweyan education, teachers exercise control not by fighting or overwhelming students' natural tendencies, but by creating social and physical circumstances designed to elicit and encourage students' natural desires and capabilities to learn. Student interest is 'controlled' not by external threats or rewards but because they find themselves engaging with others in solving the problems that various lessons present.

The changes Dewey enacted in his own school and proposed for education generally required more than a change in educators' habits; physical structures, too, required adjustment. One need only compare how much more inquisitive children are *out* of school than in school to appreciate how insensitive traditional schools have been to how the physical environment stimulates (or dampens) curiosity. 'The physical equipment and arrangements of the average schoolroom', Dewey writes, 'are hostile to the existence of real situations of experience . . . Almost everything testifies to the great premium put upon listening, reading, and the reproduction of what is told and read' (MW9:162). In conjunction with teachers and school administrators, architects and engineers can help reimagine what a physical school could be. At a minimum, new pedagogical flexibilities can be enabled by moveable desks, kitchens, and even laboratories. 'There must be more actual material, more stuff, more appliances, and more opportunities for doing things, before the gap [between children's in-school and out-of-school experience] can be overcome' (MW9:162).

In contemporary society, it is still commonplace to assume categorical distinctions between education and the rest of life ('school' *versus* 'real life', 'ivory tower' *versus* 'practical world'). Sometimes, the comparison is to the school's detriment; one is 'too cool for school' because school is primarily a place of rote and routine demands. At other times, it is 'real life' which suffers in comparison, since 'real life' connotes an arena of brutal competition and merciless consequences.

Such attitudes, while caricatures of school and 'real life', stem from well-established incongruencies between what happens in and out of schooling. School and society are distinct and, in many ways, opposing worlds. Education's fundamental task, Dewey believes, is to heal the school–society divide because 'the school cannot be a preparation for social life excepting as it reproduces, within itself, typical conditions of social life' (MW4:272).

Readers may wonder why it is so important for Dewey to connect school and society. His motivation is not just pedagogical but ethical. Because ethical responsibilities are themselves manifested in a social world, individuals can only become capable of assuming those responsibilities *if* their educational training bears some semblance to social life.

> There cannot be two sets of ethical principles, one for life in the school, and the other for life outside of the school. As conduct is one, so also the principles of conduct are one. The tendency to discuss the morals of the school as if the school were an institution by itself is highly unfortunate. The moral responsibility of the school, and of those who conduct it, is to society. The school is fundamentally an institution erected by society to do a certain specific work, – to exercise a certain specific function in maintaining the life and advancing the welfare of society.
>
> (MW4:269)

While Dewey writes here about children, his point may be set in relief by considering higher education. Over the years, many in the West have accepted the division between 'practical education' and 'education for its own sake'. As pre-professional course offerings and degrees have mushroomed, humanities educators have adjusted by appending so-called 'liberal arts' courses to the pre-professional program. Under the assumption that these courses will make them 'well-rounded', pre-professional students take just an uncoordinated sampling of humanities classes. This reveals, in effect, that universities are psychologically unable to renounce explicitly their age-old mission of 'educating the whole person'. In actual practice, however, this mission *has* been relinquished. The education of a *whole person* –

that is, educating students about facts and values transcendent of narrow vocational objectives – has been relegated to vitamin-like supplements of humanities and science courses for pre-professional degree seekers.

Such trends in education may seem innocuous, mere responses to *society's* preference for buying and selling. But society needs and wants more than economic activity. The formation of an educated and ethical person requires a diverse curriculum, which does not predispose one to construe 'welfare' in exclusively pecuniary terms. For welfare also includes artistic innovation and moral resourcefulness; it requires intelligence, the ability of new generations to reason intrepidly about their future. On Dewey's view, the proper measure of a school's 'service to society' would be this: the active representation, in microcosm, of the plurality of values (economic, aesthetic, moral) that its students will find themselves engaged with for the rest of their lives.

Dewey's mandate that education become relevant to the needs and conditions of society addresses the excesses of traditionalists and romantics. Both of those approaches are undermined by their assumption that there is such a thing as 'education in itself'. Dewey is arguing that 'education in itself' is impossible as long as the school is kept connected with the society it inhabits. In contrast to other theoretical approaches to education, Dewey assumes no 'ideal learners'. There are, in the actual world, only learners who bring some particular 'reference to social life or membership' to their education (MW4:271–22).

In a culture where school and society saw one another as part of the same enterprise, debates over what 'the moral mission' of schools should be would dissolve. This is because, Dewey writes,

Apart from participation in social life, the school has no moral end nor aim. As long as we confine ourselves to the school as an isolated institution, we have no directing principles, because we have no object . . . Only as we interpret school activities with reference to the larger circle of social activities to which they relate do we find any standard for judging their moral significance.

(MW4:271)

Some, such as Alan Ryan, have criticized Dewey's emphasis on the socializing and future-oriented function of the school as oppressive to some students: those who are individualistic nonjoiners or those who approach education with conservative attitudes about traditional values would find little accommodation of their perspectives in Deweyan schools.[9] Dewey might reply that his educational philosophy ensures room for these students, too, because the school's mission was *not* to socialize individuals toward a certain particular social type, but to enable each student to have the fullest possible experience of their own autonomy, which will of course be meaningful only within a larger social context.[10] I suspect, however, that there is a more difficult problem here for Dewey than my reply can presently address.

Education for democracy

The school's aim, then, is complex. It is not simply vocational training, intrinsic flourishing, or even civics; in actual life, the child inhabits all these roles – he is a voter, family member, community activist, friend, worker, and recreational player. Accordingly, the school must educate the child to accomplish and grow in all these endeavors. Schools failing to do this prevent the child from living a social life as 'an integral unified being' and condemn her to 'suffer loss and create friction' (MW4:269).

Schools' training of leadership deserves special emphasis. Students must be trained with the self-reliance needed for intelligent leadership along with a constructive sense of their membership in the society they are inheriting. In this regard, the school is the most important institution in a democracy. In a 'democratically constituted society', social life predominantly consists of interests that are not wholly foreign to one another, but are 'mutually interpenetrating' (MW9:92). Progress, in such a society, is measured by how effectively citizens can adjust to changing conditions and problems. For example, as science develops new ways of prolonging life, citizens would discuss and debate the challenges to values implied by the research. What is gained and what is lost, and from which perspectives? How can the benefits and detriments, appreciated from various points of view, be translated into the best course of action? The challenge for education in a democratically constituted society is to train children to avoid framing social problems from only *one* particular perspective – from the point of view of business, or science, or religion, for example. This is a burdensome but necessary requirement. 'A democratic community', Dewey writes, 'is more interested than other communities have cause to be in deliberate and systematic education' (MW9:92–3).

It is safe to say that education's most valuable contribution to democracy is the creation of what Dewey calls a 'total' attitude.[11] The need for such an attitude stems from the conflicts that arise between individuals and groups. For example, when the interests of medicine conflict with those of a religion (in end-of-life care, say) or when developers' property interests conflict with the aesthetic interests of homeowners, there is, Dewey writes, 'a stimulus to discover some more comprehensive point of view from which the divergencies may be brought together, and consistency or continuity of experience recovered' (MW9:336). While there may be many very different perspectives with which one can interpret experience, we should not conclude that this entails permanent disagreement among plural-istic groups. For, Dewey reminds us, even among the most disparate groups 'in certain fundamental respects the same predicaments of life recur' (MW9:337). There is almost always common ground between diverse groups, and this fact offers continuing hope that challenges can be confronted as a unified public, no matter what other differences might remain outstand-ing. Progress toward such an ideal demands more than just strategic politics; it demands an education which is both practi-cal and philosophical:

> [E]ducation offers a vantage ground from which to penetrate to the human, as distinct from the technical, significance of philo-sophic discussions . . . The educational point of view enables one to envisage the philosophic problems where they arise and thrive, where they are at home, and where acceptance or rejec-tion makes a difference in practice.
>
> (MW9:337–8)

Education of a 'total attitude' enables people, at their best, to build communities. It also makes possible the creation of 'communal perspectives', which can transcend parochial bound-aries to address new conflicts. When aiming for these goals, education utilizes activities that are conjoint, consciously shared, and communicative. Participants in the process learn strategies for open communication and free inquiry; they strive to be 'objective' in a manner consistent with sympathetically seeing 'an other's perspective' rather than striving for a perfectly neutral point of view.

Any pluralistic society which seeks to be democratic must figure out how to prevent those with parochial, even anti-democratic, views from fomenting factionalization or even violence. By what criteria is a group 'too parochial'? This is a political question as well as an educational one, and Dewey takes it up in *Democracy and Education*. There he uses the example of a gang (or clique) to discuss his basis for criticizing parochialists. In even the most hermetic of groups, we must first recognize that they: (1) hold some interests in common among themselves, and (2) have some interaction and cooperation with other groups. These two traits, found throughout human societies, allow us to ask about such groups: 'How *numerous and varied* are the interests which are consciously shared? How *full and free is the interplay* with other forms of association?' (MW9:89, emphasis mine). Measured against these criteria, a group need not be criminal to possess traits that, while not inherently immoral, are likely to engender conflicts and internecine strife. Dewey writes,

> The isolation and exclusiveness of a gang or clique brings its antisocial spirit into relief. But this same spirit is found wherever one group has interests 'of its own' which shut it out from full interaction with other groups, so that its prevailing purpose is the protection of what it has got, instead of reorganization and progress through wider relationships . . . The essential point is that isolation makes for rigidity and formal institutionalizing of life, for static and selfish ideals within the group . . . On such a basis it is wholly logical to fear intercourse with others, for such contact might dissolve custom. It would certainly occasion reconstruction.
>
> (MW9:91, 92)

In our day as in Dewey's, the ability to exclude others remains an important source of group identity. As a result, factionalization increasingly dominates Western cultural formations – in how people live, sell, shop, politick, educate, and communicate, to name just a few. By permitting the creation of ever more parochial groups we eliminate risks but also experience little growth. Conflicts become more intractable as forms of life become anti-educational.

The rise of techniques creating factionalization stand in marked opposition to the democratic ideal as Dewey conceives it. On Dewey's view, 'democracy is not an alternative to other principles of associated life. It is the idea of community life itself' (LW2:328). Democratic life, then, rests upon the qualitative character of a society's constituent social groups. If we recall Dewey's two criteria for assessing the democratic character of groups (mentioned above), we find (1) that social groups embody the democratic ideal when they push beyond their narrower 'interests' to seek out 'more numerous and more varied points of shared common interest' with other groups. They recognize that navigating social conflicts requires 'the recognition of mutual interests' rather than the aggrandizement of differences.

We also find (2) that the democratic ideal is fostered when 'freer interaction between social groups' is sought. The challenges presented by more diverse social interaction tends to produce in groups a 'change in social habit' and an improved ability to readjust to new situations (all quotes from MW9:92). In other words, groups faced with inter-group dialogue become more democratic once they stop hunkering down ('rallying their base' as contemporary political strategists call it) and engage instead with those less like themselves. The result is that their character *as a group* becomes broader and more adaptable.

While it is obvious that many groups do not *in fact* do this, Dewey's point is a hypothetical one based on the idea that we *want* to get along. Unless groups can discover new mutual interests or ways of interacting with other groups, there is little chance of escaping anti-democratic antagonisms and struggles for factional power.

Conclusion

In the end, education determines whether democracy flourishes or falters. Education determines the kind of habits we develop for investigating beliefs and situations, and how we communicate along the way. While any culture seeks to pass on its values and beliefs to the next generation, Dewey argues that it is critical that we distinguish between education that encourages interaction and creative hypothesizing from those which celebrate parochialism and dogmatism.

Among Americans, Dewey found a general cultural tendency to fix belief with methods that rest upon sheer authority. Such anti-empirical habits of mind were not isolated to isolationist communities, but were the result of popular pedagogical methods and communicative practices outside the school. The unfortunate result was that many citizens could not understand or evaluate complicated political and scientific explanations. One cause of this, bad schooling, has been discussed in this chapter. But Dewey points to another cause, worth considering in the twenty-first century. He writes,

> There is a considerable class of influential persons, enlightened and liberal in technical, scientific and religious matters, who are only too ready to make use of appeal to authority, prejudice, emotion and ignorance to serve their purposes in political and economic affairs. Having done whatever they can do to debauch the habit of the public mind in these respects, they then sit back in amazed sorrow when this same habit of mind displays itself violently with regard, say, to the use of established methods of historic and literary interpretations of the scriptures or with regard to the animal origin of man.
>
> (MW15:50)

As a contemporary example, one might think for a moment of the American broadcasting elite who, despite their excellent educations, barrage viewers with the kind of bad logic and hyperbolic rhetoric that leads to good ratings but also to diminished public understanding. Alternatively, one might consider the ferocity with which advertisers colonize space in schools and textbooks – under the cover of 'efficiency' and the 'free market'. These influential persons, powerful modelers of disingenuous inquiry, are deeply complicit in debauching the public's ability to reason. As they blur the distinction between argument and persuasion, they contribute to public skepticism about the legitimate claims of scientists, philosophers, educators, and advocates of sound public policy. The blame for public ignorance, then, must be spread beyond society's usual charlatans to educated individuals. By caving in to careerism and self-gain, they fail to exercise the moral and intellectual discipline needed to model responsible inquiry, and so compromise the potential for democracy.

The lesson Dewey wanted educators to take from such phenomena is: if genuine democracy resides in 'the idea of community life itself' but actual conditions show that community life is being undermined by deceptive or authoritarian methods of fixing belief, then another way must be found to educate citizens. Since democracy is more than just a technique of governing but is 'primarily a mode of associated living, of conjoint communicated experience', then education becomes vital to democracy *only once it provides individuals with the intellectual habits not only for rejecting authoritarianism, but for critically evaluating everyday persuasion and trickery.*

This brings us to the second and final way education enables democracy to flourish, through the instruction of communication. Communication makes cooperative inquiry possible. Inquiry provides citizens with an alternative to knee-jerk reactions; it allows us to examine events logically and investigate alternatives with imagination and art. Inquiry and communication allow experimentation with meanings, which may be able to mitigate social isolation and factionalization. Against such problems we find in education 'the only possible solution: the perfecting of the means and ways of communication of meanings so that genuinely shared interest in the consequences of interdependent activities may inform desire and effort and thereby direct action' (LW2:332). The more impoverished our communication, the less able we are to navigate around incongruent values toward common ground and acts of cooperation. Ideally, education trains students to be imaginative and experimental, and to see inquiry as a fallible process which may, in the future, revise the meaning of present judgments. By definition this process is exclusionary of dogmatisms, and Dewey certainly did intend this value to be inculcated.

6

Aesthetics: creation, appreciation, and consummatory experience

Art is the living and concrete proof that man is capable of restoring consciously, and thus on the plane of meaning, the union of sense, need, impulse and action characteristic of the live creature. The intervention of consciousness adds regulation, power of selection, and redisposition. Thus it varies the arts in ways without end. But its intervention also leads in time to the idea of art as a conscious idea – the greatest intellectual achievement in the history of humanity.

(LW10:31)

Introduction

Few areas of human endeavor inspire as much passion and admiration as the arts. Arresting photographs, inspirational chorales, heartbreaking poems, and mouthwatering canapés are just a few examples of the kind of transformative experience only art can provide. Because the arts have typically interwoven reason with powerful emotions, philosophy has often taken an ambivalent attitude toward art's philosophical legitimacy. As guardians of both rationality and reality, philosophers have acted ingeniously to rationalize away the volatile emotions and seemingly random expressions of the artist's expressive messages. At times, this has amounted to the dismissal or downgrading of the philosophical validity of human artistic endeavor.

Not so with Dewey. By challenging or transcending many traditional philosophical assumptions, Dewey liberalized aesthetic theory, and celebrated art as 'the greatest intellectual achievement in the history of humanity' (LW10:31). Art cannot be captured in the staid language of objects; art is *an event of participation* that weaves artworks and appreciators into especially satisfying experiences. Because the understanding and improvement of experience is central to Dewey's philosophy, the powerful forces of art and aesthetic experience must be investigated as one of the *most* appropriate areas of philosophical inquiry.

Dewey's interest in art and aesthetics is evident in writings on psychology, education, and metaphysics.[1] In later years it was fostered by travel and by his growing friendship with Albert C. Barnes, a Philadelphia physician and pharmaceutical manufacturer who amassed a significant collection of French paintings (notably Pierre-Auguste Renoir, Paul Cézanne, Pablo Picasso, Henri Matisse) in Merion, Pennsylvania. Barnes's own interest in art's educational uses led him to enroll in one of Dewey's seminars at Columbia; they became lifelong friends, with Barnes contributing significantly to Dewey's own education about art and aesthetics.

Over his career, Dewey came to believe that art and aesthetics were central, not peripheral, to philosophy. The following are four substantive ways in which he believed aesthetics are centrally important to philosophy. First, there is aesthetics itself: the nature of aesthetic experience, artworks, interpretation, and the historical development of aesthetic values and criticism. Second, there are art's ethical functions in shaping character (personal and communal) by the symbolization of present identity and the imaginative idealization of the future. Third, there are art's political functions: particularly the way art can function to shape communication that manipulates states, countries, and markets (through, e.g., propaganda and advertising). Fourth, there is metaphysics: aesthetic experience exemplifies the most vivid and condensed example of experience at its most integrated or 'consummatory'. Such a degree of fulfillment represents life – including intellectual inquiry – at its most satisfactory.

Art as experience

Dewey's study of art, *Art as Experience* (1934), grew out of 'Art and the Aesthetic Experience', a series of lectures he gave in 1931. While undoubtedly one of the four or five most important expressions of Dewey's own philosophy, the wider impact of *Art as Experience* on the field of aesthetics has been episodic.[2] Dewey's unique approach to art is announced by the title of the book's very first chapter: 'The Live Creature'. (Compare, for example, the title 'What is Art?' found in aesthetician Clive Bell's influential 1913 book, *Art.*) No theory of art could begin with analytic definition of an object, Dewey believed, because no object is ever meaningful standing alone, but only in relation to particular interpreters. To avoid committing the 'philosophic fallacy' (treating eventual functions as starting points of experience) philosophers of art are obligated to discover how art *functions in experience*. They must investigate the multifaceted continuities between art, aesthetics, and the rest of lived experience.

Thus, *Art as Experience* inquires into how art functions, first by looking at the organic sources of art: the physical, sensory, and psychic functions many creatures, including humans, share. As with simple sensations (discussed in chapter 1), experiences with art result from the transaction of an organism with its environment over a period of time. Such transactions adjust the state of the organism for survival and, more importantly, growth: 'In a growing life', Dewey writes, 'the recovery [of unison with the environment] is never mere return to a prior state, for it is enriched by the state of disparity and resistance through which it has successfully passed' (LW10:19). Though rooted in simple biology, such facts 'reach to the roots of the esthetic in experience', for when life is able to survive and grow, 'there is an overcoming of factors of opposition and conflict; there is a transformation of them into differentiated aspects of a higher powered and more significant life' (LW10:20). In other words, concepts and fine-grained meanings emerge out of the ongoing and rhythmic adjustments of sense. This fact establishes the naturalistic basis for all aesthetics, and prescribes success conditions for a theory of art: namely, to explain how meaningful artistic and aesthetic phenomena are already implicit in the constructive rhythms of everyday experience – and how, therefore, such positive experiences might be capable of expansion.

Dewey's novel thesis – that aesthetic theory reflects living functions and continuities connecting creature and world – was probably harder for philosophers to accept than for artists. Many artists, to be artists, must commute constantly between imaginative conceptual planning and intimate sensory contact with the sights, sounds, and smells of materials. Thus, they must be alive to the ways that blood can redden, trains can moan, or rain can perfume evening air; such electric consciousness of the qualitative dimensions of experience is connected with their purpose of communicating through art. Artists could never afford to take the philosophical position that qualities are simply, radically, 'out there' apart from the perceiver; this view practically implies that art making is impossible. For an artist, as for any other living creature, qualities enter experience only as they are actively 'taken up' emotionally, imaginatively, and purposefully. Such engagement is a prerequisite to art's communicating at all.

These organic connections help presage a topic we will consider shortly, namely Dewey's urgent insistence on art and artists' potential to benefit everyday life. For at their best, art and artists forge new connections between sense perceptions and cultural meanings; these new connections are often exactly what individuals and societies need to regain a healthy balance after periods of violence or disease.

Let us turn to a synopsis of the main components of *Art as Experience*. The fundamental problem of aesthetics, in Dewey's view, is not conceptual or definitional – how to define art, expression, or value. Rather, the problem is fundamentally practical: How has the ordinary person become so distanced from the arts? Why have so many aspects of daily life become so thoroughly unaesthetic? In other words, Dewey sees in culture a widespread tendency to view art's objects and events as radically different from those common to everyday life. Artists, too, are set apart as special, possessing insight or genius foreign to others. Fundamental to such misconceptions is a presumption that aesthetic experience is categorically different than other kinds of experience. The reconstruction of aesthetic theory – and experience – depends, then, upon a critique of misconceptions, diagnoses concerning the sources of these misconceptions, and a positive argument to recover 'the continuity of esthetic experience with normal processes of living' (LW10:16).

One important component of Dewey's argument regards the ecological connectedness of conduct and communication. Details about that connectedness have been described in previous chapters; here, it is sufficient to add that aesthetic and everyday experiences are also extensively connected because they draw upon the same fundamental biological and psychological conditions. Whatever differences arise to distinguish them as types of experience, it remains true that they are based in the same ecological transactions that fund all types of experience (including moral, cognitive, and religious experience).

A second component of the argument is methodological, and concerns the starting point of inquiry into aesthetic phenomena. As discussed earlier (in connection with, for example, stimulus and the reflex arc), theories that start from rigidly preestablished categories or definitions result in inquiries that fail to understand the phenomena that initiated the questions. Aesthetic theories which start from academic definitions, compartments, and lists of 'accepted' examples of art all result, Dewey writes, in 'a conception of art that "spiritualizes" it out of connection with the objects of concrete experience' (LW10:17). In contrast, a practical starting point – a radically empirical attitude toward experience – entails that aesthetic inquiry go 'back to experience of the common or mill run of things [to] discover the esthetic quality such experience possesses' (LW10:16). This approach not only corrects the errors described before as the 'philosophic fallacy' but also clues philosophers in to something that great artists have *always* known: that art's purpose is never mainly to build upon someone's *knowledge* but to provoke and shape whole *experiences*. If philosophy could adopt for itself this broader mission, it might illuminate sources of the beautiful and the benumbing in experience so ordinary life could more effectively recover a deeper, more meaningful sense of the aesthetic.

A third component of the argument is rhetorical. To help readers shift away from their preconceptions, they needed to imagine what aesthetic experience could be *apart* from traditional artistic contexts (museums, music halls, theaters) and the associated concepts unconsciously at work in thinking about them (fine/useful, art/craft, beautiful/practical, aesthetic/ordinary). These conventional contexts and concepts block one's ability to see, with fresh eyes, the aesthetic aspects of life. To reconsider the meaning of sophisticated artistic products in a radically empirical way, Dewey argues, we have to forget them for a while and attend to their source, ordinary experience, which is usually not considered aesthetic at all. 'In order to *understand* the esthetic in its ultimate and approved forms', Dewey writes, 'one must begin with it in the raw; in the events and scenes that hold the attentive eye and ear of man, arousing his interest and affording him enjoyment as he looks and listens: the sights that hold the crowd:

> the fire-engine rushing by; the machines excavating enormous holes in the earth; the human-fly climbing the steeple-side; the men perched high in air on girders, throwing and catching red-hot bolts . . . [one must notice] how the tense grace of the ball-player infects the onlooking crowd; . . . the delight of the housewife in tending her plants, and the intent interest of her goodman in tending the patch of green in front of the house; the zest of the spectator in poking the wood burning on the hearth and in watching the darting flames and crumbling coals.
>
> (LW10:10–11)

These homespun examples are poignant *and* mundane; they drive home the point that aesthetic experience is not a categorically distinct type of experience. Rather, 'it is an inherent possibility of most experience; it is concerned with the fulfillment of *meaning*, not truth' (Alexander 1987, 7). This means, at the very least, that we should stop opposing the aesthetic and the useful.[3] Additionally, Dewey uses numerous examples of aesthetic objects from other cultures to help point out that the aesthetic/useful distinction is culturally constructed, not absolute. Turkish rugs and African tribal dances, for example, have both use and beauty, but those qualities are not distinguished, conceptually, by the cultures employing them. If we want to understand art, artists, and aesthetic experience we must demythologize them. This process begins with noting and describing how the aesthetic dimension grows out of the transactions that make up ordinary events.

The dualisms and misconceptions just mentioned have had a powerful influence in shaping the way both intellectual elites and everyday people view art and aesthetic experience. The effect for most people is that they view the arts as foreign or irrelevant to their interests; for aesthetic theorists and philosophers, the incorporation of these misconceptions into their theories renders them impotent to connect great artistic works with the human need for more extensive aesthetic experience. These ideas have amassed such an impact because they have been actively affirmed and promulgated by cultural and economic forces, especially the museum. To help readers fully divest their minds of these misconceptions, Dewey undertakes a concentrated diagnosis of how museums have encouraged a conception of art isolated from the rest of experience – as, for example, 'pure', 'high', or 'fine'.

What, then, is the 'museum conception' of art? Consider some 'typical' works of art: Da Vinci's *Mona Lisa* (a.k.a. *La Gioconda*), Michelangelo's *Pietà,* or the Parthenon of Athens. One powerful influence on the definition of these things as typical works of art is the museum view that 'art' consists of classic objects. A 'classic object', it is assumed, has fine and noble characteristics distinguishing it from practical objects; moreover, these characteristics should be obvious regardless of where the object is displayed. Dewey argues that this view commits two major errors. First, it assumes that we can make judgments about the aesthetic nature of art objects despite the fact that they have been removed from the historical and cultural contexts that formed them. This obscures a long history of aesthetically expressive objects serving multiple functions: a beautiful prayer rug aids supplication, a dynamic tribal dance appeals for rain, finely wrought pottery supplies a ceremonial vessel for communal drinking, festive plays and songs memorialize a community across generations. Dewey's point is that contemporary disregard of original functions impoverishes aesthetic theories' appreciation of the ties between art's meaning and its socio-historical functions in experience. The second, perhaps more serious, error of conceiving of art using museum criteria is that this depreciates the power an artwork can exercise in future experience. The more an artwork is decontextualized and elevated as 'beautiful' in a narrow sense, the more art becomes dependent on museums alone for their status. Deprived of wider sources of cultural acclaim, art objects become *bijoux:* prestigious with those who value money or social prestige, but largely disconnected from wider influence on human aesthetic experience.

What causes the museum conception of art? Why have people placed art on a pedestal and awarded it a nearly exclusive possession of aesthetic qualities – at the expense of ordinary experience? One very general cause (affecting but not limited to aesthetics) is a general intellectual tendency toward compartmentalization. In the course of managing the flux and chaos of life, we invent concepts or compartments; these are habits of thought useful for solving problems. 'Art' is one such compartment; 'morality' and 'religion' are others. Complications arise when we forget that these created compartments are *not* permanent or discrete kinds of things, but were invented for pragmatic reasons. Laboring under the assumption that they *are* permanent, we find ourselves stuck with impossible conflicts (such as science *versus* religion, serious *versus* popular art) and concepts that we feel *must* fit actual experience, but for some reason will not.

Other factors, less philosophical, also separate art and the aesthetic from ordinary life, for example, ambitious self-aggrandizement that affects nations, classes, and individuals alike. A country will fill its museums with war booty to boast of national power and destiny; it erects opera houses, museums, and galleries as sanctimonious testaments to its cultural power. Within a society, social class reputation can be similarly burnished by art collecting. These practices commodify art and internationalize its trade. Dewey's main concern with commodification is that it weakens or destroys 'the connection between works of art and the *genius loci* of which they were once the natural expression' (LW10:15). The more invasive and magnetic the pull of commodification and trade upon an indigenous art-making community, the more rapidly the intimate and social functions responsible for art deteriorate. In place of those organic functions there is imposed an impersonal world market which reduces artworks to 'that of being specimens of fine art and nothing else' (LW10:15).

Some critics have argued that Dewey overstates the influence of the museum conception on viewers of art. Monroe Beardsley (1982) argues that museum visitors bring their culture with them when they enter a museum and their interpretation of the meanings of works is mediated by much more than whatever influences are exercised by curatorial presentation. In response, Dewey might argue that this might be true about some works of art – created with museums and its patrons in mind – but his thesis is about the long-term effects on cultural perceptions of art more generally when the *idea* of art is put on a pedestal. Now it seems almost beyond doubt that the public has come to view artworks as rarefied objects requiring knowledge for them to be enjoyed. Given the impression that art is essentially intellectual, many avoid engagement with it; they excuse their participation in jazz or opera, for example, by saying, 'I don't know enough about it.' Dewey's hope is that by defeating this prejudice more people will be able to find beauty in the fluttering trills of a Mozart sonata or the graceful pruning of a weekend gardener. He is seeking to lessen the ideological influence of the museum over the value judgments 'fine' and 'beautiful', because he believes this in turn can expand the degree to which everyday experience actually becomes aesthetic.[4]

Consummatory experience (an experience) and anesthetic experience

We have been considering obstacles which Dewey believed prevent people from having a more meaningful experience with both art and everyday life. His name for this form of experience is consummatory experience, or '*an* experience', as he also referred to it. This idea is of the greatest importance to Dewey's aesthetics. I shall try a backdoor route to explaining *an* experience by considering what is opposite to it. Entertain, please, this typical domestic scenario:

> While feeding the cat, the phone rings; conversation is perfunctory and half-attended to because kitty is meowing, insistent on her food. Anxious to remain faithful to the day's agenda, the call is terminated abruptly. A moment later, my child trips, falls, and starts to cry. The day has officially begun.

Many have days which unfold in this way. Such experience is 'anesthetic'. (More on this shortly.) Dewey writes, 'There is distraction and dispersion; what we observe and what we think, what we desire and what we get, are at odds with each other' (LW10:42). There is experience, but events do not make up *an* experience.

We can start to understand what *an* experience is by considering when life is the opposite of random, chaotic, or fragmentary. Entertain, in contrast, a few examples of *an* experience:

> A piece of work is finished in a way that is satisfactory; a problem receives its solution; a game is played through; a situation, whether that of eating a meal, playing a game of chess, carrying on a conversation, writing a book, or taking part in a political campaign, is so rounded out that its close is a consummation and not a cessation.

(LW10:42)

All of these experiences are examples of *an* (consummatory) experience. In each case, experience is of a consciously experienced, deeply meaningful unity or whole, one whose character is so unique and self-sufficient that we can clearly recognize it as separate and special. Consummatory experiences are not confined to interactions with art (note the diverse range of activities Dewey chooses as illustrations); there can be consummatory experiences in situations of all kinds: ordinary, recreational, communicative, scholarly, even political. In addition, consummatory experience can be tremendous (a quarrel with a lover, a last-minute rescue) or slight (watching a flock of geese nestle cozily on a riverbank); it may be enjoyed (that Parisian meal which memorialized what food may be) or suffered (the Atlantic storm whose fury summed up what a storm can be) (LW10:43). This last example may confound some common assumptions about aesthetic experience. For Dewey, consummatory experience can have either a positive or negative value; again, what marks out this experience as special is its self-integrated nature, its unity. As Alexander puts it, 'In *an* experience the conclusion is not merely a terminus or an ending, but a moment which brings a process to fulfillment: it is the outcome of a guided process of action which organizes and unifies the experience' (Alexander 1987, 199–200).

Several have criticized Dewey's requirement that aesthetic experiences with works of art be 'unified' or 'integrated'. Marshall Cohen (1965, 119) offers the example of cinematic montage which, while clearly art, is characterized by the 'gappy, "breathless", or discontinuous quality that Dewey assigns to practical experience'. Noel Carroll (2001) cites John Cage's silent piece 4' 33" as another counterexample – while possessing neither qualitative unity nor integrated consummation it is nevertheless art. In defense of Dewey, Richard Shusterman (1992, 76–7) and Philip Jackson (2000) have pointed out, in essence, that while contemporary artworks may be filled with 'jarring fragmentation and incoherencies' (or even silence), such aspects must be understood not simply in relation to the artwork as an isolated object/event, but to the 'more complex forms of coherence' that arise 'within a larger coherent totality of meaning' in the experienced situation that frames the work.[5]

In sum, to have *an* experience is to undergo a series of events which hang together (have unity), exhibit character (have a theme or pervasive quality), and end with some drama (consummating, not just terminating). *An* experience stands out as unique and results not merely from exertion or accident but from a coordination of doings and undergoings. *An* experience may blossom in many mediums (linguistic symbols, smells, tastes, sounds, ideas, textures, etc.) and may in retrospect be evaluated as either a zenith or nadir of good.

Dewey's account of consummatory experience is meant to explain why certain episodes in life, including encounters with art, are aesthetic. But it also diagnoses specific ways in which life is often *not* aesthetic – 'non-aesthetic' or 'anesthetic', in Dewey's terms. This is useful for making daily life more meaningful because too often we unthinkingly allow the anesthetic 'to be taken as norms of all experience' (LW10:47).

What is 'anesthetic' experience like? Consider two homely examples. Your Sunday picnic is unexpectedly cancelled due to rain; carefully planned arrangements are suddenly useless and meaningless. Gathered picnickers are crabby and at loose ends; the day stretches ahead with 'nothing to do'. Or perhaps you are working in a mailroom during the holiday season. This is a scene of intense pressure and automatic movement. A relentless conveyor belt of new mail hums as an anxious supervisor paces back and forth, making sure no one slows down or takes a break. You feel like an appendage to the machines, pressing yourself to work as efficiently as your abilities permit. These two examples illustrate two opposed extremes of experience, *both* anesthetic. At one extreme is aimlessness, a 'loose succession' that begins and ends nowhere in particular; at the other extreme is arrested, constricted motion like that of a machine. Thus, Dewey writes,

> The enemies of the esthetic are neither the practical nor the intellectual. They are the humdrum; slackness of loose ends; submission to convention in practice and intellectual procedure. Rigid abstinence, coerced submission, tightness on one side and dissipation, incoherence and aimless indulgence on the other, are deviations in opposite directions from the unity of an experience.
>
> (LW10:47)

Dewey's intent is to help us realize the variety of ways in which potentially aesthetic experiences of everyday life can be ruined or preempted by experiences which are anesthetic. Unified aesthetic experience may be preempted or dissolved by (1) *interruption* (phone calls, computerized alarms, advertising, or even a sneeze during a romantic kiss); by (2) *hyperactivity* (over-caffeination, incessant multi-tasking, demanding bosses); and by (3) *passivity* (habits of laziness, procrastination, the desire to 'be entertained'). To flourish, aesthetic experience must attain unity and integration; it must be granted the conditions that make possible a natural back-and-forth of doing and undergoing. Such a rhythm can shape an overall experience with its thematizing, emotional quality.

Making and appreciating artworks

As we have seen, life contains both aesthetic and anesthetic kinds of experience. The purpose of art, in Dewey's view, is to create especially aesthetic experiences. What must artists do to create works with such effects? And how must appreciators actively interact with art to have consummatory experiences?

To address such issues, Dewey must help readers overcome the traditional and radical separation of the 'artistic' from the 'aesthetic' (that is, 'artists' from 'appreciators'). To understand what happens at these different phases of an artwork's career, one must dispense with the notion that artists merely make and appreciators merely perceive. This picture essentially imposes (on art making/appreciating) the same mistaken stimulus–response model Dewey rejected in psychology. In both cases, the error is to separate and oversimplify a complicated and transactional set of processes. Of course artists *do* things with materials to make artworks of various types; of course appreciators *perceive and undergo* the effects initiated by art. What an understanding of art as participatory experience requires is that we avoid reducing art to making or appreciating and see how *both* phases are central to the experiences of artist and appreciator.

Let us begin with artists. 'To be truly artistic', Dewey states, 'a work must also be esthetic – that is, framed for enjoyed receptive perception' (LW10:54). What does this tell us about the experience of artmaking? One thing it tells us is that making is a process of both doing and undergoing. The artist *alternates* between doing (for instance, applying paint), undergoing (stepping back and looking), and then doing again (blending lines, and so on). The communicative aspect of art complicates this rhythm. The artist never just 'dashes off' a work for an unimagined viewer (any more than an appreciator allows a work simply to 'wash over' her). To make art means to be deeply engaged with the materials at hand (paint, canvas, light) while also attempting to form a sympathetic and imaginative projection of what appreciators will experience later on. Besides possessing technical skill and a sensitivity to material qualities, an artist must both know his own mind and embody 'in himself the attitude of the perceiver while he works' if he wishes to communicate meaningfully (LW10:55).[6]

Artmaking is a transformative process, both for the marble or pigment and for the personality of the maker. Just as factory workers are dulled by repetitive labor, artists too are shaped by their work. As physical materials of artistic expression (paint, marble, dance) are worked and reworked, so too are the emotions, concepts, and the imaginative vision of the artist himself. To engage in artmaking, Dewey writes, is to partake in 'a prolonged interaction of something issuing from the self with objective conditions', and this is 'a process in which both of them acquire a form and order they did not at first possess' (LW10:71).

Just as with artmaking, the appreciation of art involves a rhythmic alternation between doing and undergoing. 'Receptivity', Dewey writes, 'is not passivity. It, too, is a process consisting of a series of responsive acts that accumulate toward objective fulfillment' (LW10:58). The active engagement characteristic of aesthetic experience thus entails much more than passive recognition and reaction to a work's scheme or form. In aesthetic experience the appreciator (1) resonates sympathetically with an artwork's perceptual qualities and conceptual meanings and also (2) actively reconstructs these elements.

In this way every appreciator is *also* a creator – a writer of the novel they read, a painter of the canvas they view. This creativity requires an imaginative synthesis of the various elements of experience such as perceptions, emotions, memories, and associations. There are limits, however, to the appreciator's experience. In a genuinely aesthetic work, the appreciator creates and orders experience along lines *roughly similar to the artist's own process.*[7]

> There is work done on the part of the percipient [appreciator] as there is on the part of the artist . . . For to perceive, a beholder must create his own experience. And his creation

must include relations comparable to those which the original producer underwent. They are not the same in any literal sense. But with the perceiver, as with the artist, there must be an ordering of the elements of the whole that is in form, although not in details, the same as the process of organization the creator of the work consciously experienced.

(LW10:60)

Why must the appreciator's experience be roughly comparable to the artist's? The reason is that art, like language, is a communicative medium. Dewey believes, as did Peirce before him, that communication is a three-way function and includes speaker, thing said, and someone spoken to. Therefore, the experience of art requires that artists and appreciators be attuned to one another as they shape experience. To see this in practice, consider how a talented food critic, Ruth Reichl, highlights a meal's aesthetic quality by using the perspectives of both maker (chef) and appreciator (diner).

The meal began with cold hors d'oeuvres surrounding an edible landscape, in which pandas carved out of vegetables cavorted around a gelatin lake. Eight cold plates were set around it: crisp slices of pig's ear in hot oil crunched pleasantly when you ate them. Dried bean curd was cut into noodles and tossed with fava beans. Pork kidneys had been soaked in many changes of water until they were pure texture, little clouds under a hailstorm of Sichuan peppercorns. Fish was richly smoked. Jellied pâté rivaled anything on the Champs-Élysées.[8]

This description shows that the meal (artwork) is an aesthetic success because there is attunement of the chef (artist) to his patron (appreciator). Reichl's review shows how the diner's experience is informed by sympathy with the chef's processes of making ('bean curd was cut into noodles' and 'pork kidneys had been soaked in many changes of water'); it also indicates how the chef arranged details in anticipation of the diner's experience ('pandas carved out of vegetables cavorted around a gelatin lake' and kidneys served like 'little clouds under a hailstorm of Sichuan peppercorns'). Reichl understands, as Dewey puts it, that 'without an act of recreation the object is not perceived as a work of art. The artist selected, simplified, clarified, abridged and condensed according to his interest. The beholder must go through these operations according to his point of view and interest' (LW10:60).

Defining art

Much debate in aesthetics has revolved around the question 'What is art?' Definitions have varied tremendously. One fundamental dividing line separates 'essentialist' and 'anti-essentialist' approaches to definition. Essentialism seeks to define art by listing the necessary and sufficient property (or properties) all share in common. Candidates for such properties have included the ability of works to depict reality, express an artist's emotions, trigger emotion in the viewer, convey moral ideas, display beautiful form, and so on. Because such definitions have been infamously vulnerable to counterexamples, anti-essentialism developed as an alternative approach. Anti-essentialists argue that art cannot be defined using a set of essential properties, and that other ways to designate things or events as art must be found. Here, too, approaches vary greatly. Some say art gains its identity depending on the purposes it serves; others argue that art arises through certain procedures or processes of making, and how well they fulfill the requirements of the context (e.g., a museum) that receives them. Others would point to the way art is subjectively received – its ability to have a certain effect upon an individual.

Dewey's view may be considered anti-essentialist, since he believes that art cannot be simply located in isolated subjects, objects, or events; for Dewey, 'art' denotes the result of a process, the *interaction* of a thing (for example, a painting) and an appreciator (viewer). He distinguishes 'art products' and 'works of art'. For too long, common sense and philosophy have conflated the 'works' with the 'products' of art.

> The product of art – temple, painting, statue, poem – is not the work of art. The real work of art is the building up of an integral experience out of the interaction of organic and environmental conditions and energies . . . The work takes place when a human being cooperates with the product so that the outcome is an experience that is enjoyed because of its liberating and ordered properties.
>
> (LW10:70, 218)

For Dewey, 'art products' means the *things* (or commodities) most commonly associated with art – paintings, sculptures, etc. – such things are 'physical and potential'. 'Works of art' ('artworks') more accurately suits Dewey's aesthetic position. 'Artworks' are 'active and experienced . . . what the product does, its working' (LW10:167). They involve both physical and conceptual elements in active relation. Of course, a physical object *may* be the initiating cause of the appreciator's aesthetic experience; nevertheless, identifying 'art' with a physical, static object neglects two fundamental facts about art as experience. First, the overall process actually includes *both* physical and conceptual aspects. The changes which art initiates happen both to the material and to the experiences of artist and appreciator. Second, art is not static, but 'a cumulative series of interactions' that take time (LW10:223).

There have been many criticisms of Dewey's criteria for identifying art. Perhaps the strongest line of argument maintains that Dewey's attempt to reconstruct the identity of art (by divorcing it from physical things and marrying it to aesthetic experience) results in an account that is too subjective – and so too uninformative. D.W. Gotshalk, for example, argues that Dewey's separation of the 'work' from the 'product' drives art away from the definite objects made for appreciation by artists into nebulous potential things which always await some consumer's actualization of it. This is too vague and tentative as a criterion of art. The result, writes Gotshalk, is to make 'the crucial difference between the physical and the artistic . . . lie in the seclusive and esoteric and private experiences of individual percipients. This is idealism come home to roost with a vengeance' (Gotshalk 1964, 135). More recently, Richard Shusterman raised related difficulties with aesthetic experience as a defining characteristic of art. Dewey's text, he argues, implies that aesthetic experience is *both* definable and yet, ultimately, indefinable.[9] But if aesthetic experience is indefinable, then it has no explanatory power – and cannot do the practical work of separating 'art' from 'non-art'.

Dewey's reply to this line of argument will be unsatisfying to anyone seeking what Shusterman cleverly calls 'a traditional wrapper theory of art'. Such wrapper theories aim at step-by-step procedures or necessary and sufficient conditions to determine whether something is art, but Dewey's pragmatism has foregone this type of approach to conceiving art. Instead, as Shusterman puts it, Dewey's theory aims 'at bringing us closer to achieving more and better concrete goods in experience' by 'reminding us that *experience* (rather than collecting or criticism) is ultimately what art is about' and by helping us 'recognize and valorize those expressive forms which provide us aesthetic experience' but which are still denigrated by the prejudices promulgated by the institutions of 'fine art' (Shusterman 1992, 57). As was true in every other area of his philosophy, Dewey's philosophy did not aim to improve upon definitions but to liberate and enrich human experience.[10]

Expression and form

Dewey's theory of artistic expression is a novel and important part of his aesthetic theory. It is sometimes conflated with Romantic expression theories, such as those of R.G. Collingwood and Benedetto Croce. Expression theory argues that artists create art (in various media) by giving articulate expression to feelings and emotions. On this model, artistic creation begins with an inchoate emotional state (such as the artist's grief at his child's death) and engages in a process of self-exploration using an artistic medium (language). The discoveries of the artist are externalized in the artwork (poem), which conveys to the reader a clarified and encapsulated form of the artist's inner emotion (grief).[11]

In contrast to expression theory, Dewey believes that expression in art is not reducible to the use of a medium to convey or externalize the artist's initial emotion. What someone 'gets' when they have a consummatory experience with a work of art cannot be equated with a sympathetic vibration to the artist's own feeling. In what way, then, is artistic expression more than the conveyance of emotion, according to Dewey? First, it can be acknowledged that expression often *begins* with an impulsive emotion such as grief or revulsion. But a genuine artist will then take up that emotional impulse using a medium able to articulate it in terms understandable by the larger social and cultural world in which he lives. For Dewey, 'the task of the artist is to make the medium expressive so that the appreciator who encounters it will interact with it in such a way as to have an organized as well as an emotional response – the emotion must be articulated as well as evoked by the medium' (Alexander 1987, 221). Artmaking requires more than provoking audiences' emotions; and appreciation of art, the having of consummatory experience, requires more than a mere parroting of emotional exclamations.

Emotion is an indispensable part of expression; but its role in artistic expression is as an organizing force. In the work of art, Alexander notes, 'emotion is not what gets expressed; it is the manner of expression' (Alexander 1987, 222). Talented artists, then, are not simply conveying an emotion. They are clarifying, ordering, and modulating their initial emotional impulsions with careful and creative uses of their chosen media to express meaning. Deftness with media is also a crucial component in expression. Whereas most people rely upon language to express meaning, artists master many more media, and with greater precision. 'Sensitivity to a medium as a medium', Dewey notes, 'is the very heart of all artistic creation and esthetic perception' (LW10:203). So, for example, a film director like Stanley Kubrick could utilize the medium of film to express emotions in meaningful ways. Consider how his film *The Shining* takes a simple sequence like walking down a hotel hallway and transforms it into a scene pregnant with supernatural iridescences and potentially horrible consequences. This mastery of expression takes commonplace sequences and passes them 'through the alembic of personal experience', infusing their meaning with emotion and unique perspective (LW10:88). Learning to appreciate deeply Kubrick's techniques and emotional perspective amounts to seeing the world through his mind's eye. This education awakens 'new perceptions of the meanings of the common world' that transcend just the watching of films (LW10:88). We become 'acculturated', so to speak, in a way that makes experience more generally aesthetic and meaningful.

In terms of expressive abilities, artist and non-artist differ not because the artist has some especially 'sensitive soul' or 'flicker of creative genius' but because of the artist's developed capacities for disciplined expression. The artist, Dewey writes,

> has the power to seize upon a special kind of material and convert it into an authentic medium of expression . . . [He]

sticks to his chosen organ and its corresponding material, and thus the idea singly and concentratedly felt in terms of the medium comes through pure and clear.

(LW10:204)

The result of artistic expression, then, is not the delivery of an emotion but a transformation of an experienced situation.

Philosophy has long puzzled over how artworks can appear so much more compelling, vivid, and permanent than the confused jumble of events that make up everyday life. A variety of attempts have sought to explain why arranging materials (paint, stone, bodily motion, sounds, words) in certain ways – into a *form* – should result in the effect or end we call 'art'.[12] Most have sought to explain how the forms responsible for art derive from imitation of something else: worldly objects, authorial emotions, even transcendent universals or ideals (for example Beauty). Dewey rejects such imitation theories as further examples of the intellectualist fallacy. Since art is a process, a way of experiencing, it cannot be explained by a subject–object correspondence any more than knowing can.[13]

Nevertheless, form is an important part of Dewey's aesthetics; it describes *the manner* in which aesthetic expression is successfully carried off, from artist through appreciator. In Dewey's aesthetics:

> Form reflects the capacity of the art product and the responsive perception of the appreciator to work successfully together . . . Form is the energetic process of organizing the material of experience into a funded, meaningful, consummatory event which does not transcend life but fully actualizes it. Form is the dynamic process of shaping experience by means of a medium so that it becomes expressive.

(Alexander 1987, 237, 234)

Typically, we think of form as something definite – a cupola's sweeping vault, a tragedy's narrative arc – and expect that form can be simply located at a point in time or space. In Dewey's process-based account of art, form cannot be so located in just the artist's mind, art object, or audience's mind. Form operates across all phases of a work's history, from the creator's interaction with his materials, to the resulting art object, to the interaction of the audience with the work.[14] To make this less abstract, consider how dynamic form might operate in a viewer's experience of Michelangelo's statue, *David*:

> As the appreciator approaches *David*, she notices how his lips and eyes relate to one another, how the delicacy of their detail is accentuated by the statue's grand scale. She lingers on how the hands radiate with sensuality and power. As she views these features, she draws upon memories of her youth, her contests in courage. Present vision, memory, and emotion culminate; there is a consummatory *ahh* of aesthetic enjoyment.

The form of the statue is the way it works on this viewer – the way it compels and shapes the perceptual and conceptual ingredients into an integral whole – a consummatory experience. A work's form never simply points back to the physical object itself; it illuminates the work's meanings for the appreciator in ways that carry her experience to fulfillment.[15]

Some have criticized Dewey's account of form for being too subjective or relativistic. (Gotshalk's criticism, mentioned above, criticized Dewey for this fault.) Dewey's position claims that artworks are *collaborative* (involving maker, work, and appreciator) but this suggests that a work can have *many* possible audiences. If there is a different individual form at work in each situation, then there is *no* stable and identifiable entity that is *the* artwork. Besides eliminating the work, Dewey's account also eliminates all criticism – because now there is no longer a stable subject matter for criticism!

Dewey can reply to these charges in two different ways. First, Dewey's naturalism does not allow the presumption behind the objection – it denies that there are subjects existing in radical isolation from objects. We experience an objective world in the only senses 'objective' can have. Aesthetic experience is the cumulative outcome of various interrelated factors, *many of which we do not constitute or control* through individual whim. Thus, some stability in aesthetic judgment is derived from forces and qualities beyond our control. At the same time, there must be a response for art to be art, and that response is undertaken by an autonomous appreciator. Together, object *and* interpretation combine to make meaning. Second, Dewey could also point out (*a la* Shusterman's rebuke of the 'wrapper theory' of art mentioned earlier) that the *point* of criticism is not the isolation of art objects or forms, but empirically to highlight what aesthetic experience is and can be. Yes, audience interpretation and reception to *David* has changed over the centuries. But on a pragmatist theory of language and meaning it *has* to change; creatures and their cultures adapt and grow, and so do the meanings they assign to cultural artifacts. What a critic identifies as formally significant in a work is always indexed to the system of meanings and values relevant to that critic's history and culture. The forms he identifies as 'timeless' are not literally so; rather, he is expressing his faith that there is something enduringly meaningful in the way that art works on us, meaningful in a sense that is broader and deeper than this narrow cultural moment.

Aesthetic criticism

Besides seeking definitions of art and explanations of aesthetic experience, aesthetics develops theories about the value and meaning of art. It asks questions such as, why do some works deserve to be called 'good' or 'beautiful'? What distinguishes 'art' from 'entertainment'? What does a work like Monet's *Water Lilies* mean? Are interpretations of aesthetic meaning or value mere subjective opinion or are they, somehow, more objectively grounded?

For a long time, traditional aesthetics maintained that objective criticism of art is possible because definitions of art can be discovered. Any essentialist (or universalist) theory that develops criteria for the nature of art can also posit ways to judge the value and meaning of artworks. So, for example, theories which argue that art is essentially imitative (mimetic) will typically posit criteria of evaluation for works based upon how accurately they imitate; if a theory states that art is essentially expressive of the artist's emotions, then criteria of evaluation for specific works will revolve around how well they capture those emotions. The twentieth century's shift of interest in aesthetics toward abstraction and formal structure did not initially change criticism's aspiration to universality. Formalism, to mention one important school to which Dewey reacted, thought that criticism should evaluate artworks based on whether they possessed certain formal properties (whether they were, for example, 'graceful', 'elegant', 'unified', and 'skilful'). Two influential formalists, Clive Bell and Roger Fry, argue that there is one quality all works of visual art share: 'significant form'. This quality combines certain forms and relations (line, color, etc.) in ways that stir a special 'aesthetic emotion' in viewers.

Dewey rejects universalist/essentialist approaches to criticism for reasons similar to ones mentioned earlier (connected with debates over 'what is art'). If art is a process of genuine interaction, created and enjoyed by actual people, then any theory about the nature, meaning, and value of art cannot be grounded in an abstract essence or universal. Art must be understood as a phenomenon of human communication, taking place in a biological, historical, and cultural context. Artworks are expressive not through artists' mere imitation or representation of abstract universals, but by them 'selecting and ordering the energies in virtue of which things act upon us and interest us' (LW10:189). It is consideration of *the audiences' potential experience* that guides talented artists to eliminate from artworks those 'forces that confuse, distract, and deaden' while deploying 'order, rhythm and balance' for maximum aesthetic effect (LW10:189).

There is truth in the old idea that 'the artist aims at what is universal'. However, for Dewey, this does *not* mean that artists capture or represent preexisting forms in their work. Rather, they work 'by selecting those potencies in things by which an experience – any experience – has significance and value' (LW10:189). A universal, at best, is 'universally effective' in producing aesthetic experience, rather than universal in any deeper or metaphysical sense. Dewey's contemporaries Fry and Bell miss this point, and their account of significant form starts from the theoretical presumption that someone's aesthetic experience with an expressive work of art must be traced back to some static, universal thing. Dewey unsurprisingly assumes a practical starting point. The painter approaches his subject with an active mind, filled with biases, tendencies, and past experiences. So does the viewer. If a work's shapes, lines, and colors are expressive, it is not because they reproduce an eternal 'significant form' but because 'they are integrated into a general body of coordinated, funded responses' (Alexander 1987, 230). This fundamental notion about the starting point applies not just to Formalism, but to any critical school under consideration. It must be remembered that both art and criticism are situated and historical processes. Attempts of aestheticians to universalize judgments about them have led to excessively abstract theories, liable to counterexample and, more importantly, impotent to transform ordinary into aesthetic experience. They should be abandoned.[16]

Pragmatist aesthetics approaches criticism experimentally. As in cases of other kinds of judgment (moral, logical, etc.), aesthetic judgment must look to practical experience for its subject matter, criteria, and the experimental validation of its conclusions. In effect, this repudiates the practice of relying exclusively on authorities (museum curators, art journal critics, etc.) for what to consider aesthetically good or beautiful. Evaluative judgments about aesthetic merit will be effective in guiding future aesthetic experience only if those judgments are based on a process of inquiry deeply mindful of how concrete and active our particular perspectives are. By listening to practical experience, pragmatist criticism steers around many of the economic and metaphysical prejudices present in conventional views of art (such as the 'museum conception'); by making the function of art in experience its overriding concern, pragmatist criticism remains especially open-minded toward new forms of art.

Pragmatist method differs from those of formalism or structuralism. Those approaches draw boundaries around artworks to permit close analyses of *internal* grammar and qualities. Pragmatism rejects such boundary-drawing and insists upon consideration of biographical, historical, and cultural factors as relevant to judgment. Artworks, after all, are only meaningful through their transactions with people, and people's sense of meaning arises through historical and cultural experience. Nevertheless, the pragmatist critic must be cautious *not* to let these 'external' sources of information overshadow the central experience with the artwork. Such information helps enrich our experience of a work, but it should not be allowed to displace the importance of the immediate and qualitative encounter with that work.[17]

Let us now consider what a pragmatist critic should be capable of. First and foremost, a talented critic must always be a sensitive *perceiver* — not a theorist looking for examples to justify his or her abstractions. 'Since the matter of esthetic criticism is the perception of esthetic objects', Dewey writes, 'natural and artistic criticism is always determined by the quality of first-hand perception; obtuseness in perception can never be made good by any amount of learning, however extensive, nor any command of abstract theory, however correct' (LW10:302). Following up on such fine-grained perceptions, the critic must *describe* the properties of the object that could account for the experience she just had, whether it was an opera, a painting, or an encounter with an old friend. These perceptions and descriptions are preliminary and do not issue any final evaluations about the work. As preliminary, they must remain closely tied to the artwork itself, 'with the objective properties of the object under consideration – if a painting, with its colors, lights, placings, volumes, in their relations to one another' (LW10:312).

Once she has carefully perceived and described her experience of an artwork, she can *analyze* it; she may categorize 'the properties of a work of art by such names as symmetry, harmony, rhythm, measure, and proportion' (LW5:251). These categories are posited provisionally, and are meant to help 'effect a heightening and deepening of a qualitative apprehension' (LW5:252). For example, a pragmatic critic's comment that a Mozart piano sonata has a 'poignant but repetitive melody' is not a declaration that a permanent property of the sonata has been discovered. Rather, her proposition is tentatively estimating how that sonata is entering into her aesthetic experience. It is a pregnant clue for the further organization of her critical assessment.

The final phase of criticism is the expression of aesthetic judgment. Aesthetic criticism is a form of inquiry; it is empirical and ends in judgment. Since pragmatic criticism repudiates the *matching up* of an object with a form existing (somehow) apart from experiences, judgment necessarily reflects the critic's perspective. Dewey writes, 'Criticism is judgment. The material out of which judgment grows is the work, the object, but it is this object as it enters into the experience of the critic by interaction with his own sensitivity and his knowledge and funded store from past experiences' (LW10:313). Art criticism, in short, is never done from a God's-eye point of view.

Some have worried that Dewey's pragmatist criticism is relativistic. It offers nothing objective with which to evaluate art; consequently, we can never know when aesthetic judgments are just idiosyncratic opinions of critics and when they are actually *true*. Here are two reasons that this fear of relativism in pragmatist criticism is unfounded. First, while pragmatists allow that the values and personality of the critic (including her social and historical context) influence aesthetic analyses, the art object is still part of the mix. Because that object exhibits stable qualities which are physically perceived, there is resistance to the critic's interpretative whim. Further parameters on the range of interpretation are imposed by the critic's own habits (physical, linguistic, emotional, and social). Such factors, Dewey argues, favor a moderately realist view of criticism, not a relativist one.[18] In the end, the test of truth for aesthetic criticism lies not in correspondence but in its instrumental ability to enrich the quality and extent of future aesthetic experience. In these regards, criticism is subject to corroboration or correction by the experimental testing of others.

What did Dewey as art critic conclude, generally, about aesthetic criteria? What makes a work of art bad or good? How can evaluative judgments about levels of aesthetic quality be done using the language of function and experience? What distinguishes art from entertainment?

Let us begin to understand his schema with bad or non-art – works that fail to evoke any aesthetic experience at all. What has gone wrong? Sometimes art fails because it lacks authentic feeling; one feels manipulated by the writer or filmmaker. Rather than being invisibly moved by the story or characters, one becomes consciously aware of the strategic devices of the arts. One cannot look through the glass because it is so full of fingerprints, so to speak. When such contrivances become so overt, they prevent a work from hanging together properly. 'The facets of the work', Dewey writes, and 'the variety so indispensable to it, are held together by some external force' and when the ending arrives, it feels 'foisted upon us by something . . . from outside the movement of the subject matter' (LW10:74). Such works may not lack emotion, but the emotion present fails to organize the elements to achieve a coherent effect.[19]

While one finds criteria in Dewey's work for demarcating 'great' art, it must be noted that these cannot be used to establish any *ultimate* ranking for works of art. Value judgments are perspectival, and art functions expressively at given times and places through interactions with unique people possessing particular cultural backgrounds. These facts together entail that no ranking of '*the* great works' is possible. However, just as there are enduring mathematical and logical principles, one may also discover artworks that endure: Homer's *Iliad*, Dante's *Inferno*, Velasquez's *Las Meninas*, Bach's *Brandenburg Concertos*, or Whitman's *Leaves of Grass* make good first examples.

What makes artworks 'great', 'universal', or 'timeless'? Such designations cannot rest upon some intrinsic property possessed, nor can it simply be that we are accustomed to regard them this way. Dewey believes the qualities responsible for making a work 'universal' or 'timeless' are best understood by reference to an evolutionary framework; it is better, that is, to ask how these works *function* so successfully in experience. In Dewey's aesthetics, as Alexander notes, a work's timelessness is 'less like the timelessness of a Platonic essence [and more like] . . . the timelessness of a species which is highly adaptable to a variety of environments' (Alexander 1987, 237). An artwork's adaptive fitness is demonstrated by its enduring expression of meaning to individuals and societies over generations. Formally, such works typically possess 'an intimacy of the relations that hold the parts together', and those parts 'have the unique end of contributing to the consummation of a conscious experience' (LW10:121,122). We call such works 'beautiful'.

Besides having intimately related parts, great art has a balance between order and disorder. It's all in the mix: while appreciators need the serenity of order, we disdain the ennui of repetition; while the novelty injected by disorder adds spice, we denounce the confusion of chaos. Artworks engender experience that is aesthetic (or consummatory) when they provide a measured ratio of these energies. Put another way, great art utilizes unity and variety to evoke experience that involves us because it seems so *alive*: 'The ballet girls of Degas', Dewey writes, 'are actually on tiptoe to dance; the children in Renoir's paintings are intent upon their reading or sewing. In Constable, verdure is moist; and in Courbet a glen drips and rocks shine with cool wetness' (LW10:182).

Subject matter of sufficient scope and weight may also account for an artwork's greatness. Again, no ultimate list of 'artful' subject matters can be derived from Deweyan aesthetics, since significance is a function of personal and cultural context. Nevertheless, one may observe how war, romance, birth, and death show tenacious longevity, and so discover no empirical reason to suspect the imminent expiration of these topics' significance.

Perhaps most important in making an artwork 'great' is its *enduring* capacity for intensifying and enlivening ordinary life. Such works afford 'continuously renewed delight' and engender further consequences that are 'indefinitely instrumental to new satisfying events' (LW1:273, 274). This latter point deserves emphasis. The fact that an artwork produces a sparkling epiphany is nevertheless *not* a sufficient reason to call it 'great'. A great work must also lend itself to other, future uses. Dewey writes, 'A genuinely esthetic object is not exclusively consummatory but is causally productive as well . . . The "eternal" quality of great art is its renewed instrumentality for further consummatory experiences' (LW1:274). This final criterion for 'great' art – endurance – will probably seem controversial or unacceptably old-fashioned. Temporary art, site-specific works, or works that depend almost entirely upon striking a certain cultural note at just the right moment, cannot be 'great'.

Dewey's criterion of 'enduring causality' gives us a principled way of discriminating between 'entertainment' and 'art'. Entertainment stimulates quickly and dissipates quickly, with little lasting effect:

> Some esthetic products have an immediate vogue; they are the 'best sellers' of their day. They are 'easy' and thus make a quick appeal; their popularity calls out imitators, and they set the fashion in plays or novels or songs for a time. But their very ready assimilation into experience exhausts them quickly; no new stimulus is derived from them. They have their day – and only a day.

> (LW10:172)

In such works there is stimulation but not growth.[20]

Again, Dewey's criteria do not permit the construction of *ultimate* lists of specific cultural products which are definitively 'art' or 'entertainment'. In fact, Dewey's own book, *Ethics*, erroneously dismisses artistic media (film and jazz) which many today could argue, on Deweyan grounds, to have produced 'art'. Such judgments were certainly premature. Today, no one doubts that film or jazz are media expressive enough to be called art. But despite Dewey's rash remarks, his general criterion is still useful. That is, one may make discriminating aesthetic valuations within a medium (and across media) by observing whether or not an art form effects enduring growth both in other artworks and in the experiences of appreciators. Works designated as 'entertainment' fail to be 'art' because they fail to create and recreate consummatory and growing experiences.

Dewey's criticisms of commercial entertainment applies to political art (e.g., socialist realism or class-conscious art) as well.[21] While I cannot defend this claim at length here, I believe that his aesthetics rules out the ability of such genres to produce a genuinely aesthetic experience mainly because they are *primarily* designed to communicate a narrow message to a specific audience. 'If the artist desires to communicate a special message', Dewey writes, 'he thereby tends to limit the expressiveness of his work to others – whether he wishes to communicate a moral lesson or a sense of his own cleverness.' (LW10:110.)

Political art's overweening emphasis on political message – its dedicatedly 'informational' function – gives it a function more scientific and practical than expressive. Because it is designed to convince, it is insufficiently expressive; it does not engage perception or feeling to a degree required of *an* experience. It is here that the similarities of political art and entertainment meet, disqualifying both from categorization by Dewey as 'art'. For whether a work's primary intention is to offer quick pleasure or affirm an ideological point, the result is the same: ephemeral stimulation that does not express enduring meaning and ages quickly with the passage of time.

Art critics are not priests. They are not gatekeepers of Beauty and Meaning, charged to guide the philistine masses toward works of artistic genius. Dewey is a pluralist and a perspectivist – there is no singular, true meaning which everyone must 'get' from an artwork; indeed, meanings must vary from person to person, and over time. But in our culture, in love with prescriptive rankings of what is good, art criticism still has a role. For Dewey, it is a reconstructive and educative role. Done properly, it empowers its students to appraise art themselves:

> The function of criticism is the reeducation of perception of
> works of art; it is an auxiliary in the process, a difficult process,
> of learning to see and hear . . . The individual who has an

enlarged and quickened experience is one who should make for himself his own appraisal. The way to help him is through the expansion of his own experience by the work of art to which criticism is subsidiary.

(LW10:328)

The pragmatic critic reeducates by pushing students (readers, public) away from 'conventional wisdom' toward active, experimental engagements with art. As Alexander notes, 'criticism is a pluralistic enterprise having a number or tasks. Instead of seeking to provide fixed, pure methodologies, it can understand itself as genuinely experimental and hermeneutic' (Alexander 1987, 276). Dewey calls such critical education 'moral' because it removes prejudice, encourages open-mindedness, and generally enriches the capacity to experience life.[22]

Thus, pragmatic aesthetic criticism assumes several pedagogical tasks: to retrain the eye and ear, heighten sensitivity to the actual presence and play of artworks' qualities, and elucidate the ways in which an artwork emerges and responds to the cultural arenas producing it. It may be true, as Dewey claims, that 'art breaks through barriers that divide human beings, which are impermeable in ordinary association' but it is the job of the critic to place such art in the front and center of public consciousness, to enable active participation, and hopefully to 'restore continuity between the refined and intensified forms of experience that are works of art and the everyday events, doings, and sufferings that are universally recognized to constitute experience' (LW10:249, 9). Thus, the art critic potentially may develop the sympathetic attitudes (of people and groups) both within and between cultures as well.[23] Ultimately, critics can help repair and revitalize community *if* their criticism draws acutely upon the moral life which they notice is sustaining or draining them.

Conclusion: the existential importance of art

'At its height', Dewey writes, experience 'signifies complete interpenetration of self and the world of objects and events' (LW10:25). Potentially, art can evoke the highest and most synthetic form of experience, *consummatory* experience. Obviously, this is not like ordinary life. In contemporary life,

> Zeal for doing, lust for action, leaves many a person, especially in this hurried and impatient human environment in which we live, with experience of an almost incredible paucity, all on the surface. No one experience has a chance to complete itself because something else is entered upon so speedily. Resistance is treated as an obstruction to be beaten down, not as an invitation to reflection. An individual comes to seek, unconsciously even more than by deliberate choice, situations in which he can do the most things in the shortest time.

> (LW10:51)

Such words may evoke Plato's Cave, but Dewey attributed these experience-diminishing conditions not to human nature, but to a variety of modern economic, technological, and communicative developments. Many of these developments reflect our choices about how to engineer the pace and rhythm of daily life; therefore, the potential to re-engineer design for better living also exists. Artists and critics can contribute to such change by illuminating which living conditions are destructive of aesthetic experience. They can help their various publics to see how life's harried pace fragments attention, defeats natural impulses toward inquiry, and coerces the worship of dangerously simplistic efficiencies. They can help show how our reactions to harried life – often retreats into passive recreation or hyped-up levels of activity – also fail to produce genuinely meaningful aesthetic experiences. Then, constructively, they can promote life's more enriching possibilities through the examples of art.

In the end, art and art criticism are concerned with something of momentous value. For the overarching impact of present life's dysfunctional routines is a deadening of the live creature and a profoundly felt loss of meaning. As we give up a healthy balance between doing and undergoing, life alternately races and drags. It passes, but without accumulating meaning, as present, past, and future seem increasingly disconnected. Such living conditions deserve, as much as anything else, the label 'existential'. While many modern artists urged that attention be paid to man's existential plight – for example, Arthur Miller's *Death of a Salesman* – Dewey urged philosophers to improve conditions by helping the public reconsider art's nature and function. Changes in public perceptions of art could enable artworks to intermix more boldly with the routines of contemporary life, while simultaneously enlarging the public vision of how ordinary routines can be made more aesthetic. These are the keys to a better future. 'Only imaginative vision elicits the possibilities that are interwoven within the texture of the actual. The first stirrings of dissatisfaction and the first intimations of a better future are always found in works of art' (LW10:348).

If philosophers could see the capacity of experience for meaning, they would see why art represents a zenith of human accomplishment. They would understand why art holds such promise for the betterment of daily life. If Dewey is right to think that philosophy's objectives are fundamentally tied up with those of everyday people, then it becomes incumbent upon philosophers to do aesthetic criticism which contributes to the reconstruction of ordinary life in aesthetic directions.

7

Religion: religious experience, community, and social hope

There is such a thing as passionate intelligence, as ardor in behalf of light shining into the murky places of social existence, and as zeal for its refreshing and purifying effect. The whole story of man shows that there are no objects that may not deeply stir engrossing emotion. One of the few experiments in the attachment of emotion to ends that mankind has not tried is that of devotion, so intense as to be religious, to intelligence as a force in social action.

(LW9:52–3)

Introduction

As this book has hopefully shown, pragmatism can do an extraordinary job criticizing and reconstructing central areas of philosophical concern. But for a pragmatist like Dewey, religion posed a problem. One the one hand, his pragmatic approach is empirical and naturalistic. This means that seeking the satisfactory accounts of an event or entity means, in most cases, following the methods of natural science: observe, gather evidence, test with experiment, and never forget that one's conclusions are, at best, probable and useful hypotheses, not absolute truth. On the other hand, consider the central belief of most Western religions: God is revealed to be transcendent, eternal, unobservable empirically – and yet present and active in mundane affairs.

The problem for Dewey is, then, given his pragmatic naturalism, how can he explain the widespread meaningfulness of religious practice? Such practices are, after all, part of most people's ordinary experience, and so Dewey the empiricist cannot simply dismiss or ignore their existence. At the same time, most religions are sustained by non-empirical methods (such as revelation or intuition) which insist on the existence of non-natural (eternal and transcendental) objects. In short, the phenomena of religious life exhibit two poles in tension for pragmatism. One pole, the institutions of religion, supports metaphysical entities and epistemological methods of inquiry that directly oppose core views of pragmatism; the other pole, religious experience, is a lived and immediate experience which many people report having and which pragmatists, committed to a radically empirical starting point, must not dismiss out of hand. How can a naturalist and pragmatist like Dewey explain the meaning of both opposed poles?

Because most views about religion begin from deep and personal roots, a few facts about Dewey's religious background are appropriate. Dewey was raised in a religious family, and was engaged with religious practices for the first few decades of his life. His father, Archibald Sprague Dewey, was a grocer, and not particularly strict about religious matters; Dewey's mother, Lucina, in contrast was a kind and generous woman but also 'narrow and strict in her views of morals and religion' (Dykhuizen 1973, 6). The pressures she placed on her sons to be religious probably contributed to Dewey's later observation that

> religious feeling is unhealthy when it is watched and analyzed
> to see if it exists, if it is right, if it is growing. It is as fatal to be

forever observing our own religious moods and experiences, as it is to pull up a seed from the ground to see if it is growing.

(EW1:91)

In addition to his mother, Liberal Evangelicalism influenced Dewey's thinking in church and at the University of Vermont. It proved to be a form of Christianity more acceptable to him, and teachings of figures such as Reverend Lewis O. Brastow probably provided him with early motivations to undercut dualisms such as flesh vs. spirit and ordinary vs. divine.[1]

At twenty-one, while living and teaching in Oil City, Pennsylvania, Dewey reportedly had a 'mystic experience'. Dewey reported the experience to Max Eastman, which Dykhuizen relates:

> The essence of [Dewey's] experience was a feeling of oneness with the universe, a conviction that worries about existence and one's place in it are foolish and futile. 'It was not a very dramatic mystic experience,' Eastman continued. 'There was no vision, not even a definable emotion – just a supremely bliss-ful feeling that his worries [about whether he prayed in earnest] were over.'

(Dykhuizen 1973, 22)

Dewey belonged to congregations for about the first thirty-five years of his life and was active both pedagogically and in a research capacity. Dewey's most emphatic turn away from organized religion probably occurred in 1894, when he left a teaching position in Ann Arbor, Michigan, for one in Chicago. There, Dykhuizen reports,

> Democracy in all its phases – political, economic, social, cultural – came to claim Dewey's strongest allegiance and to command his deepest loyalties; interest in social aid and social reform groups began to replace his interest in the Church. Thus

it is not surprising that Dewey's formal connection with
organized religion ended when he left Ann Arbor.

(Dykhuizen 1973, 73)

Constructing a common faith

Dewey returned to the issues of religion, in a concentrated
and philosophical way, in the 1930s. His challenge was to
apply his fully developed, naturalistic view of human experience
to the phenomena of religion and religious experience. In
what ways are religious experiences natural ones? How could
religion, a predominantly cultural and political institution, be
made more democratic? How radical a reconstruction would he
have to recommend – that is, how much of traditional religious
conceptions could be preserved, and how much would need to
be discarded?

In 1930, four years before he published his major work on
religion, *A Common Faith*, Dewey stated clearly where he stood.
'What I Believe' argues passionately for a new kind of 'faith',
one which was not just a belief in something, but faith as a
'tendency toward action'. The intent of this action-oriented
faith was for meaningful experiences, available to *everyone*, and
found in *this* world: 'Faith in its newer sense signifies that *experience itself is the sole ultimate authority*' (LW5:267, emphasis mine).[2]
This notion of faith, as Dewey explains at greater length in
A Common Faith, differs markedly from more traditional
notions. Typically, faith is an allegiance to a definite collection
of conceptual propositions, based on divine authority, which are
recited and adhered to. 'Jesus was born to a virgin', or, 'The
sinful are punished eternally in Hell' to take two examples.
The referents of these propositions are eternal and unchanging
objects: the Real, the True, the Good. None of these objects,
however, can be attained in earthly life; all human conduct

can do is imitate or approach them. Experience, as presented by religion, suffers by invidious comparison. It is presented as inferior – as illusion, flux, confusion, uncertainty, evil, a veil of tears. In contrast, religion's objectives are raised up as superior alternatives – as fixed, eternal, intrinsically valuable, certain, and ensuring mental tranquility. Given that religion insists dogmatically that the superior must be pursued, no matter how impossible it is to attain them in this life, Dewey became convinced that much of traditional religion (and philosophy, for that matter) amounted to a cynical disparagement of human experience.

The religious standpoint is one of distrust. It probably came into being for good reasons; after all, for much of human history, people *have* been at the mercy of natural elements, and chance has been our cruellest foe. While this distrust (and its creation of a two-realm metaphysics) may have aided survival in the past, there is little reason to believe it does now. It is irrational, in other words, dogmatically to extend the ancient picture past its period of usefulness. We know, for example, that experience is not pure chaos – it is characterized by patterns and regularities that provide the bases necessary for comprehension, prediction, and control of our world. In addition, human development of technological instruments – both physical tools and the scientific method – has significantly improved living conditions and odds of survival amid nature and fate. We can afford to rely upon experience with a less fearful (if still wary) eye. Moreover, insofar as blind faith in dogma *increases* our ignorance of the actual conditions in which we act, living a moral life requires that we shift away from religious dogma so that our actions can become more intelligent and, also, more moral.

A Common Faith (1934) is Dewey's most comprehensive statement about religion and religious phenomena. The book grew out of three Terry Lectures given at Yale University. Looking back, Dewey wrote that he did *not* mean to address either (1) believers still content with supernatural religious traditions or (2) religious liberals trying to preserve religion by postulating two realms – a realm science can study (nature), and one it cannot (spiritual). Rather, he was writing 'to those who have abandoned supernaturalism, and who on that account are reproached by traditionalists for having turned their backs on everything religious' (LW14:79–80). They can take heart that *all* the elements that make the religious attitude valuable exist *in experience*, and these elements do not require either a traditional religious framework or supernaturalism.

Because he can find no evidence for the supernatural, Dewey proposes that instead we try supposing that religious human experience occurs *within* the natural and social spheres. Indeed, he felt it *vital* that religious experience be 'emancipated' from the anachronistic beliefs and practices impeding it.[3] Take this approach, Dewey is saying, and there is hope that 'what is genuinely religious will undergo an emancipation' so that 'for the first time, the religious aspect of experience will be free to develop freely on its own account' (LW9:4). The benefit to such freedom in religious experience would be more meaningful lives for both individuals and communities.

While the label of 'atheist' is roughly descriptive of Dewey, it should be noted that he rejected the 'militant atheism' of his day. Militant atheism held that belief in religious experience was insupportable given man's condition: alone in a hostile and alien world. Dewey rejected this view because it lacked what he called 'natural piety', a felt sensitivity to one's place in a larger environment. This is a piety all humans can cultivate, and one which Dewey argues is necessary for moral growth. Dewey's task, then, was to find a way between militant atheists and traditional theists and reconstruct common conceptions of the religious along naturalistic lines. In contrast with most conventional religions, he needed to show how experience could be 'religious' without being supernatural.

Dewey begins his emancipation of religious experience from the supernatural by distinguishing 'religion' from 'religious'. He notes the problems encountered merely by seeking a cogent definition for 'religion'. Even if he generously defines religion as, say, the human recognition of some unseen and higher power which controls destiny and is due obedience, reverence, and worship, problems immediately crop up. For in reviewing a wide spectrum of religions, one finds an incommensurable mix of the 'unseen powers' of various deities as well as incompatible prescriptions for worship (what to worship, how to worship, the purposes of worship, and the motives of worship). If one attempts to give an essential definition by stripping away the inconsistencies (such as the philosophical, social, and cultural differences), very little religious significance is left. In short, because no clear and univocal meaning for 'religion' can be found 'we are forced', Dewey writes, 'to acknowledge that concretely there is no such thing as religion in the singular. There is only a multitude of religions . . . [and] the differences among them are so great and so shocking that any common element that can be extracted is meaningless' (LW9:7).

While all human cultures may be said to have developed a religion, this fact does not prove that this collection of practices has displayed anything universal or essential about religion. At best, 'religion' is an umbrella term for various human social and political institutions. But note: this is merely a sociological defin- ition, not a theological one.

The concrete and irreconcilable differences between actual religious practices suggest, Dewey argues, that what is meaning- ful about religion be sought by looking into the nature of religious experience. For comparison, consider the project of defining 'art'. Because it was impossible to find an essential, defining property for all 'aesthetic' objects and events, the quest for a definition of 'art' was set aside, and instead the *functions* in experience responsible for the aesthetic was taken up. This same method is applied by Dewey to the case of 'religion'. He wants to understand the nature of religious experience by asking, How does it function? As with art, this type of inquiry does not seek out a particular *entity* responsible for religious experience; rather, it seeks out an account of the qualities and relations in play in particular situations.

Because the phrase 'religious experience' has such strong connotations for us, it will be useful to make clear what religious experience is *not* for Dewey. First, it is *not* part of a proposal for a new religion. In fact, as mentioned earlier, Dewey's redescription of religious experience is meant to enable people to shed themselves of the hindrances of traditional religions.[4] Secondly, religious experience *cannot* be proof of supernatural objects. The experience has the qualities it has; it feels like it feels, so to speak. The project of connecting some *cause* to the experienced effects (i.e., interpreting it) is an entirely separate and subsequent matter. One can no more prove that an experience is supernaturally caused by pointing at the experience itself than one can prove that a law is just by simply pointing at it in a book.[5] Finally, religious experience is *not* exclusive of other experiences. It is something which may pervade or color many other kinds, such as aesthetic, moral, or political. The religious coloration of, say, an aesthetic experience does not make the experience less aesthetic; rather, it increases our sense of connection to the artwork because we now *also* grasp how this aesthetic experience is contained in a universe which makes it possible.[6] Just as 'good' can apply to many different things – friendships, meals, arguments, even bets – 'religious' as a quality 'can be had equally well in the ordinary course of human experience in our relations to the natural world and to one another as human beings related in the family, friendship, industry, art, science, and citizenship' (LW9:224).

Turning now to Dewey's positive statements about religious experience, we find that he refers to it as an 'orientation', an 'outlook', and those 'attitudes that lend deep and enduring support to the processes of living' (LW9:15). To make this more concrete, Dewey asks us to compare three different ways people cope with life's obstacles: accommodation, adaptation, and adjustment. Sometimes we deal with immovable conditions by *accommodation* – by 'grinning and bearing it', as they say. Whether the problem is hot weather or extended unemployment, we cope by tamping down expectations and resign ourselves to the situation; change is made *in us*, not in our conditions. In other cases, we deal with problems through *adaptation,* by changing *conditions* to make our situation better. For example, deserts were adapted to food needs by advances in irrigation and agriculture; pollution in cities is being adapted by changes in the way cars are powered. But sometimes the challenge to cope is met by changes which are religious in kind. In cases of *adjustment* we make changes *both* in *ourselves and conditions*. Such changes are 'inclusive and deep seated' and they transform our attitude in 'generic and enduring' ways (LW9:12,13). We *adjust* ourselves (wants, aims, ideals) and the relevant conditions surrounding us, but this time the changes revise our identity in a more fundamental way than the first two types of coping. These changes, Dewey writes,

> relate not to this and that want in relation to this and that condition of our surroundings, but pertain to our being in its entirety. Because of their scope, this modification of ourselves is enduring. It lasts through any amount of vicissitude of circumstances, internal and external. There is a composing and harmonizing of the various elements of our being such that, in spite of changes in the special conditions that surround us, these conditions are also arranged, settled, in relation to us.
>
> (LW9:12–13)

In adjustment, there is an act of 'submission' by the present self to its own evolution; but what is important is that this is voluntarily and consciously undertaken as a wholesale, not momentary, act of will. The change taken comes from the 'organic plenitude of our being' (LW9:13). Examples of adjustment can come from many arenas; testimony of people overcoming racist outlooks, accepting their sexuality, or even taking responsibility for wrongdoing can all fulfill Dewey's description of such religious attitude. For me, fatherhood fits this description nicely. It has caused dramatic changes in my desires and ideas as well as in the conditions of my living environment. Most important, however, is the way my own commitment to these new ideals has transformed my identity. My whole self has been revised as I have come to a deeper appreciation of my place in a larger universe.

With so little time on earth to observe and reflect, how do human beings 'leap' and evolve to a new self? By what miracle can one orient their actions toward a new paradigm for their identity? Rather than attribute the power of adjustment to something divine, Dewey argues that these shifts or leaps are facilitated by the human imagination. Imagination has the ability to project beyond observation and reflection, toward a new whole that includes both self and world. 'The whole self is an ideal', Dewey writes, 'an imaginative projection. Hence the idea of a thoroughgoing and deep-seated harmonizing of the self with the Universe . . . operates only through imagination' (LW9:14).

The imaginative projection of who we should become may be called an 'epiphany', the sudden revelation of the meaning of something. The tradition has dealt with epiphany by attributing its origin to 'external' causes; in religious thought, such causes were usually divine; philosophy has typically called the causes Reason, or Nature. Dewey agrees that there must be something external which goads the imaginative-religious achievement; but he argues that 'external' need not imply something *transcendental* to experience. Like the army poet goaded by the colors, smells, and emotions stirred up by his near-fatal service on the battle-field, we draw our epiphany about who we must become not only from our own resources, but from the *transactions* in which we and the world are engaged.

It is startling to consider that the human imagination has the awesome power Dewey describes to create new ideals for both self and universe. After all, many of us learned to think of the imagination as a kind of 'theater of the mind', which can entertain children or provide adults with incidental recreation. But if one considers for a moment the height and range of human creativity it is easy to see that Dewey's belief in the much larger role of imagination is not at all far-fetched. 'Imagination', he writes, 'may play upon life or it may enter profoundly into it' (LW9:13). In its more profound work, imagination intervenes in life, synthesizing and extending experience so as to project new ideals that may be made actual. *Religious experience* is the process of adjustment in which imagination extracts from the actual the ingredients necessary for whole new ideals.

One critic of Dewey's account of religious experience was J.H. Randall, who argued that Dewey's specific project of describing religious experience in a purified and 'generic' way was inconsistent with his philosophy's professed commitment to see experience as embedded in its cultural environment.[7] In other words, it is just as impossible to free religious experience from religion (in some institutional form) as it is to free musical experience from all musical instruments. In fact, what Dewey unconsciously does in his philosophy, Randall says, is reinscribe his own liberal Protestant view under the disguise of a generic, empirical description.[8] In his defense of Dewey on this point, Michael Eldridge points out that Randall and others had missed Dewey's essential point about the separation of religious from the religion. It is possible to separate out the religious aspects of experience because their functions and qualities can be observed at work in experiences not laden with religious content. (Several examples were mentioned above.) Because religious experience is not a separate kind of experience but one which supervenes (or informs) many types, it is not restricted to the sphere of culture normally designated as 'religion'.[9]

For his naturalization of religion and religious experience to succeed, Dewey had to critique traditional notions of faith and God. For many, 'faith' is the opposite of reason; it does not demand extensive inquiry or verification; it is a trust in the 'evidence of things not seen' because such things subsist in a realm permanently inaccessible to finite and fallible humans. Thus, Dewey writes, 'religious faith is . . . given to a body of propositions as true on the credit of their supernatural author, reason coming in to demonstrate the reasonableness of giving such credit' (LW9:15). Because religious propositions are typically very abstract, theologies develop to show how such propositions apply to specific and worldly situations.

Let me mention two criticisms Dewey makes of traditional religious faith. First, the traditional meaning given to faith closely identifies it with *intellectual* acceptance of propositions (such as 'God exists and loves mankind'). However, there are other kinds of faith, such as moral faith. Moral faith, Dewey argues, is *not* primarily intellectual, but practical. It occurs when one acknowledges that the ideal one has in mind is worthy enough to modify one's present desires, purposes, and conduct. It is a practical ideal that exists potentially, not an already existing reality that draws our faith like a magnet. The key question is how to make that ideal a living reality. In other words, moral faith is pragmatic – it is a tendency toward action, not reflective contemplation. When traditional religions portray faith as intellectual recognition, the impetus to inquiry and struggle wanes. Those with faith, for example, in God's love, can trust that this eternal ideal of love is 'already embedded in the existent frame of things', and that 'only our senses or the corruption of our natures prevent us from apprehending its prior existential being' (LW9:15–16).

A second problem generated by religious faith is the tendency to hypostatize or oversimplify the phenomena of human life. For example, the decision to go to war is explained and justified by an 'evil' enemy; homosexuals' lobbying for equal legal treatment is dismissed because of a so-called 'sinful' lifestyle; we resign ourselves to practices which are cruel to animals because they were 'not created in God's image'. These magic labels, or hypostatizations, frustrate and even preempt inquiry and debate. They resolve problematic and anxious situations by an appeal to absolute categories and ideas whose certainty all derive from the same source: a realm disconnected from the physical and social environment we actually inhabit. The resolution of fearful situations by such methods constitutes, for Dewey, the very model of the 'unreligious' attitude. 'Fear', Dewey writes, 'never gave stable perspective in the life of anyone. It is dispersive and withdrawing . . . The essentially unreligious attitude is that which attributes human achievement and purpose to man in isolation from the world of physical nature and his fellows' (LW9:18). Fear, of course, is a natural human reaction. And for much of human history, life has been dangerous and short. Even today, for Westerners ensconced within a manifold of technological security, hurricanes happen. So do cancer and disastrous economic cascades. But while fear may coerce one to accept a faith connected to the supernatural, this faith diverts one from having to arduously examine the practical requirements of morality. This choice is immoral because it leads one to be less effective in securing those values supposedly cherished. It is this inherent contradiction between the end one professes and the means one adopts that makes traditional religious faith *un*religious.

Dewey called his view of a truly religious faith 'natural piety'. It is grounded not in a realm of supernatural, unseen powers but in a 'just sense of nature as the whole of which we are parts' and our recognition that as parts we are 'marked by intelligence and purpose, having the capacity to strive by their aid to bring conditions into greater consonance with what is humanly desirable' (LW9:18). 'Faith', as Dewey understands it, is grounded in 'natural piety' because it accepts that 'experience itself is the sole ultimate authority' (LW5:267). On Dewey's view, faith is not a God-given assurance of intellectual propositions; rather, one has faith in, say, 'justice' when one is mentally and physically *disposed toward working* for the ideal of justice. Such a faith exhibits the tendency or disposition to carry out plans, strategies, and actions that create more justice in this world. The civil rights leader who says 'I have faith we'll get equal pay' is not announcing his blind trust in an external power; he is expressing his practical intent to change society.

So far I have been using examples of moral faith to illustrate what Dewey found missing from traditional religious faith. One may naturally wonder what, if anything, distinguishes religious faith from moral faith. On Dewey's view, religious faith is one kind of moral faith. That is, there may be moral faiths and objectives that are pursued without much emotion and which do not transform one's character. Distinguishing the moral and religious Dewey writes,

> The religious is 'morality touched by emotion' [as Matthew Arnold put it] only when the ends of moral conviction arouse emotions that are not only intense but are actuated and supported by ends so inclusive that they unify the self. The inclusiveness of the end in relation to both self and the 'universe' to which an inclusive self is related is indispensable . . . This comprehensive attitude, moreover, is much broader than anything indicated by 'moral' in its usual sense. The quality of attitude is displayed in art, science and good citizenship.
>
> (LW9:16,17)

Some moral acts do not effect any change in participants – those with moral faith that discrimination is wrong can protest and effect negotiated change without undergoing anything like a religious experience. What is characteristic of religious faith is the presence of ends and emotions that stir up and then unify the self in an enduringly transformative way. The ideal pursued is expansive enough to engender 'adjustment' rather than just 'accommodation' or 'adaptation'. Consider as an example the actions of American civil rights activist, Rosa Parks. In Montgomery, Alabama, in 1955, Ms Parks was ordered by a bus driver to vacate her seat for a white passenger. She refused as an act of civil disobedience, was arrested and tried. Years later she recalled that, 'When that white driver stepped back toward us, when he waved his hand and ordered us up and out of our seats, I felt a determination cover my body like a quilt on a winter night.'[10] Parks had a religious experience: she acted for *moral ends* (on behalf of dignity and equality) that were *inclusive* (of the general set of conditions responsible for denying civil rights to all), *intensely emotional*, and *transformative* of Parks's lifelong identity. Her intelligence and knowledge of the situation were not irrelevant to what she chose to do, or why, but they were ingredients in something more than just an act of moral faith. Let us turn now from faith to God.

'God is dead. God remains dead. And we have killed him', a character of Nietzsche's famously said. Many would likely accuse Dewey's philosophy of rendering a similar judgment. Insofar as 'God' means a single being or personality responsible for the cosmos and its inhabitants, such an accusation is surely correct. Belief in such a being is neither warranted nor advisable. But as we have seen in the cases of 'faith', and 'religious experience', Dewey would prefer to reconstruct the concept of 'God' rather than eradicate it.

If God is not a particular supernatural being or force, what does 'God' mean? To understand Dewey's definition, one must first set aside the reflex to think of God as one thinks of other singular objects (like a person). Think instead of other familiar descriptions of God: 'God is goodness', 'God is wisdom', or 'God is love'. Those descriptions bring out aspects of God representative of our highest ideals. Now some philosophers have defined God as 'perfection' itself, where perfection means 'a being possessing all possible ideals'. If one removes the idea of a possessor of ideals from this traditional notion, one can begin to grasp Dewey's 'God'. He writes,

> 'God' represents a unification of ideal values that is essentially imaginative in origin when the imagination supervenes in conduct . . . The unification effected through imagination is not fanciful, for it is the reflex of the unification of practical and emotional attitudes. The unity signifies not a single Being, but the unity of loyalty and effort evoked by the fact that many ends are one in the power of their ideal, or imaginative, quality to stir and hold us.
>
> (LW9:29–30)

In other words, when our whole personality is engaged and transfixed by an ideal (such as equality), imagination conceives of how a multitude of ends unify so as to call out from us the loyalty and effort necessary for achieving that ideal. This unification cannot be a merely whimsical or intellectual arrangement of ideal values; ideals only enter into experience if they are unified according to constraints present in actual lives. These constraints include our practical and emotional attitudes as well as conditions present in the natural and social world.

> [T]his idea of God, or of the divine, is also connected with all the natural forces and conditions – including man and human association – that promote the growth of the ideal and that

> further its realization . . . *It is this active relation between ideal and actual to which I would give the name 'God'.*

(LW9:34, emphasis mine)

Because this notion of God is still very abstract, consider how another grand ideal, that of 'democracy', can express the way Dewey's model works. Democracy was and remains an immensely important moral ideal for America and much of the world. If democracy can be said to be 'alive', it is not simply because people keep discussing it but because it is a persistent factor that shapes and is shaped by human events. The ideal of democracy influences practical life: human agents use the ideal to guide them as they prescribe future conduct (such as voting technology, civil rights, legal judgments about privacy). In addition, various practical implementations of the ideal – its 'real life testing' – feeds back into it, adding to its coherence and relevance as a working principle. The ideal of democracy, then, modifies and is modified by experience, and both are enriched in reliability and meaning. Democracy, of course, is just one ideal; one's active faith in the unity of *all* these ideals is what Dewey meant by 'God'.

Reconstructing religion as a force of social intelligence

Religion, as most have known it, is permeated by a narrative structure (beginning, middle, and end) that dramatically describes the origin and fate of humans and the universe. The purpose of the narrative is to orient believers with a framework that indicates how they might play their part in the drama; by fulfilling this role, believers discover what they were meant to do and be during life on earth. Dewey understands that his critique of the supernatural undermines the prescriptive function of religious narratives, and he knows that for an audience to accept his radical reconstructions (of 'faith' or 'God'), they would have to surrender the traditional and meaningful supports of their faith for a new view of life. They would naturally want to know, 'What comes next?'

What Dewey proposes should come next is not the replacement of religious institutions with new ones. The emancipation of religious experience, in other words, must construct a new faith in the power and glory of passionate intelligence not in old defining lines of sect, race, and class. Fundamentally, Dewey is urging people to reconsider how, as religious persons, they think and associate. If religion is truly supposed to address the problems and struggles of everyday people, religious habits must be reconstructed toward (1) free and open inquiry and (2) more expansive and natural forms of association. Let us examine each of these in turn.

Dewey's reconstruction of religion demands, first, that several key habits of religious inquiry be surrendered. These are habits concerned with what knowledge is and how it should be sought. Typically, religions have claimed their own special way of knowing. Though there is some variation among religions, knowing generally includes (1) a *content*: a body of propositions (specific intellectual beliefs, asserted to be true intellectually) that are separated out as 'religious', (2) a *method*: particular interpretative strategies for decoding the content (a doctrinal apparatus: prayer, revelation, mystical experience, etc.) which believers must accept, and (3) a divine *guarantee*: of the infallible truth of both content and interpretative methods. Dewey's 'common faith' argues that this model of knowing must be given up; instead, the pursuit of cherished religious knowledge and value should utilize *inquiry*, also known as the scientific method (if taken in its most generic sense).

Why should the religious pursue answers with inquiry? One reason is that inquiry is by nature an open and public process; no special or private beliefs are necessary and no beliefs are protected from criticism. As a method, inquiry pursues answers through hypothesis formation, observation, conceptual and physical experiment, and action. Its assumptions are not dogmatic or fixed in advance but are instead fallible and hypothetical. Anyone who questions the validity of a judgment can test it by trying the experiment themselves and seeing what they find. This leads, over time, to results which are more openly accepted and, thus, socially stable.

Despite the stark opposition between traditional religious knowing and scientific inquiry, Dewey believes that a more full-fledged adoption of inquiry would not require a complete change of mental habits for most people. The methods of inquiry are largely commonsensical, so Dewey is not proposing a wholly unfamiliar process. What *is* critical is that religious persons become more aware that methods of inquiry (which they already possess and use) can be extended to enhance religious experience and values. Dewey writes,

> The positive lesson is that religious qualities and values if they are real at all are not bound up with any single item of intellec-tual assent, not even that of the existence of the God of theism; and that, under existing conditions, the religious function in experience can be emancipated only through surrender of the whole notion of special truths that are religious by their own nature.
>
> (LW9:23)

Only by removing the epistemological quarantine around religious experiences and values can intelligence work to expand and secure those goods.

Dewey's call for a methodological shift (from traditional religious knowing to the scientific inquiry) requires another, complementary, change in the habits of human association. In many traditional religions, much emphasis has been placed on determining who is chosen (or 'elect') and who is not. The power of those chosen to speak for God and identify others chosen has been a source of grievous division for many human societies. What must replace such division, Dewey thinks, are the integrating bonds characteristic of the human community.

The connections of community are almost timeless; they reach back into the past and can extend far into the future. If it can be appreciated that many of our most celebrated achievements have been directly facilitated by a *human community* (and not by God), then community may provide a powerful source of inspiration for this new, common faith. The challenge is to make our celebration of the fruits of community explicit.

> The things in civilization we most prize are not of ourselves. They exist by grace of the doings and sufferings of the continuous human community in which we are a link. Ours is the responsibility of conserving, transmitting, rectifying and expanding the heritage of values we have received that those who come after us may receive it more solid and secure, more widely accessible and more generously shared than we have received it. Here are all the elements for a religious faith that shall not be confined to sect, class, or race.
>
> (LW9:57–8)

Unfortunately, the stubborn links between religion and supernaturalism makes appreciation of community more difficult. First, it makes awareness of communities' constructive powers more difficult insofar as each religion inculcates beliefs meant to maintain the competitive claim *their* sect has over others. Second, religion encourages expectations that crucial ends will be accomplished by supernatural intervention (miracle) rather than through cooperative inquiry into actual conditions. Rather than forging connections necessary to solving problems communally, isolated groups wait for salvation. Finally there is excessive attention paid to *individual* salvation (at least within Christianity) that overemphasizes the *individual* possession of sins or failings rather than looking more expansively (and empirically) at how natural and societal conditions can also be sources for these problems.

Dewey's overarching goal in reforming the habits of thought and association of supernaturalistic religions is practical and moral. These religions have spent their time on 'sinfulness of man, the corruption of his heart, his self-love and love of power' rather than addressing afflictions of our social fabric such as political corruption and economic injustice, to name just two (LW9:51). Wittingly or not, religious institutions' lack of open and inclusive methods of inquiry has resulted in a rigid conservatism; this conservatism has tacitly lent support to society's status quo, including those with vested interests injurious to the common good. As a meliorist, Dewey cannot abide this. For religion and society to survive and flourish, they must recognize that religious experience and values are *best* pursued with cooperative methods of inquiry.

Conclusion: toward a common faith

When Nietzsche wrote 'God is dead' in *The Gay Science* he was both announcing that religion had become largely irrelevant to cultural life and that this fact had gone largely unrecognized. Writing decades later as an American, Dewey affirms and elaborates upon Nietzsche's observation in *A Common Faith* by chronicling what he calls a shift in the 'social centre of gravity of religion' (LW9:41). For most of history, religion mediated the social fabric of human relationships. It organized humans' view of themselves, their communities, and the cosmos itself; it guided the daily norms and rituals of domestic, political, and economic life. One did not choose a religion but inherited it from older generations.

Now, for the first time in history, religion no longer provides an overarching ethos but is just one particular institution within a larger and dominant secular Western culture. Enormous social changes have displaced religion as a central organizing force of culture, changes which may be traced back not only to the expanded independence of the state's legal authority, but to the vast number of human associations which have evolved in contemporary life and which now occupy a much greater part of our interest than religion can. These new forms of human association (in, for example, business, recreation, or community politics) have effectively changed how people prioritize their time and resources. In short, they represent new values, and are in competition with older, religious values – even among religious believers. 'The essential point', Dewey writes, 'is not just that secular organizations and actions are legally or externally severed from the control of the church, but that interests and values unrelated to the offices of any church now so largely sway the desires and aims of even believers' (LW9:44).

It was clear to Dewey, as it is to us today, that the marginalization of religion provokes counter-reactions, such as the aggressive reassertion of 'traditional' values by fundamentalist religions. Such reactionary tactics represent losing propositions. Instead, the time was ripe to try the natural hypothesis that 'all significant ends and all securities for stability and peace have grown up in the matrix of human relations' and the goods we experience are had 'in the concrete relations of family, neighborhood, citizenship, pursuit of art and science' (LW9:47). The values of religious and secular people, many of which overlap, can be more effectively secured and expanded by investigating, empirically, the human and natural realms, rather than the supernatural ones.

The shift to a naturalistic framework for values amount to the adoption of what Dewey calls 'a humane point of view'. It insists upon (1) the application of intelligence to social problems rather than the appeal to supernatural institutions or dogmatism; (2) the proposition that moral values (and moral inquiry) are empirically available within experience; (3) the fact even our most difficult problems arise from the same world as our goods – and that labels attempting to segregate problems from lived experience (e.g., by calling them 'evil') actually *harm* our chances at improving life; and finally (4) that a shift to the humane point of view is an affirmation of democracy.

This last point deserves elaboration, for it connects a theme present in Dewey's philosophy of education, ethics, and politics with his naturalistic view of religious experience. What, then, is the connection between religious experience and democracy? In a word, the connection is intelligence. Both the emancipation of religious experience and the flourishing of democratic life depend upon the free and cooperative exercise of inquiry that is connected – radically, empirically – to lived experience. The supernatural, by definition, is remote from experience and consequently, from inquiry. Therefore, Dewey's exhortation that religious faith be abandoned for empirical intelligence is part and parcel of his championing of democracy.

A widespread expansion of intelligence would not necessarily destroy churches or other religious institutions, but it would demand they transform themselves to remain relevant. The transformation would require the adoption of an empirical creed in place of old, dogmatic ones; it would require that religious leaders see their institution not as exceptional, but as unique, in concert with a more 'comprehensive community of beings' (LW9:56). An empirical creed would pledge allegiance to the fallible, cooperative, and communal aspects of inquiry; it would demand the surrender of exclusive and authoritative claims to truth. It would necessitate the invention of new symbols, new metaphors, and new narratives which placed mundane trial and tribulation at the *center* of religion's concerns. While some have wondered if the empirical creed Dewey promotes is itself just another dogmatism, it must be remembered that the spirit in which this creed would be tried is experimental and fallible. It must self-terminate if it fails the tests of experience.

In Dewey's view, all these changes represent the last best hope for the survival of traditional religions. At the same time, they express the construction of a common faith that draws upon the very real existence of human religious experiences – the special but not mystical ability humans have to pursue a 'thoroughgoing and deep-seated harmonizing of the self with the Universe'.

Conclusion: philosophy as equipment for living

> Respect for experience is respect for its possibilities in thought and knowledge as well as an enforced attention to its joys and sorrows. Intellectual piety toward experience is a precondition of the direction of life and of tolerant and generous cooperation among men. Respect for the things of experience alone brings with it such a respect for others, the centres of experience, as is free from patronage, domination and the will to impose.
>
> (LW1:392)

In 'The Need for a Recovery of Philosophy', Dewey urged philosophy to become more than a contemplation of the present or analysis of the past. It should seek instead to become 'equipment for living', capable of making future life better.[1] Philosophy does this by creating theories with meanings amenable to testing by application to human practices. Some practices may include direct, physical action; others may be more indirect and discursive. Nevertheless, at some point, philosophies which are authentic should be able to demonstrate meaningful connections to human needs and purposes.

Why, then, should Dewey still be read? What makes his work relevant to the twenty-first century? One reason is that Dewey offers unique, penetrating, and humane insights about philosophical topics still being debated today: consciousness, social justice in a pluralistic democracy, the source of moral values, the aims of education, the conflict between scientific and religious explanation, to name just a few.

Another perhaps more persuasive reason is that Dewey's philosophical method – his practical and experimental naturalism – is proving extraordinarily useful for interpreting contemporary problems in productive and interesting ways. Indeed, in recent years a diverse range of fields outside philosophy have taken up Dewey (and pragmatism) because of just such a promise; they include: architectural theory, art criticism, biomedical and healthcare ethics, economics, education, environmental studies, feminism, legal theory, literary criticism, political science, psychiatry, public administration, race theory, and religious studies. What each field (and researcher) finds useful varies, but new enthusiasts typically cite Dewey's conceptions of method (experience-based), inquiry (communal and experimental), warrant (fallible), democracy (communicative and participatory), or selfhood (socially transactive).

So to conclude this book on a pragmatic note, here are three brief sketches of how Dewey's ideas are making a difference in the areas of medicine, environment, and feminism. These contemporary applications, along with others, provide perhaps the best possible testimony for the living vitality of Dewey's thought.

Healthcare and medical ethics

Pragmatism, and Dewey in particular, have become increasingly influential in the areas of healthcare and medical ethics.[2] Dewey's experimental and fallibilistic logic offers medical decision-makers a flexible yet justified way to work through dilemmas which initially seem deadlocked. 'Dewey', bioethicist Glenn McGee writes, 'found moral investment in the existential context of the social situation itself, not in the narrow notions of acceptability and condemnation that we bring to every problematic area. In this way Dewey articulated not a relativism, but a careful and subtly contextual ethics' (McGee 1999, 28). McGee points out that a pragmatic and experimental approach to problem-solving often relieves the destructive pressure practitioners feel to arrive at 'final' answers. Once decision-making is understood pragmatically, it becomes natural to allow that *any* present solution can become problematic in the future; for that reason, solutions should build in some flexibility (McGee 1999, 28–9).

Also useful to healthcare issues are Dewey's account of the social nature of habits and the mutually-constituting dependence of individual and society. Micah Hester, for example, applies Dewey's distinction between 'habits' and 'habituations' to explain and criticize the way medical institutions perpetuate the unreflective practices of personnel. Frequently motivated by efficiency and profit, institutional training often inculcates the practice of seeing patients as 'cases' rather than as unique persons having significant experiences. This practice, along with similarly impersonal approaches to bedside manner ('enlightened paternalism'), creates a damaging divide between professionals and patients that prevents truly healthy living.

Finally, Dewey's experimental and naturalistic conception of inquiry – which aimed to heal the divide between science and art, fact and value – has helped inspire new visions for psychiatry in the twenty-first century. David Brendel, a Harvard psychiatrist, argues that psychiatry's self-understanding is at a crossroads, unsure about whether it is a science (of brain functioning) or an art (of understanding the mind in a socio-cultural context).[3] Utilizing dominant features of pragmatist philosophy (particularly its 'practical, pluralistic, participatory, and provisional' aspects), Brendel develops an approach to clinical diagnosis, treatment, training, and research called 'clinical pragmatism'. Only clinical pragmatism, he argues, can enable psychiatrists to heal their patients (by recognizing the complexity of their suffering) while maintaining current academic standards and scientific rigor.

Environmental ethics

Over the past several decades a broad range of topics has become categorized as 'environmental ethics'. The general objective of this philosophy (as opposed to the political movement) has been to devise justifications for extending protection (or care) over more of the environment, including non-human animals. Recently, classical pragmatism's ideas and figures (including Dewey) have offered new and productive proposals for difficult theoretical deadlocks. Here, I shall just mention two.

First, why should we value the environment? Answering this question has spawned a long-running debate between anthropocentrists and eco-centrists. The latter believe that humans must protect environmental systems because they possess *intrinsic* value; the former argue that *human interests* are, in fact, the root of all value. These views are exclusionary – they seek to derive *all* value from humans *or* nature. In contrast, Dewey's naturalism starts with the observation that humans are continuous with nature; we subsist in transaction with nature. Thus, the traditional philosophical conflict derives from a presumed – and erroneous – discontinuity. Nature, like any other concept, is more profitably understood situationally and functionally – not metaphysically and absolutely.[4] 'Nature', to put it crudely, is both *what we have made of it* (a construct of culture) and *that which resists and surprises us*. Its value, therefore, is that it cannot be identified with 'what we say it is', or 'what it is in itself'. On Dewey's view, nature's value, like the meaning of 'nature' itself, must be discovered through ongoing and cooperative inquiry.

Second, deadlocks over how to value and justify animal welfare have been injected with new life by Deweyan ideas. His pragmatist ethics both critiques and proposes an alternative to the two dominant (antagonistic) approaches. These approaches, most famously held by utilitarian Peter Singer and rights-theorist Tom Regan, are universalistic and rationalistic; they propose a single, general principle to decide all particular cases of animal welfare. The utilitarian-vs.-rights debate has proved difficult to resolve, and the theories have proven difficult to put in practice. Dewey's alternative strategy for extending animal welfare has gained traction because it is not ultimately tied to rational analysis of a creature's traits. In addition to rational analysis, any moral inquiry *must* *also* be permitted to include the emotions and sympathies one feels. To inquire about the moral status of a cow, for example, is to inquire as a *full* person, not as a cold, calculating machine.[5] Moreover, the results of moral inquiry cannot amount to universal prescriptions; moral inquiry, like all other kinds, is historically and culturally situated. However firmly we embrace its results, it must be understood as open to revision by experimental and democratic processes.

Feminism

Like the fields mentioned above, 'feminism' names not a single area of inquiry but clusters of areas.[6] Dewey's ideas have provided feminism with concepts and resources for argument that can be briefly mentioned.

Two ideas useful to feminism are Dewey's experiential method (or practical starting point) and his theory of inquiry. Women's voices have traditionally been excluded or marginalized in many societies, particularly in legal, economic, and political spheres. Dewey's radically empirical method validates women's experience *as a logical basis* for criticisms of existing societal ideologies.[7] At the same time, Dewey's conception of the purpose of inquiry – the resolution of problems – lends force to the argument that a higher priority must be assigned to the problems affecting women, as well as other marginalized or oppressed groups.[8]

In political theory, feminists dissatisfied with traditional social contract theories have made use of Dewey's rejection of atomic individualism. Dewey views the self as one whose actions and identity are governed by relations with others; this self is 'a dynamic and social individual with multiple ties and projects in the world' (McKenna in Seigfried 2002, 137). Once the self is conceived in this way, the self – and women – have a fulcrum on which to mount arguments against blind economic or technological forces, or the automatic re-enforcement of patriarchal customs.

Notes

Introduction

1. Dewey was president of the Eastern Division of the APA in 1905; he gave the Carus Lectures, Gifford Lectures, William James Lectures, and Terry Lectures.
2. As a product of the culture of New England, Dewey writes that he felt 'an inward laceration' from its intellectual bequests; in particular the 'divisions by way of isolation of self from the world, of soul from body, of nature from God, brought [him] a painful oppression' (LW5:153). Study of Hegelianism with George Sylvester Morris afforded Dewey personal and intellectual healing.
3. While in Michigan, Dewey developed long-term professional relationships with James Hayden Tufts and George Herbert Mead. In 1886, he married Harriet Alice Chipman; they had six children and adopted another. Two of the boys died tragically young (at the ages of two and eight).
4. See the careful historical work by Ryan 1995 and Westbrook 1991.
5. 'There are', Dewey writes, 'two kinds of demonstration: that of logical reasoning from premises assumed to possess logical completeness, and that of showing, pointing, coming upon a thing' (LW1:372).

Chapter 1

1. Was Dewey a 'behaviorist'? I think not. While supportive of behaviorist criticisms of introspectionism, Dewey strenuously rejected behaviorist attempts to explain complex, situated actions in terms of simple elements such as stimuli. Such reductionistic explanations oversimplify behavior, isolating it from its more comprehensive cultural, linguistic, and pragmatic contexts. See MW11:13.

2. Dewey's dissatisfaction stemmed from idealism's presumption that reality is essentially unified and perfect. The upshot of such a presumption poses a practical obstacle to our ability to make moral judgments empirically, experimentally, and thus, with real conviction. The pragmatic consequence of idealism, for Dewey, is an unacceptable pessimism. See Alexander 1987, 51.

3. Dewey writes, 'The older dualism between sensation and idea is repeated in the current dualism of peripheral and central structures and functions; the older dualism of body and soul finds a distinct echo in the current dualism of stimulus and response' (EW5:96). What replaces that dualism – experience – is most fully stated in his 1925 masterpiece, *Experience and Nature*.

4. We should say, instead, that the 'qualities never were "in" the organism; they always were qualities of interactions in which both extra-organic things and organisms partake' (LW1:198–9).

5. Such labels, erroneously treated as evidence for realities existing antecedent to the activity of perception, are in fact the intellectual signs of cognitive discrimination and abstraction, which we undertake for pragmatic purposes. See 'A Naturalistic Theory of Sense Perception' (LW2:51) and *Experience and Nature* (LW1:198–9).

6. About this process of reciprocal adjustment see MW9:346.

7. For example, primitive man acted *selectively* in choosing how to satisfy his instinctive hunger; this selectivity created the conditions necessary for a more elaborate *interest* in how food tasted; eventually customs of dining and arts of cuisine with complex *meanings* evolved.

8. Even a philosopher like Hume, who wisely reinvigorated discussions of habit to help explain how our 'impressions' of sensation could somehow add up to enduring things and events, still referred to habit as a 'mysterious tie' largely possessed at the narrow level of the individual. However, Dewey writes, 'The development of biological knowledge has now done away with the "mysterious" quality of the tie' (LW12:244).

9. About this, Alexander writes, '[Habits] are general paths of integration and interpretation. As such they . . . become the basis for the

continuity between the biological and social worlds' (Alexander 1987, 142).

10. Reflection, on this picture, is a response to disturbance: 'the painful effort of disturbed habits to readjust themselves' (MW14:54).

11. Emotions are intentional in the sense that they are '*to* or *from* or *about* something objective, whether in fact or in idea' and not just reactions 'in the head' (LW10:72).

12. See 'The Theory of Emotion' on this point (EW4:182).

13. Dewey underscores the fact that sentient beings are not 'adding' feeling to a world of objects. Rather, the ability to feel develops out of a being's interaction with the world. The result is a wholly changed being and world.

14. Dewey decried the attempts of his day to reduce accounts of mind to brain function. While more sophisticated than earlier attempts to explain the connection between mind and body, he saw contemporary efforts as repeating the erroneous attempt to place mind *in* body as marbles are *in* a box. See LW1:224–5.

15. The idea that language can create 'objects as objects' may tempt some to conclude that Dewey was an idealist or relativist, believing that mind makes world. This interpretation would be mistaken. It is better, I believe, to see Dewey as a realist insofar as he believes that beings with language frame a 'world' outside their experience, where 'world' simply means 'sources of experience yet independent of us'.

16. James's substitution of a 'stream of consciousness' for a series of discrete elementary states was, Dewey says, an enormous advance, which over the years 'worked its way more and more into all my ideas and acted as a ferment to transform old beliefs' (LW5:157).

17. No private language is possible for Dewey. While a mind's meanings might be privately entertained, they are not therefore invented by a private, subjective consciousness; meanings are social, emerging from symbol systems developed through communication and collective action. See LW1:147.

18. In Dewey's view, human sociality is primordial and mental interiority is a much later development. See LW1:178–9.

19. Here is one very cogent and important statement Dewey makes of the two kinds of experience: '[E]xperienced situations come about in two ways and are of two distinct types. Some take place with only a minimum of regulation, with little foresight, preparation and intent. Others occur because, in part, of the prior occurrence of intelligent action. Both kinds are had; they are undergone, enjoyed or suffered. The first are not known; they are not understood; they are dispensations of fortune or providence. The second have, as they are experienced, meanings that present the funded outcome of operations that substitute definite continuity for experienced discontinuity and for the fragmentary quality due to isolation' (LW4:194).

20. Dewey's continuity narrative uses the language of process: events, interaction, organization, function. This language helps explain the emergence of live feelings from dead events. For the differences between things which are inanimate, animate, and feeling, see LW1: 197.

Chapter 2

1. Such as the metaphysical assumption that epistemology's questions are rooted in two-tiered reality consisting of a realm of changing appearances and another of permanent, unchanging ideas. Though his shift away from traditional epistemology strikes at the heart of philosophy's sentimental appeal, Dewey argues that philosophy must relinquish the idea that knowledge springs from simple 'human wonder' and instead we should try to understand knowing as an activity that permits us to cope with those actual problems which stop us in our tracks.

2. See *Reconstruction in Philosophy*: 'When experience is aligned with the life-process and sensations are seen to be points of readjustment, the alleged atomism of sensations totally disappears. With this disappearance is abolished the need for a synthetic faculty of super-empirical reason to connect them'(MW12:131–2).

3. *The Quest for Certainty* (LW4) lays out Dewey's extensive account of how Western epistemologies grew out of Western history and culture.

4. See *Experience and Nature*: 'Suppose however that we start with no presuppositions save that what is experienced, since it is a manifestation of nature, may, and indeed, must be used as testimony of the characteristics of natural events. Upon this basis, reverie and desire are pertinent for a philosophic theory of the true nature of things; the possibilities present in imagination that are not found in observation, are something to be taken into account' (LW1:27).

5. Dewey's extensive treatise on logic is entitled *Logic: The Theory of Inquiry* (LW12).

6. On Dewey's view, a sign (say 'apple') is as natural an object as the things to which it refers (this apple). This is not, of course, to say that their qualities are identical.

7. It is clear that as early as 1900, Peirce's ideas about inquiry had become central to Dewey's instrumentalism. See MW1:272.

8. Peirce's 'The Fixation of Belief' (1877) and 'How to Make Our Ideas Clear' (1878) are widely considered to be the two earliest explications of pragmatism's tenets. See Peirce 1992.

9. This description combines two similar accounts of inquiry. See 'Analysis of Reflective Thinking' (LW8) and *Logic* (LW12).

10. Again, because of the 'intellectualism' of traditional philosophy, many philosophers have neglected or dismissed this early and felt phase of reflection.

11. On the contribution of feeling to inquiry, see 'Qualitative Thought' (LW5), especially p. 248.

12. Dewey's notion that hypotheses can only be tested in experience has roots in Peirce, particularly in 'How to Make our Ideas Clear' (Peirce 1992), which champions the pragmatic method of clarifying the meanings of terms and propositions.

13. 'Problems', for pragmatists, denote not only the mundane or physical but intellectual problems as well. See 'What Pragmatism Means by Practical' (MW4:98–115).

14. Taking the practical starting point about judgment means abandoning the idea of perfect, neutral objectivity in judgment. It is to admit that one has a perspective and that judgment is an art, not a science; it involves habit and technique but is not reducible to an algorithm.

Chapter 3

1. Regarding the terms 'ethics' and 'morality', I will be using these terms interchangeably, taking my cue from Dewey's *Ethics* (written in collaboration with James Tufts). See MW3:40.

2. According to Kant, because human nature is only free to the degree that it is rationally autonomous, our moral choices must not be determined by desires or indeed by any emotion; morality of choice rests on a rational being's respect for the moral law (which itself is rational), and nothing else.

3. In her fine book, Jennifer Welchman writes that Dewey thought ethical philosophy 'must become the theoretical wing of a practical science largely conducted by professional experimental scientists . . . As the theoretical wing of the social sciences, philosophy has a twofold vocation: critical [analyze and critique human objectives] and constructive . . . [acting to] assist in the design of new institutions and practices by which new ideas and powers can be put to humanly fruitful use' (Welchman 1995, 192–3). Dewey disallows rule by philosopher kings; rather, 'The determination of what should be done is the fundamental project of society at large. Philosophy's contribution is the development of procedures and principles of assistance in the collective social construction and evaluation of ideals (ends) of human flourishing and the materials and means of their construction' (Welchman 1995, 192).

4. See LW7:179.

5. 'That men love and hold things dear, that they cherish and care for some things, and neglect and condemn other things, is an undoubted fact. To call these things values is just to repeat that they are loved and cherished; it is not to give a reason for their being loved and cherished . . . But to consider whether it is good and how good it is, is to ask how it, as if acted upon, will operate in promoting a course of action' (MW8:27, 29).

6. This same observation applies to traditional tensions between 'instrumental' and 'intrinsic' (or 'final') goods.

7. For criticisms of Dewey's use of growth as a criterion in moral theorizing, see Burke 1973 and Diggins 1994.

8. See Clarence Irving Lewis, review of *The Quest for Certainty*. *The Journal of Philosophy*, Vol. 27, No. 1 (1930) and George Santayana, 'Dewey's Naturalistic Metaphysics', *The Journal of Philosophy*, Vol. 22, No. 25 (1925).

9. This fact is made painfully evident when one experiences the sudden death of a loved one. I am not 'who I was' before the loss; I am disoriented, at a loss. A hole has been ripped in the fabric of my identity.

Chapter 4

1. See, for example, *The Public and its Problems* (1927), *Individualism, Old and New* (1930), and *Liberalism and Social Action* (1935).

2. For example, we enforce property rights with the authority of law; laws are legitimated by their process of creation (by fairly elected representatives of the public).

3. Rice-Oxley 2004.

4. I follow Jaggar (1983) here.

5. This sense of 'liberal' should not to be confused with the more local, political descriptor attached to wings of specific political parties, such as the liberal wing of the Democratic party in America. While such liberals can certainly trace their roots back to many principles of the classical liberal tradition, their positions also reflect fundamental divergences.

6. John Rawls's theory of the liberal welfare state is widely acknowledged to have done the most systematic and influential work in this area.

7. In 'The Priority of Democracy to Philosophy', Rorty writes, 'Those who share Dewey's pragmatism will say that although [liberal democracy] may need philosophical articulation, it does not need philosophical backup. On this view, the philosopher of liberal democracy may wish to develop a theory of the human self that comports with the institutions he or she admires. But such a philosopher is not thereby justifying these institutions by reference to more fundamental premises, but the reverse: he or she is putting politics first and tailoring a philosophy to suit' (Rorty 1991, 178).

8. For a less abstract example of how ideals that are immune to inquiry can impair inquiry, imagine the following illustration: your young daughter is being bullied by boys at her school. On consultation with teachers and the boys' parents, you receive a variety of excuses but all amount to this: 'boys will be boys'. Such an appeal (to the ideal of 'boys') would be unsatisfactory because it does nothing to address an unacceptable situation. A chief reason it is so ineffective is that it incorporates a standard – 'boy' – which is impervious to further inquiry or argument (human nature is unchangeable, after all). As long as self-evident ideals are allowed in this inquiry, you cannot help your daughter. And once inquiry is blocked, practice is blocked. It is just this kind of blockage that makes Deweyan intelligence integral to a renascent liberalism.

9. See Niebuhr's 'The Pathos of Liberalism', where he writes that Dewey's liberalism 'does not perceive the perennial and inevitable character of the subordination of reason to interest in the social struggle. Its ideal of a "freed intelligence" expects a degree of rational freedom from the particular interests and perspectives of those who think about social problems which is incompatible with the very constitution of human nature' (Niebuhr 1935, 303).

10. Social problems (divorce, for example) are often defined much more nebulously than physical ones; often they require a prior knowledge of similarly nebulous components (e.g., sexual drive). In addition, it is often difficult to find a language with which to characterize the results of social inquiry that is neutral with regard to cultural and historical meanings (e.g., discussing divorce neutrally in a culture with diverse religious preconceptions about marriage or the value of procreation).

11. The experimental method, Dewey writes, is germane across the sciences and beyond. All share the same starting point – experience as encountered – and the same pragmatic test. See LW11:293. On policy, see LW12:502.

12. In 'What I Believe', Dewey argues that the existential malaise of contemporary economic arrangements infect multiple classes and

professions. See Ryan 1995, 317 and Dewey, LW5:274–5. Here I follow Campbell (1995, 172–4).

13. The inchoate nature of the public is made worse, not better, by much of what counts as 'news', Dewey thought. The explosion of information fomented by the telegraph, penny newspapers, telephone, and radio created a glut of material which, while entertaining, contained few items on which the public could act. The goal of a self-conscious public could not be pursued without a serious reexamination and reconstruction of some of the main organs of public communication – which today we simply call 'the media'. See LW2:347.

14. For a discussion of the apathy criticism, see Campbell 1995, 226–8; for the moral flaw argument, see Niebuhr 1935.

15. Dewey quite explicitly rejects the notion that 'more information means more democracy', seeing face-to-face interactions as productive of sympathy [and regard for others' intelligence] and personalities. See LW7:329.

16. Comparing his idea of democracy with that of the ideal state, Dewey writes, 'To be realized [democracy] must affect all modes of human association, the family, the school, industry, religion' (LW2:325).

17. Robert Talisse pointed this out to me in an electronic mail exchange (6 September 2006). See also Talisse 2007.

18. Dewey's conception of a political program must be understood as situational (determined by actual social conditions and needs), flexible, and hypothetical (no single formulas, partial, tentative, always revisable). See Campbell 1995, 207.

Chapter 5

1. See MW9:377 and LW5 for these self-appraisals by Dewey.

2. For major statements about this debate see *The School and Society* (1899) and *The Child and the Curriculum* (1902).

3. About traditional methods Dewey writes, '[Such learning] shapes the mind to look backward; to rob it of power to see and judge what is actually going on around us' (LW17:463).

4. While Dewey was often hastily labeled (and disparaged) as a leader of 'progressive education', his educational views were genuinely his own and he never accepted the main tenets of the progressive education movement: the rejection of pedagogical authority and celebration of student enthusiasms. See, e.g., 'How Much Freedom in New Schools' (LW5:320).

5. By placing the 'stimulus' completely outside the human organism, psychologists' behavioral model neglected the profound effect that anticipation and memory have in prefiguring one's encounters with novel events.

6. Adler's attack on the valueless 'positivism' of Dewey and others was delivered as a speech entitled 'God and the Professors'. See Westbrook 1991, 519–21.

7. Katherine C. Mayhew and Anna Camp Edwards, *The Dewey School,* 312. Cited in Westbrook 1991,101.

8. Dewey notes that in education, language offers tremendous power through abstraction. Language and symbolization can imaginatively extend the limits of the physical environment, enable the sharing of the remote human past, and project possible situations. *Overuse* of the symbolic – long monologues by teachers, memorization of facts, a singular focus on definitions – can inure students and cultivate passivity, thus eliminating any motivation they might have to reengage.

9. Dewey, Ryan writes, 'emphasized the importance of tradition, but only as something to use, and there is certainly one form of intellectual conservatism that sees tradition as something which we immerse ourselves in and test ourselves by rather than as a mere stock of useful resources' (Ryan 1995, 148). In addition, Ryan adds, 'the introspective nonjoiner gets rather short shrift in Dewey's universe . . . That ethical individualism, that ability to stand out against the crowd, is something Dewey never sufficiently emphasized in his educational writings' (Ryan 1995, 148).

10. On schools' ethical and social responsibility, see MW4:271.

11. On 'total attitude' see Hildebrand 2006.

Chapter 6

1. See Dewey's *Psychology* (1887) on the connection of art with creative imagination and aesthetic feeling; see *The School and Society* (1902) and *Democracy and Education* (1915) on art, pedagogy, and the enrichment of ordinary experience. *Experience and Nature* (1925) discusses metaphysical connections between art and experience.

2. While *Art as Experience* has been influential and strongly praised – in 1966 Monroe Beardsley called it 'the most valuable work written in English (and perhaps in any language) on aesthetics so far in our century' – the rise of analytical approaches to aesthetics in the 1950s contributed to a widespread disinterest in Dewey's aesthetics until the 1980s (Beardsley 1966, 332; see also Leddy 2006).

3. The *completeness* of the experience is crucial to its aesthetic quality: 'An angler may eat his catch without thereby losing the esthetic satisfaction he experienced in casting and playing. It is this degree of completeness of living in the experience of making and of perceiving that makes the difference between what is fine or esthetic in art and what is not' (LW10:33).

4. About this expansion of the aesthetic, Dewey writes that the 'limitation of fineness of art to paintings, statues, poems, songs and symphonies is conventional, or even verbal. Any activity that is productive of objects whose perception is an immediate good, and whose operation is a continual source of enjoyable perception of other events exhibits fineness of art' (LW1:374).

5. The important point to understand here about consummatory experience (including unity and integration) is that the framework for meaningfulness is larger than the event or object ingredient to the generation of the consummatory experience.

6. It is typical to think of the artist as a 'sensitive' type; but this is not a sensitivity that is detached from the natural world or other persons. It must be an intimate and anticipatory connection between matter and form, between self and audience. Part of the intimacy must be with one's own character. No artist starts from a pure or neutral standpoint when making a work; rather, he starts

from where he is, fully funded with his history, culture, and passions. See LW10:93.

7. This does not imply that the appreciator/perceiver go through exactly the same relations – that is impossible; but they must be, Dewey argues, comparable.

8. Ruth Reichl, 'Critic's Notebook; The Vanishing Haute Cuisine' ('Dining In, Dining Out' column, *New York Times*, 17 June 1998) http://select.nytimes.com/search/restricted/article?res=F70E16F E38590C748DDDAF0894D0494D81 (accessed 21/7/06).

9. Dewey, Shusterman points out, lists numerous characteristics of aesthetic experience (implying it can be defined), but also states that the unifying feature of aesthetic experience (pervasive quality) is immediate and ineffable (in effect, indefinable). See Shusterman 1992, 55–6.

10. See Shusterman 1992, 58.

11. This account of expression theory follows Steven Mulhall's entry 'Expression', in *A Companion to Aesthetics*, ed. David Cooper (Oxford, UK: Blackwell, 1992).

12. Early theories of art, such as those of Plato and Aristotle, focused upon 'mimetic' capacity – art's ability to imitate or represent something more real than itself. What art was said to imitate varied, but could include physical objects, actions, and ideal types. In their view, the artist's chief talent, like that of the craftsman, was reproductive: the ability to produce a close 'likeness' of a more real entity. Later theories of art, such as those of romantics and idealists (such as Coleridge, Schopenhauer, Bosanquet, and Schelling) sought to take the essence of aesthetic activity back from the superhuman world and place it in the realm of spirit and self. Ultimately, for them, art reveals the self to itself through its creative acts. In this scheme, the artist's chief talent is creative, the ability to penetrate to the vital sources of a reality ultimately spiritual in nature and express it in painting, poetry, music, etc.

13. All these different imitation theories make the common methodological mistake described in earlier chapters as 'the intellectualist fallacy'. See LW10:142.

14. See Alexander 1987, 235: 'Form doesn't illuminate itself or point to a timeless Platonic object; it illuminates the material, that is, the world. It achieves this through the unfolding of a history; form reveals the ways the various parts of phases temporally work together so as to establish a meaningful whole. Form is the . . . working of the work.'

15. This collaborative view of art implies that artworks require an audience to be art because all art has form, and form (as Dewey defines it) is a relational process necessarily including maker and appreciator. 'Art' cannot simply be in an object. Nor can it be in only the artist's mind. An artwork is not complete until it communicates, and that requires others besides the artist: 'The external object, the product of art, is the connecting link between artist and audience' (LW10:111).

16. Though a great diversity of aesthetic theories exist, they have shared a common flaw: a theoretical starting point. These systems, Dewey writes, have 'superimposed some preconceived idea upon experience instead of encouraging or even allowing esthetic experience to tell its own tale' (LW10:279). See also LW10:293, 295.

17. 'Historical and cultural information', Dewey writes, 'may throw light on the causes of their production. But when all is said and done, each one is just what it is artistically, and its esthetic merits and demerits are within the work. Knowledge of social conditions of production is, when it is really knowledge, of genuine value. But it is no substitute for understanding of the object in its own qualities and relations' (LW10:320).

18. Those who dismiss aesthetic criticism by saying 'There's no disputing about matters of taste', ignorantly presume, Dewey contends, 'that likings cannot be gone behind, or be made subject to inquiry as to their productive causes and consequences' (LW2:95–6). But if experience is not subjective and isolated from the world, it *can* be analyzed, debated, and even reconstructed.

19. In other instances an artwork may fail because there is too much emotion or the emotions are hackneyed and stale. Sentimental art

fails, in part, because it does not permit the appreciator sufficient 'room' to respond; its effusiveness suffocates.

20. Works can fail in multiple ways to engender growth; we may call such failures aesthetically dead, melodramatic, even pornographic. See LW10:182.

21. See Jackson 2000.

22. 'The moral function of art itself', Dewey writes, 'is to remove prejudice, do away with the scales that keep the eye from seeing, tear away the veils due to wont and custom, perfect the power to perceive. The critic's office is to further this work, performed by the object of art' (LW10:328).

23. We cross cultural barriers not simply by acquainting ourselves with the art of other individuals or cultures, but by what we might call a 'live entering'. Only then do we see things from another perspective and, thus, enlarge ourselves. See LW10:337.

Chapter 7

1. See Dykhuizen 1973, 7. See Eldridge 1998, chapter 5 passim, and especially pp. 146–7.

2. Again, 'experience' for Dewey was no shallow or narrow thing – experience is broad and deep. It is ultimate insofar as it possesses the resources necessary for meaning and happiness: 'Such happiness as life is capable of comes from the full participation of all our powers in the endeavor to wrest from each changing situation of experience its own full and unique meaning' (LW5:272).

3. Dewey's comments about religious experience echo those made about aesthetic experience. Both could be deployed far more universally so as to transform ordinary experience; see LW9:11. The identification for many (theists and atheists) of 'religious' and 'supernatural' hinder morality as well as religion. Efforts to comprehend and secure cherished values (such as justice, compassion, generosity) in daily life is difficult enough. But the additional requirement of grounding moral conduct in the supernatural complicates our task, for it 'diverts attention and energy from ideal

values and from the exploration of actual conditions by means of which they may be promoted' (LW9:13).

4. Traditional religions have had a deleterious impact on human life insofar as they have promoted a 'body of beliefs and practices that are apart from the common and natural relations of mankind' and thus 'weaken and sap the force of the possibilities inherent in such relations' (LW9:19).

5. When someone – a Taoist, a Christian, or even a scientist working on a theory – has a 'religious experience' they report its effects, such as a greater feeling of wholeness, peace, or security. But experiencing a sequence of effects should not be conflated with their interpretation, nor with a judgment about their cause or its nature. See LW9:10.

6. About cases of aesthetic experience that are infused with religious feeling, see LW10:199.

7. Dewey, Randall writes, 'sets out from the conviction that what is genuinely religious in life, once purified of all that has grown up about the idea of the supernatural, will then . . . be "free to develop freely on its own account"' (Randall 1940, 136–7). However Dewey's talk 'about ridding religious experience of "all historic encumbrances" [is] an aim hardly appropriate from one usually so insistent on the continuity of human institutions and cultures' (Randall 1940, 136–7).

8. See Randall 1938, 137–8.

9. See Eldridge 1998, 176–7.

10. In Williams and Greenhaw, *The Thunder of Angels: The Montgomery Bus Boycott and the People Who Broke the Back of Jim Crow* p. 48.

Conclusion

1. I take 'equipment for living' from Kenneth Burke, who held what might be called a pragmatic view of literature. Literature and poetry, Burke said, '*is* produced for purposes of comfort, as part of the *consolatio philosophiae*. It is undertaken as *equipment for living,* as a ritualistic way of arming us to confront perplexities and risks.' See *The Philosophy of Literary Form* (Berkeley: University of California Press, 1974), 61.

2. For example, pragmatism has been applied to areas involving biotechnology, clinical ethics, stem cells, managed and end-of life-care, mental illness, and genetic testing.

3. 'The field [of psychiatry] continues to be torn apart by strong and divergent pulls toward a science that studies brain functioning and a humanism that studies the mind in its broad social and cultural context' (Brendel 2006, 3).

4. As Larry Hickman put this third alternative, 'As a committed evolutionary naturalist, Dewey accepted and argued for the view that human beings are in and a part of nature, and not over and against it . . . Nature-as-nature and nature-as-culture are not ontologically separate, but only functionally so' (Hickman in Light and Katz 1996, 51, 57).

5. About Dewey's starting point for this issue, James Albrecht writes, 'For Dewey, emotionally felt obligations to other beings are a fundamental, naturally occurring aspect of our associated existence as human beings; as such they are legitimate starting points in the moral dissatisfactions that trigger the process of moral reflection, action, and change' (Albrecht in McKenna and Light 2004, 20).

6. Deweyan pragmatism is informing not just theories about gender and economic justice for women, but feminist approaches to science, epistemology, and economics.

7. About this new experiential starting point Shannon Sullivan writes, 'Because John Dewey's pragmatism puts epistemology and its standards to work in the service of life, however, it can provide feminist standpoint theory with non-foundational justification for its emphasis upon women's lives' (Sullivan in Seigfried 2002, 219).

8. On Dewey's value to feminism, see Seigfried, 2002, p. 51.

Bibliography

Works by Dewey

The following abbreviations are used for references to John Dewey's work as found in the critical edition by Southern Illinois University Press. Citations give text abbreviation, followed by volume number and page number.

EW   *John Dewey: The Early Works*, 5 vols (Carbondale: Southern Illinois University Press, 1969–72)

MW   *John Dewey: The Middle Works*, 15 vols (Carbondale: Southern Illinois University Press, 1976–88)

LW   *John Dewey: The Later Works*, 17 vols (Carbondale: Southern Illinois University Press, 1981–91)

Books

Art as Experience, LW10
The Child and the Curriculum, MW2
A Common Faith, LW9
Democracy and Education, MW8
Ethics, MW5 and LW7
Experience and Education, LW13
Experience and Nature, LW1
How We Think, MW6 and LW8
Human Conduct and Nature, MW14
Individualism, Old and New, LW5
Liberalism and Social Action, LW11
Logic: the Theory of Inquiry, LW12
Psychology, EW2

The Public and Its Problems, LW2
Quest for Certainty, LW4
Reconstruction in Philosophy, MW12
The School and Society, MW1.
Science and Society, LW6
The Study of Ethics: A Syllabus, EW4
Theory of Valuation LW13

Articles

'American Ideals (I): The Theory of Liberty vs. the Fact of Regimentation', LW9
'The Bearings of Pragmatism upon Education', MW4
'Between Two Worlds' (unpublished), LW17
'Brief Studies in Realism', MW6
'Conduct and Thought', LW5
'Context and Thought', LW6
'Creative Democracy: The Task Before Us', LW14
'Democracy in Education', MW3
'Does Reality Possess Practical Character?', MW4
'Education as a Necessity of Life', MW9
'Ethics', MW3
'Experience and Objective Idealism', MW3
'Experience, Knowledge, and Value: a Rejoinder', LW14
'From Absolutism to Experimentalism', LW5
'The Future of Liberalism', LW11
'The Interpretation of the Savage Mind', MW2
'Introduction to Essays in Experimental Logic', MW10
'How much Freedom in New Schools?' LW5
'Liberalism and Equality', LW11
'The Logic of Judgments of Practice', MW8
'The Lost Individual', LW5
'The Moral Training Given by the School Community', MW4
'My Pedagogic Creed', EW5
'A Naturalistic Theory of Sense-Perception', LW2
'The Need for a Recovery of Philosophy', MW10

'The New Psychology', EW1
'Philosophy and Civilization', LW3
'The Place of Religious Emotions', EW1
'Psychology as Philosophic Method', EW1
'Qualitative Thought', LW5
'Realism without Monism or Dualism', MW13
'The Reflex Arc Concept in Psychology', EW5
'Religion and Morality in a Free Society', LW15
'Science, Belief, and the Public', MW15
'The Search for the Great Community', LW2
'Some Stages of Logical Thought', MW1
'The Theory of Emotion', EW4
'Three Independent Factors in Morals', LW5
'The University Elementary School', MW1
'What I Believe', LW5
'What Pragmatism Means By Practical', MW4

Works by others

Albrecht, James M. 2004. '"What Does Rome Know of Rat and Lizard?": Pragmatic Mandates for Considering Animals in Emerson, James, and Dewey'. In *Animal Pragmatism: Rethinking Human-Nonhuman Relationships*, Erin McKenna and Andrew Light, eds. Bloomington, IN: Indiana University Press

Alexander, Thomas M. 1987. *John Dewey's Theory of Art, Experience, and Nature: The Horizons of Feeling*. Albany: State University of New York Press

Beardsley, Monroe C. 1966. *Aesthetics from Classical Greece to the Present: A Short History*. New York: Macmillan

—— 1982. *The Aesthetic Point of View: Selected Essays*. M. Wreen. and D. Callen, eds. Ithaca: Cornell University Press

Boisvert, Raymond D. 1998. *John Dewey: Rethinking Our Time*. Albany: State University of New York Press

Brendel, David H. 2006. *Healing Psychiatry: Bridging the Science/Humanism Divide*. Cambridge, MA: MIT Press

Browning, Douglas. 1998. 'Dewey and Ortega on the Starting Point'. *Transactions of the Charles S. Peirce Society*, vol. 34, no. 1, pp. 69–92

Burke, Kenneth. 1973. *The Philosophy of Literary Form: Studies in Symbolic Action,* 3rd edn. Berkeley: University of California Press

Campbell, James. 1995. *Understanding John Dewey: Nature and Cooperative Intelligence.* Chicago and La Salle, Ill.: Open Court

Carroll, Noel. 2001. 'Four Concepts of Aesthetic Experience'. In *Beyond Aesthetics: Philosophical Essays.* Cambridge: Cambridge University Press

Cohen, Marshall. 1965. 'Aesthetic Essence'. In *Philosophy in America*, Max Black, ed. Ithaca: Cornell University Press

Darwin, Charles. 1901 [1873]. *The Expression of Emotions in Man and Animals.* 2nd edn. 1873. London: John Murray

Diggins, John Patrick. 1994. *The Promise of Pragmatism: Modernism and the Crisis of Knowledge and Authority.* Chicago: University of Chicago Press

Dykhuizen, George. 1973. *The Life and Mind of John Dewey.* Carbondale and Edwardsville: Southern Illinois University Press

Eldridge, Michael. 1998. *Transforming Experience: John Dewey's Cultural Instrumentalism.* Nashville: Vanderbilt University Press.

Fesmire, Steven. 2003. *John Dewey and Moral Imagination.* Bloomington: Indiana University Press

Gotshalk, D.W. 1964. 'On Dewey's Aesthetics'. *The Journal of Aesthetics and Art Criticism*, vol. 23, no. 1, *In Honor of Thomas Munro*, pp. 131–8

Hester, Micah D. 1999. 'Habits of Healing'. In *Pragmatic Bioethics*, Glenn McGee, ed. Nashville: Vanderbilt University Press, pp. 45–59

Hickman, Larry A. 1996. 'Nature as Culture: John Dewey's Pragmatic Naturalism'. In *Environmental Pragmatism*, Andrew Light and Eric Katz, eds. New York: Routledge, pp. 55–72

——, 1998 edn. *Reading Dewey: Interpretations for a Postmodern Generation.* Bloomington: Indiana University Press

Hildebrand, David. 2003. *Beyond Realism and Antirealism: John Dewey and the Neopragmatists.* Nashville: Vanderbilt University Press

——. 2006. 'Does Every Theory Deserve a Hearing? Evolution,

Creationism, and the Limits of Democratic Inquiry'. *Southern Journal of Philosophy,* vol. 44, no. 2, pp. 217–36

Jackson, Philip W. 2000. *John Dewey and the Lessons of Art.* New Haven, CT: Yale University Press

Jaggar, Alison M. 1983. *Feminist Politics and Human Nature.* Totowa, NJ: Rowman & Allanheld

James, William. 1890. *Principles of Psychology* Vol. II. New York, NY: Dover Publications, Inc.

——. 1895. 'The Knowing of Things Together'. In *The Writings of William James: A Comprehensive Edition,* J. J. McDermott ed. Chicago: University of Chicago Press, 1977, pp. 152–68

Krutch, Joseph Wood. [1953] 1962. *The Measure of Man: On Freedom, Human Values, Survival and the Modern Temper.* Indianapolis: Bobbs-Merrill

Leddy, Tom. 2006. 'Dewey's Aesthetics'. In *Stanford Encyclopedia of Philosophy* (online). plato.stanford.edu/entries/dewey-aesthetics (accessed 28 September 2007)

Light, Andrew and Katz, Eric, eds. 1996. *Environmental Pragmatism.* New York: Routledge

McGee, Glenn, ed. 1999. *Pragmatic Bioethics.* Nashville: Vanderbilt University Press

McKenna, Erin. 'The Need for a Pragmatist Feminist Self'. In *Feminist Interpretations of John Dewey,* Charlene Haddock Seigfried ed. University Park: The Pennsylvania State University Press, pp. 133–59

McKenna, E. and Light, A., eds. 2004. *Animal Pragmatism: Rethinking Human-Nonhuman Relationships.* Bloomington, IN: Indiana University Press

Mayhew, Katherine C. and Edwards, Anna Camp. 1936. *The Dewey School.* New York: D. Appleton-Century Co.

Niebuhr, Reinhold. 1935. 'The Pathos of Liberalism'. *The Nation,* 141, 11 September

Pappas, Gregory. 1998. 'Dewey's Ethics: Morality as Experience'. In *Reading Dewey: Interpretations for a Postmodern Generation,* Larry A. Hickman ed. Bloomington: Indiana University Press

Peirce, Charles S. 1992 [1878]. 'How to Make our Ideas Clear'. In *The*

Essential Peirce: Selected Philosophical Writings (1867–1893).
Bloomington, IN: Indiana University Press, pp. 124–41

———. 1992 [1877]. 'The Fixation of Belief'. In *The Essential Peirce: Selected Philosophical Writings (1867–1893).* Bloomington, IN: Indiana University Press, pp. 109–23

Randall, John H., Jr. 1940. 'The Religion of Shared Experience'. In *The Philosopher of the Common Man*, Sidney Ratner ed. New York: G.P. Putnam's Sons, pp. 106–45

Rice-Oxley, Mark. 2004. 'Big Brother in Britain: Does More Surveillance Work?' *Christian Science Monitor*, 6 February

Rorty, Richard. 1991. 'The Priority of Democracy to Philosophy'. In *Objectivity, Relativism, and Truth: Philosophical Papers*, Vol. 1. Cambridge: Cambridge University Press

Ryan, Alan. 1995. *John Dewey and the High Tide of American Liberalism.* 1st edn. New York: W.W. Norton

Shusterman, Richard. 1992. *Pragmatist Aesthetics: Living Beauty, Rethinking Art.* Cambridge, MA: Blackwell Publishers

Seigfried, Charlene Haddock, ed. 2002. *Feminist Interpretations of John Dewey.* University Park: The Pennsylvania State University Press

———. 2002. 'John Dewey's Pragmatist Feminism'. In *Feminist Interpretations of John Dewey*

Sullivan, Shannon. 2002. 'The Need for Truth: Toward a Pragmatist-Feminist Standpoint Theory'. In *Feminist Interpretations of John Dewey*, Charlene Haddock Seigfried, ed. University Park: The Pennsylvania State University Press, pp. 210–35

Talisse, Robert B. 2007. *A Pragmatist Philosophy of Democracy.* New York: Routledge

Tiles, J. E. 1988. *Dewey.* New York: Routledge

Welchman, Jennifer. 1995. *Dewey's Ethical Thought.* New York: Cornell University Press

Westbrook, Robert B. 1991. *John Dewey and American Democracy.* Ithaca: Cornell University Press

Williams, D. and Greenhaw, Wayne. 2005. *The Thunder of Angels: The Montgomery Bus Boycott and the People Who Broke the Back of Jim Crow.* Chicago: Chicago Review Press

Further reading

For readers wishing to pursue Dewey in more detail or from other perspectives, the following is a very short and hopefully useful list of secondary literature, arranged by subject matter.

General works on Dewey

Bernstein, Richard J. 1966. *John Dewey*. New York: Washington Square Press

Boisvert, Raymond D. 1998. *John Dewey: Rethinking Our Time*. Albany: State University of New York Press

Campbell, James. 1995. *Understanding John Dewey: Nature and Co-operative Intelligence*. Chicago and La Salle, Ill.: Open Court

Talisse, Robert. 2000. *On Dewey*. Wadsworth

Tiles, J.E. 1988. *Dewey*. London and New York: Routledge

Biographical

Coughlan, Neil. 1976. *Young John Dewey: An Essay in American Intellectual History*. New York: Free Press

Dykhuizen, George. 1973. *The Life and Mind of John Dewey*. Carbondale and Edwardsville: Southern Illinois University Press

Martin, Jay. 2003. *The Education of John Dewey: A Biography*. New York: Columbia University Press

Rockefeller, Steven C. 1991. *John Dewey: Religious Faith and Democratic Humanism*. New York: Columbia University Press

Experience and inquiry

Alexander, Thomas M. 1987. *John Dewey's Theory of Art, Experience, and Nature: The Horizons of Feeling.* Albany: State University of New York Press

Burke, F. Thomas, Hester, D. Micah and Talisse, Robert B., eds. 2002. *Dewey's Logical Theory: New Studies and Interpretations.* Nashville: Vanderbilt University Press

Burke, Tom. 1994. *Dewey's New Logic: A Reply to Russell.* Chicago: University of Chicago Press

Hickman, Larry A. 1990. *John Dewey's Pragmatic Technology.* Indianapolis: Indiana University Press

Hook, Sidney. 1927. *The Metaphysics of Pragmatism.* Chicago: Open Court Publishing Co.

Shook, John R. 2000. *Dewey's Empirical Theory of Knowledge and Reality.* Nashville: Vanderbilt University Press

Sleeper, Ralph W. 1986. *The Necessity of Pragmatism: John Dewey's Conception of Philosophy.* New Haven: Yale University Press

Ethics and politics

Campbell, James. 1992. *The Community Reconstructs: The Meaning of Pragmatic Social Thought.* Urbana: University of Illinois Press

Caspary, William R. 2000. *Dewey on Democracy.* Ithaca: Cornell University Press

Fesmire, Steven. 2003. *John Dewey and Moral Imagination: Pragmatism in Ethics.* Bloomington: Indiana University Press

Gouinlock, James. 1972. *John Dewey's Philosophy of Value.* New York: Humanities Press

Lekan, Todd. 2003. *Making Morality: Pragmatist Reconstruction in Ethical Theory.* Nashville: Vanderbilt University Press

Pappas, Gregory. 2008. *John Dewey's Ethics: Democracy as Experience.* Indianapolis: Indiana University Press (forthcoming)

Ryan, Alan. 1995. *John Dewey and the High Tide of American Liberalism.* New York: W.W. Norton

Seigfried, Charlene Haddock. 1996. *Pragmatism and Feminism: Reweaving the Social Fabric*. Chicago: University of Chicago Press

Welchman, Jennifer. 1995. *Dewey's Ethical Thought*. New York: Cornell University Press

Westbrook, Robert B. 1991. *John Dewey and American Democracy*. Ithaca: Cornell University Press

Education, aesthetics, and religion

Alexander, Thomas M. 1987. *John Dewey's Theory of Art, Experience, and Nature: The Horizons of Feeling*. Albany: State University of New York Press

Eldridge, Michael. 1998. *Transforming Experience: John Dewey's Cultural Instrumentalism*. Nashville: Vanderbilt University Press (also valuable for those interested in inquiry)

Garrison, Jim. 1997. *Dewey and Eros: Wisdom and Desire in the Art of Teaching*. New York: Teachers College Press

Jackson, Philip W. 2000. *John Dewey and the Lessons of Art*. New Haven, CT: Yale University Press

Shusterman, Richard. 1992. *Pragmatist Aesthetics: Living Beauty, Rethinking Art*. Cambridge, MA: Blackwell Publishers

Index

abstraction(s) 14, 174, 214 n.5
  in pedagogy 222 n.8
accommodation 191, 197
act 16–17, 23–35
action 52
adaptation 191, 197
Addams, Jane 3
adjustment 191–3, 197
Adler, Mortimer 130, 222 n.6
aesthetic criticism (and
    interpretation) 170,
    179–80, 181–2
  Dewey's criticism of
    traditional view 171–3
  Dewey's reconstruction of
    226 n.18
  moral function of 180
  pragmatist 173–80
aesthetic experience, *see*
    experience
aesthetics
  Dewey's criticism of
    traditional view 151
  Dewey's reconstruction of
    110, 150
  expression theory 224–5 n.12
  importance in Dewey's
    philosophy 147–8
  mimetic theory 224 n.12
  organic sources of 149
  relevance to life 151

Albrecht, James 228 n.5
Alexander, Thomas 14, 26, 38,
    152, 157, 166, 167, 168,
    176, 180, 214 n.2, 214–15
    n.9, 225 n.14
alienation 110–11, 221 n.12
American Association of
    University Professors 1
American Psychological
    Association 1
Americans 94, 102, 113, 143
animals 210–11
appreciators (of art) 160,
    161–3, 166–7, 168, 169,
    170, 177, 225
Aristotle 69, 97, 224 n.12
art (artworks) 157
  commodification of 154–5
  definition of 148, 163–5,
    171, 189, 225 n.15
  Dewey's reconstruction of
    146, 147
  distinguished as great, good,
    bad 175–6, 176–8, 226
    n.19
  and education 223 n.1
  ethical and political function
    of 147–8, 179
  as expressive/communicative
    160, 162, 171–2
  instrumentality in 177–8

and metaphysics 223 n.1
and morality 226 n.22
museum conception of
153–5, 173
organic sources of 148–50
political 179
relevance to life 150
as a subject for philosophy
146–7
subject matter 177
vs. entertainment 178–9
vs. 'products' 151, 164, 165
Art as Experience 148, 150–2
reception of 223 n.2
artist (and artmaking) 149,
159–63, 166
not necessarily 'genius'
167–8, 224 n.6
associationism 10–11, 12
atheism 188, 226 n.3
autonomy 100–1, 138, 218 n.2

Bach, J.S. 82
Barnes, Albert C. 147
Beardsley, Monroe 155, 223
n.2
behaviorism 11, 213 n.1
belief 52–3
see also inquiry; faith
Bell, Clive 148, 171
Bentham, Jeremy 69
Boisvert, Raymond 133
Brendel, David 209, 228 n.3
Burke, Kenneth 85, 228 n.1

Cage, John 157

Campbell, James 98, 117
Carroll, Noel 157
certainty 40, 66, 70, 93, 187
Cézanne, Paul 147
character, *see* self
Cohen, Marshall 157
Collingwood, R.G. 166
Common Faith, A 186–8,
203
communication
and community 113, 114,
140, 145
in habits 25
and public 115
community
and art 180
democratic 139
Dewey's reconstruction of
113–14
and religion 202
vs. 'public' 116
consciousness 28, 32–4
socially constructed 34
stream of 215 n.16
Constable, John 177
consumerism 3, 112
Courbet, Gustave 177
criticism, *see* aesthetic criticism;
philosophy
Croce, Benedetto 166
curriculum 126, 127, 128,
137
custom 19, 20, 59, 64–5, 79,
87, 90, 226 n.22

Darwin, Charles 27, 38
Degas, Edgar 177

deliberation 68–9, 73, 77–9
  and education 78
  effect on character 90–1
  as social 78
democracy 94–5, 119, 120
  as community 142
  Dewey's criticism of
    traditional view 94–5
  Dewey's reconstruction of
    119–23, 125–6, 221 n.16
  and education 125, 128,
    138–45
  as an ideal 199
  public involvement in
    118–19, 121
  and religious experience 205
Democracy and Education 125,
  141
Descartes, René 26, 35, 53
Dewey, Alice 129, 213 n.3
Dewey, Archibald Sprague 184
Dewey, John
  biography 1–3
  Hegelianism influences on
    2, 10, 12, 14
  involvement with education
    in Chicago 128–9
  James' influences on 14
  popularity of 3
  as public intellectual 1–2, 3
  relevance of 207–8
  religious background
    184–6
Dewey, Lucina 184
Diggins, John Patrick 85, 219
  n.7
doubt 52–4, 72, 129
  see also belief; inquiry

dualism
  fact-value 105
  mind-body (psycho-physical)
    11, 12, 17, 20, 27, 100,
    185, 214 n.3
Dykhuizen, George
  185–6

Eastman, Max 185
education 57
  central to Dewey's
    philosophy 124–5
  and democracy 118–19,
    122–3, 145
  of democratic leaders 139
  Dewey's criticism of
    traditional view 110–11,
    127–8
  Dewey's reconstruction of
    83, 105
  discipline (control) in
    126–7, 134–5
  higher (university) 136–7
  and learning 18, 126–8,
    128
  liberal arts (humanities)
    136–7
  as occupation vs. vocation
    131–3
  progressive 129, 222 n.4
  and teaching 126–8, 130–1
  of total attitude 139–40
  traditionalists vs. romantic
    (progressive) 126–7
  and values 130, 136
Eldridge, Michael 193–4,
  226 n.1

emotion 26–8, 183, 215 n.11
in aesthetic experience
166–7, 226 n.19
and faith 196–8
empiricism
British 10–11, 41–4
see also radical empiricism
entertainment 175, 178–9
environment 13, 17, 149, 210
epistemology 41, 48–9, 51, 59,
61
see also empiricism; inquiry;
instrumentalism
equality
Dewey's reconstruction of
96–7
ethical theory 65, 69–72
deontological 81–2
Dewey's reconstruction of 93
as monocausal 69–72, 82
as scientific 76–7
teleological 81–2
see also morality
Ethics 178
ethics 218 n.1
environmental 210–11
healthcare/medical 208–10
evolution 12, 29, 41, 44–5,
125, 228 n.4
experience 28, 35, 63, 64, 181,
187, 216 n.19
aesthetic 150–3, 161–3, 165,
170, 172, 177, 181–2,
190, 223 n.3, 223 n.4,
224 n.9, 227 n.6
anesthetic 156, 158–9, 181
consummatory (*an*
experience) 156–9, 166,

169, 177, 179, 181,
223–4 n.5
and democracy 122
Dewey's reconstruction of
35–8, 44, 147, 207, 226
n.2
lived/everyday 14, 150,
151–2, 155, 180
moral 65, 66–7, 73–5, 82
religious 184, 186, 188–94,
197, 226–7 n.3, 227 n.5,
227 n.7
traditional view of 12, 35,
36, 37
experimental method 221 n.11
explanation
monocausal 71, 72, 73, 82,
96, 97–8
expression (artistic) 161, 166–8

faith
democratic 123
Dewey's criticism of
traditional view 186–7,
194–5
Dewey's reconstruction of
186, 195–7, 200, 202
moral 194, 196–7, 206
feeling 215 n.13
see also emotion; sentience
feminism 211–12, 228 n.8
Fesmire, Steven 78
form (in art) 168–70, 172
Formalism 171, 173
fringe 22, 34
Fry, Roger 171, 172
Functionalism 14–23

God 46, 97, 184, 194
  Dewey's reconstruction of
    197–9
Gotshalk, D.W. 165, 169
Gouinlock, James 115–16
government 95, 96, 101, 102
  Dewey's reconstruction of
    113
Grant, Roberta L. 3
growth ix–x, 17, 38, 84–5,
    121

habit(s) 23–8, 67–8, 68–9, 214
    n.8, 214–15 n.9
  and character 91–2
  and communication 25
  constitutive of situations
    25–6
  destructive of democracy
    143–4
  and emotion 28
  formative of citizens 117,
    122
  as social 25–6, 90
  vs. habituations 209
Hall, G.S. 11–12, 126
Harper, William Rainey 129
Hester, D. Micah 209
Hickman, Larry 65, 66, 73,
    228 n.4
Hull House 3
human nature 85, 93, 96,
    100–1, 121, 218 n.2
Hume, David 10, 24, 35, 77,
    214 n.8
hypothesis 55–6
  see also inquiry

idealism 14, 165, 214 n.2
ideals 220 n.8
  Dewey's reconstruction of
    97, 104, 121, 198–9
imagination 192–3, 198
impulse, *see* instinct
Individualism, Old and New 111
individuals (individualism)
    100–2, 108–12
  atomic 100, 106, 203
  Dewey's criticism of
    traditional view 106–7
  Dewey's reconstruction of
    111–12
inquiry 48, 52–61, 53–7
  in aesthetics 151, 173
  and education 132
  moral 68–9, 73–5, 75, 76,
    77–9, 86, 211
  religious 200–1
  scientific 74, 95
  social 98, 105, 114, 117,
    121–2, 220 n.8, 220–1 n.10
instinct (impulse) 8, 9, 18–20,
    23, 24, 31, 68, 79, 90, 97,
    117, 126, 130, 181, 214
    n.7
  socially constructed 19
  traditional view of 19
Instrumentalism 41–2, 44–5, 62
intellectualist fallacy, *see*
    philosophic fallacy
intelligence 40, 103–5, 137
  associationist view of 11
  as communal/social 40,
    44–5, 49–51
  Dewey's reconstruction of
    183, 205

interest 23
  satisfaction of 64
Introspectionism 10, 11, 12, 17
is-ought 81, 93

Jackson, Philip 157
Jaggar, Alison 101
James, William 2, 4, 14, 24,
    27, 32–4, 36, 44, 47, 52,
    215 n.16
judgment 57–8
  aesthetic 174–5
  Dewey's reconstruction of
    218 n.14
  ethical (moral) 82, 83
  justice 96–7

Kant, Immanuel 42, 43–4, 69,
    86, 100, 218 n.2
knowledge
  associationist view of 11,
    40–1, 47, 59–61
  and community 114
  Dewey's reconstruction of
    216 n.1
  problem of 48
  as social 117
  see also empiricism; inquiry;
    warrant
Krutch, Joseph W. 104
Kubrick, Stanley 167

Laboratory School, The 129,
    132
landscape, edible 162
Language

constitutive of mind 32
constitutive of reality 215
    n.15
constitutive of self 88
not private 215–16 n.17
see also sign
League for Independent
    Political Action 1
Lewis, Clarence Irving 86
Liberalism 99–102
  Dewey's criticism of
    traditional view 102–3, 106
  Dewey's reconstruction of
    102–4, 220 n.9
liberty 107, 219–20 n.7
  see also rights
Lippmann, Walter 118–19
Locke, John 10, 35, 53
logic 48, 60, 217 n.5
  see also inquiry
'Lost Individual, The' 108

McGee, Glenn 208–9
McKenna, Erin 212
Marx, Karl 97, 109
Mayhew, Katherine C. 131
meaning 18
  in inquiry 55–6, 99; see also
    inquiry
  organic sources of 149
  socially constructed 39,
    215–16 n.17
means and ends 81–3
media
  effect on public 116–17, 221
    n.13
Meliorism 5–6, 203

mentality (psychical) 32
  as individual 13
  as social 13
  see also mind
Mill, John Stuart 69, 100
mind 28, 30–1
  Dewey's reconstruction of
    21, 31–4, 50
  empiricist view 42
  Kant's view 43
  problem of other 47
  rationalist view 42
  not reducible to brain 215
    n.14
  as socially constructed 36
moral experience, see
    experience
moral theory, see ethical theory
morality 63–6, 196, 218 n.1
  authority of 75, 87
  customs in 79
  Dewey's reconstruction of
    66–7, 72
  experience of 65, 66–7; see
    also experience
  judgment in 85–6, 92
  law (rule) of 74–5
  progress in 84–5
Morris, George Sylvester 2,
    10, 213 n.2
museum 151, 153–4, 155, 163
  see also art
'My Pedagogic Creed' 125

National Association for the
    Advancement of Colored
    People 1

naturalism 44, 45, 49–53, 170,
    210
  and religion 183–4, 186,
    198–9
nature 37–8, 210, 228 n.4
'Need for the Recovery of
    Philosophy, The' 207
Niebuhr, Reinhold 104, 220
    n.9, 221 n.14
Nietzsche, Friedrich 197, 203

occupation, see education
organism 12, 13, 15, 18,
    148–9

Pappas, Gregory 64–6, 73
Parks, Rosa 197
'Pathos of Liberalism, The'
    220 n.9
pedagogy 83, 127, 128–9
  see also education
Peirce, Charles S. 2, 24, 52–3,
    56, 162, 217 n.7; n.8;
    n.12
perception 20–3
  in aesthetics 173–4
personality 89–90
  see also adjustment; self
Phantom Public, The 118
philosophic fallacy 18, 46–7,
    151, 154, 168
philosophy
  as criticism 1
  Dewey's reconstruction of
    62, 207, 218 n.3
  moral role of 4–6

relevance to life 182
piety (natural, intellectual) 188,
    195–7, 207
Plato 35, 77, 224 n.12
policy (public, social) 105
    managed by experts
        118–19
political philosophy
    Dewey's criticism of
        traditional view 96
    Dewey's reconstruction of
        97–8
    see also liberalism
practice 52, 56, 72, 207
Pragmatism 56, 62, 228 n.2
    as critical tool 208–12
    as existentialism 72
Principles of Psychology 14
'Priority of Democracy to
    Philosophy, The' 219–20
        n.7
property 101–2, 107
psychiatry 209–10, 228 n.3
psychology 10–13
    Dewey's reconstruction of
        12–15
    introspective 15, 17
    physiological 10, 11–14, 15,
        17
    relevance to life 38–9
    social 8, 19
public(s)
    Dewey's criticism of
        traditional view 116–17
    Dewey's reconstruction of
        114–15
    inchoate 116–17, 221 n.13
    Lippmann on 117–19

self-conscious 98
vs. community 116
Public and its Problems, The 118
Public Opinion 118

quality 21–2, 32, 149
    Dewey's reconstruction of
        214 n.4
    pervasive 54, 158, 159
Quest for Certainty, The
        217 n.3

radical empiricism 4, 44, 47,
        48
    see also starting point,
        practical
Randall, John Herman, Jr.
        193, 227 n.7
rationalism 41–4
rationality 100–1
realism 215 n.15
reality 70
    two tiered 45–6, 216 n.1
    see also supernatural
reasoning 52, 55–6, 214 n.5
    see also inquiry
reflection 47, 51, 53, 215 n.10,
        217 n.10, 228 n.5
reflex arc 14–18, 129
'Reflex Arc Concept in
    Psychology, The' 15
Regan, Tom 211
Reichl, Ruth 162–3,
relativism 209, 215 n.15
    in aesthetics 169–70, 175
    moral 84–8

religion 184, 199, 203–4,
   227 n.4
   contrasted with 'religious'
      189–90
   definition of 189–90
   Dewey's criticism of
      traditional view 187
   Dewey's reconstruction of
      200–6
religious
   attitude 188, 191
   experience, *see* experience
   feeling 184, 227 n.6
   inquiry and knowledge
      200–1, 203
   practice 184, 189
   vs. unreligious 195
Renoir, Pierre-Auguste 177
response, *see* stimulus
rights 96, 106
   affected by economic forces
      101–2, 106, 110
   Dewey's reconstruction of
      107–8,
Rorty, Richard 103, 219–20
   n.7
Rousseau, Jean-Jacques 97
Ryan, Alan 97–8, 101–2, 110,
   131, 138, 222–3 n.9

Santayana, George 86
school 125, 126, 133–6
   purposes of 138
   social atmosphere of 133–5
   and society 135–8
   no special moral aims 136–8
science 57, 105

scientific method 17–18, 53,
   105
   and religion 183–4
'Search for the Great
   Community, The'
   113–14
self (character, personality) 85,
   88–93, 191–3, 196–7, 198
   and consequences 92–3
   shaped by art 161
   as social 88–93
   see also adjustment
sensation 8, 20–3, 214 n.8
   Dewey's criticism of
      traditional view 216–17
      n.2
sensori-motor coordinations
   (coordinated circuit)
   16–17, 22, 26–7
sentience (feeling) 28–30,
   31–2,
Shusterman, Richard 157, 165,
   170, 224 n.9; n.10
sign 22, 32, 50–1
   Dewey's reconstruction of
      217 n.6
situation
   determinate 57
   indeterminate 53–4, 57
   moral 67–8, 69, 76, 77
   problematic 47, 54–5, 58,
      67, 74, 115, 217 n.13
society
   factionalization of 140–2
   pluralistic 121, 140
Society for the Advancement
   of American Philosophy x
Spinoza, Baruch 26

starting point 53
  humane 204–5
  practical 4–5, 38, 72–3,
    83, 86, 151, 172,
    184, 208, 217 n.4,
    218 n.14
  theoretical 4, 47, 86, 225
    n.16
state 97, 102
  Dewey's reconstruction of
    113, 115–16
stimulus 16–17, 50, 160, 214
  n.3, 222 n.5
structuralism 173
subjectivism 64–5, 86–8
  see also relativism
subjectivity 27, 36, 39
supernatural 216, 227 n.3
  and religion 188, 199–200
  and religious experience
    190
sustainability ix–x

Talisse, Robert 121, 122, 221
  n.17
Teachers Union movement 1
'Three Independent Factors in
  Morals' 69–72
Titchener, E.B. 11
tolerance 75
truth 59–60

see also inquiry; knowledge;
  warrant

universals (in art) 172, 176
University Elementary School
  133
Utilitarianism 69, 90, 97, 211

valuation (appraising) 80–1
value(s)
  absolute 81, 84, 101
  aesthetic 171
  communal 113
  in education 130, 136
  in experience ix, 204–5
  moral 79–88
  of nature 210
  religious 204
  valuing (prizing) 80–1
  vs. valuation 218–19 n.5
virtue 92
  see also habit
vocation, *see* education

warrant 61, 208
Welchman, Jennifer 89, 92,
  218 n.3
Westbrook, Robert B. 213 n.4
Wundt, Wilhelm 11